Imbert de Saint-Amand

France and Italy

Imbert de Saint-Amand

France and Italy

ISBN/EAN: 9783337233525

Printed in Europe, USA, Canada, Australia, Japan

Cover: Foto ©Andreas Hilbeck / pixelio.de

More available books at **www.hansebooks.com**

FRANCE AND ITALY

VICTOR EMANUEL II.

FRANCE AND ITALY

BY

IMBERT DE SAINT-AMAND

TRANSLATED BY

ELIZABETH GILBERT MARTIN

WITH PORTRAITS

NEW YORK
CHARLES SCRIBNER'S SONS
1899

COPYRIGHT, 1899, BY
CHARLES SCRIBNER'S SONS

Norwood Press
J. S. Cushing & Co. — Berwick & Smith
Norwood Mass. U.S.A.

CONTENTS

		PAGE
	INTRODUCTION	1

CHAPTER

		PAGE
I.	THE COMMENCEMENT OF 1859	8
II.	THE MARRIAGE OF PRINCE NAPOLEON	14
III.	THE PRINCESS CLOTILDE	23
IV.	THE ANONYMOUS BROCHURE	28
V.	THE SPEECH FROM THE THRONE	35
VI.	THE PARTISANS OF PEACE	42
VII.	ENGLAND AND PIEDMONT	48
VIII.	PRUSSIA AND THE GERMANIC CONFEDERATION	54
IX.	RUSSIA	61
X.	THE CARNIVAL	67
XI.	LENT	74
XII.	HOLY WEEK	81
XIII.	EASTER WEEK	88
XIV.	THE OPENING OF THE WAR	97
XV.	THE DEPARTURE OF THE EMPEROR	104

CHAPTER		PAGE
XVI.	Genoa and Alexandria	111
XVII.	Montebello	118
XVIII.	Palestro	123
XIX.	Turbigo	131
XX.	The Battle of Magenta	136
XXI.	The Morrow of Magenta	148
XXII.	The Entry into Milan	154
XXIII.	Melegnano	162
XXIV.	Before Solferino	168
XXV.	The Battle of Solferino	182
XXVI.	After Solferino	195
XXVII.	The Empress Regent	202
XXVIII.	Prince Napoleon	211
XXIX.	The Diplomatic Situation	218
XXX.	The Last Days of the War	224
XXXI.	The Armistice	230
XXXII.	The Interview of Villafranca	240
XXXIII.	The Preliminaries of Peace	247
XXXIV.	The Resignation of Cavour	256
XXXV.	The Emperor's Return	262
XXXVI.	Saint-Cloud	271
XXXVII.	The Return of the Troops	283

CHAPTER		PAGE
XXXVIII.	TUSCANY	292
XXXIX.	PARMA	303
XL.	MODENA	309
XLI.	THE ROMAGNAS	315
XLII.	SAINT-SAUVEUR	324
XLIII.	BIARRITZ AND BORDEAUX	331
XLIV.	THE CLOSE OF 1859	338

PORTRAITS

VICTOR EMMANUEL		*Frontispiece*
MARSHAL MACMAHON	*Face Page*	64
FRANCIS JOSEPH	" "	128
COUNT CAVOUR	" "	256

FRANCE AND ITALY

INTRODUCTION

OUR misfortunes occupy our minds too much; we do not think enough about our glories. Hypnotized by the memory of our disasters, we lose sight of triumphs, the record of which is, nevertheless, preeminently adapted to fortify the military sentiment which is the hope and consolation of France. We dwell too much on Sedan and Metz, not long enough on Sebastopol, Magenta, and Solferino. What would be said of the heirs of the First Empire if they insisted on talking of nothing but Leipsic and Waterloo? The utility of the Italian War may be disputed, but the heroism of those who took part in it is beyond question. Many of them are still living. With what respect we should surround them, how eagerly we should beg them to relate the history of their exploits! Surely it pertains to them to give important lessons to our young army. To act well it would merely need to imitate them.

The historians of the wars of the First Empire have been innumerable. The pens which deal with those of the Second are as yet few. Nevertheless, there has probably never been a siege comparable in importance to that of Sebastopol, and few victories have been as memorable as those of Magenta and Solferino. At present I intend to give a brief account of these two great battles, studying, meanwhile, the entire year 1859, which played so important a part in the destinies of France and Italy. This study may properly be included in the series by which I have preceded it, since a woman of the Tuileries, the Empress Eugénie, was regent during the war. At that time I was attached to the political department of the Ministry of Foreign Affairs, and I have since re-read the despatches written before, during, and after the hostilities. I have been able to follow every fluctuation of public opinion, to study the various ways in which the occurrences of the war were at first commented on at Paris by different classes of society, to note day by day the impressions, criticisms, joys, and apprehensions of the public. I was present at the *Te Deum* and the popular festivities by which the troops were welcomed home. I seem still to hear the trumpets blaring and the noise of the acclamations.

No two wars could be more unlike than those of 1870 and of 1859. The one was as long and lamentable as the other was swift and joyous. Alas! it was but too brilliant. A few wholesome reverses would have averted that overweening self-confidence which was afterwards one of the principal causes of the disasters of France. Had she experienced defeats as well as victories in Italy, she would have been compelled to recognize that her effective forces by land and sea were not such as to admit of her playing that preponderating rôle to which she aspired throughout the world, and she would not have opposed the Emperor when he desired to model our military institutions on those of Prussia. The reminiscences of the Italian War were too flattering to the national vanity. People got in the way of looking only at the bright side of military matters, the reverse of the medal was neglected, and it was through the prism of the victories of 1859 that the men of 1870 contemplated a disproportionate struggle. Alas! we have paid dear for our illusions! But how seductive they were! How they made our hearts beat! France delighted in her glory like a pretty woman in her mirror. She convinced herself that she was the superlatively great nation, as Paris was the capital of capitals. Had one ventured then to hint that our country was not absolutely invincible, he would have been scouted as an alarmist and a coward. Now, cruel experience has proved the fragility of much that was then admired for its splendor. But the memory of those days of enthusiasm and apotheosis has still a charm. Old men like to recall their youth, and in winter we dream of the radiance of spring.

The remarkable thing about the Italian War is the way in which it throws up into full light the character of Napoleon III., bringing out both qualities and defects; his energy, his strength of will, his audacity, his courage, but also his adventurous disposition, his innate tendency to conspire, and his temperament as a political gamester. Such as we beheld him at Strasburg, at Boulogne, and at the *coup d'État*, such we shall find him again in 1859, concealing his designs even from his closest confidants, preparing a war as one would organize a plot, braving the greatest dangers with imperturbable coolness, flinging himself headlong into enterprises whose consequences nobody could foresee, restrained by no objection, confiding in his star, and risking all for all like a true fatalist whom nothing can trouble or alarm.

Napoleon III. has been represented as a dreamer, irresolute, chimerical, at the mercy of events, and blindly obedient to the suggestions of his advisers. Nothing could be more unlike the truth. On the contrary, until disease had impaired his forces, the Emperor was pre-eminently a man of action, relying on no one but himself, and no political personage has possessed to a higher degree the quality of personal initiative. What other pretender has ever dreamed of such bold attempts as those of Strasburg and Boulogne? What *coup d'État* was ever so rash as that of the Second of December? What war was ever more mysteriously prepared or more imprudently engaged in than that of 1859?

Documents still unpublished will permit us to determine in a precise manner the attitude of the different powers in this European crisis. They will show the extraordinary difficulties encountered by the apostle of nationalities, not merely on battlefields, but in the chanceries, in attempting usefully to defend the Italian cause. We shall see that he stood almost alone in France in desiring the war; that he made ready for it contrary to the advice of his wife, his ministers, the Senate, the Corps Législatif, and public opinion; that he cleverly contrived to make the Emperor of Austria seem to be the aggressor, while in reality that post was occupied by King Victor Emmanuel; that in Italy he lost control of events notwithstanding his victories; that he was compelled to halt after Solferino, and that Russia would not have defended him against Germany, which was rising *en masse;* that he sincerely desired the establishment of an Italian Confederation, but found no one who would seriously support such a combination; in fine, that it was against his will and after long hesitation that he was induced to adopt a policy which resulted first in Italian unity and afterwards in that of Germany.

Doubtless the Emperor did not thoroughly accomplish his task. But, in spite of many disappointments, it cannot be denied that but for him Milan and Venice would still be under Austrian domination, nor that there was something chivalrous in his policy. It was the negation of the maxim: Might makes right. It proclaimed the doctrine that peoples should have the power to decide their own destiny. It extolled the forward march of civilization. Other ideas have gained the ascendency since his fall, and it may be that they will cause his to be longed for. Count

Albert Vandal has said so eloquently in his address of reception at the French Academy: "We have seen the powers which we placed in the hands of peoples turned against us; they have been used to strike, to wound, to pierce us to the heart; but who can say that the universal conscience will not avenge us, that it does not even now avenge us by remembering what humanity has lost since the greatness of France has diminished?"

The war of Italy, not less important in itself than in its consequences, has inaugurated a new era. It has produced profound modifications in the diplomatic situation and in international law. It has stated problems which are still unsolved, and from the triple standpoint of politics, religion, and society, it remains the object of numerous controversies. We must congratulate ourselves, however, that it has left no trace of animosity between Austria and France. Nothing separates the two nations, and if they reflect on their veritable interests, they will recognize that both are necessary to European equilibrium. The France of 1859 saluted the heroism of the Austrian army, and it may be affirmed to-day that there is not a single Frenchman who does not desire the prosperity of the Austro-Hungarian monarchy and the maintenance of its integrity. The Emperor Francis Joseph, once our brave and chivalrous adversary, is as much respected by Frenchmen as by his own subjects.

On the other hand, we are convinced that a conscientious study of the events of 1859 must have the result of inspiring salutary reflections in the two allied nations which fought heroically side by side. Italy ought not to forget that in the days of her great trials she had no friend but France, and it seems to be time for disastrous misunderstandings to cease. In March, 1871, Jules Favre wrote to M. Rotham: " With the transformation of science, two peoples who inhabit the shores of the same sea, who are united by a common origin, the exchanges of navigation, and the resemblance of manners and characters, can be enemies only through the criminal folly of their governments." A war between France and Italy would be a civil war. May such a spectacle never be presented to the patriots of both nations! At present affinities of race, religion, and language may get the better of erroneous calculations, and attempts at reconciliation may be noted. And it may be that the time is opportune for evoking souvenirs which should be indissoluble ties of amity between the two peoples. No, no; it will not be said that so much generous blood has been shed in vain, and that the Latin race has made so many heroic sacrifices absolutely without avail.

It is to the survivors of the war of Italy that we dedicate these simple pages. Should any of those intrepid men do us the honor of glancing over them, they may find some interest in reading the story of their exploits and receive the respectful homage rendered to their courage and their patriotism!

IMBERT DE SAINT-AMAND.

CHAPTER I

THE COMMENCEMENT OF 1859

ON the morning of January 1, 1859, the year that was beginning seemed as if it must be a tranquil one. In Paris, the winter season promised to be brilliant. A host of balls and soirées were in preparation. Commerce and industry were in full prosperity. No one suspected that any difficulty whatever could occur at the Tuileries during the diplomatic reception on New Year's Day. Hence, the representatives of the powers were greatly amazed when they heard Napoleon III. say to Baron Hübner, Austrian ambassador: "I regret that our relations with your government may not be so good as they have been; but I beg you to say to the Emperor that my personal sentiments have not changed."

This simple sentence, although uttered in a calm and courteous tone, resounded like a clap of thunder in a clear sky.

Business slackened, stocks fell, speculators were seriously disturbed. But the excitement soon abated. At the reception of the Empress on the following day, both she and her husband paid Baron Hübner most particular attentions, as if to efface the painful impressions of the day before. In his conversations with the representatives of the powers, Count Walewski, Minister of Foreign Affairs, sought to reduce the imperial remark to the proportions of an incident not in the least bellicose. Optimism was the fashion in official circles. No change occurred in the routine of the salons. The theatres played to full houses; balls were as numerous as in previous winters. The official journals took good care not to arouse vain fears by sounding the alarm clock too early. Anxieties were finally dispelled by the following paragraph in the *Moniteur* of January 7: "For several days past public opinion has been disturbed by alarming rumors which it is the duty of the government to put an end to by declaring there is nothing in our diplomatic relations to authorize the fears these rumors have a tendency to produce."

Now let us see how matters were considered in Austria. The French *chargé d'affaires* at Vienna, the Marquis de Banneville, on January 8, addressed the following despatch in cipher to Count Walewski: "The general excitement which for some days past seems to have prevailed in European circles, must be felt more keenly in Vienna than elsewhere, since the incidents which, rightly or wrongly, have occasioned this excitement chiefly refer to the international relations of Austria. A sort of panic was produced which the declaration of the *Moniteur* has to-day greatly allayed. Moreover, I know that Baron Hübner, in reporting the words addressed to him by the Emperor, gave them an altogether different meaning than that attributed to them for a moment by public opinion, and he added that the tone and accent in which they were pronounced rendered them still more conciliatory and friendly."

At Turin, the Prince de La Tour d'Auvergne, minister of France, had instantly appreciated the gravity of the situation. January 3, he wrote to Count Walewski: "Everybody is anxious, and public opinion looks forward more than ever to great events in a near future. The presence of the famous General Garibaldi at Turin has given rise to many comments. I know that he had a long conference last week with Count Cavour. He is said to have made a formal engagement with the president of the council, in presence of General La Marmora, to hold himself at the disposition of the Sardinian government in case of war, renouncing all alliance with the Mazzinian party, and referring altogether, so it is affirmed, to M. de Cavour, should occasion arise, the proper solution of the Italian question. Nothing more was required to authorize all manner of suppositions, and possibly it might have been cleverer on the part of Count Cavour, supposing it necessary to put himself in relations with Garibaldi, to keep the interview entirely secret."

January 10, Victor Emmanuel opened the session of the Sardinian parliament. These words in the royal speech produced a great impression: "Fortified by the experience of the past, let us go resolutely to meet the contingencies of the future. This future will be happy, our policy being founded upon love of liberty and the fatherland. Our country, whose territory is small, has acquired consideration in the councils of Europe, because it is great by means of the ideas it represents and the sympathies which it inspires. This situation is not free from perils since, while respecting the treaties, we are not insensible to the cries of anguish arising from all parts of Italy. Made strong by union, confiding in the goodness of our cause, we await with prudence and resolution the decrees of divine providence."

In a despatch of the same day, the Prince de La Tour d'Auvergne gave the following account of the session: "The latter part of the address in which His Majesty alluded to the possibilities of the future was received with hearty applause in which even the tribunes took part. The impression produced in the diplomatic body by the King's remarks, moreover, seemed to me rather favorable. It was satisfactory, under existing circumstances, to find His Majesty talking of his respect for the treaties. My colleagues of Russia and Prussia, who sat beside me, did justice to the moderation of this language. The King, on entering the Chamber as well as on leaving it, was welcomed with much enthusiasm."

The next day, January 11, the minister of France wrote another despatch: "The opinion of the members of the diplomatic corps on the speech of the crown is far from unanimous. If some of my colleagues appreciated it with kindness, the larger number seemed much affected by the phrase in which His Majesty avows that he is not insensible to the cries of anguish which reach him from all parts of Italy. Even public opinion, I must admit, appears to consider the speech rather bellicose."

In Vienna likewise, stress was laid on warlike ideas. The Marquis de Banneville was under no illusion. He expressed himself as follows in a despatch of January 14: "I have good reason to believe that the Austrian government has for some time been familiarizing itself sufficiently with the notion of a war to find relative compensations should this supreme necessity actually arise. Doubtless the chances of war are very uncertain for it, and it does not disguise the fact that its Italian provinces are at stake; but it deems its military condition sufficiently good to permit it to take these risks, without foolhardy hopes, but also without over-anxiety or discouragement. It is sustained by confidence that a war undertaken solely for the purpose of depriving it of Lombardy and Venetia would certainly bring it allies within a given time. In fine, between the possible recurrence of the revolutionary events which in 1848 menaced the Austrian monarchy with dissolution in all its provinces and an external war, it would not hesitate to choose the latter extremity. The first of these dangers outranks all others in its estimation, and it would brave the first in order to avoid the second."

Things were at this point when an item of news became known which was considered symptomatic of an approaching war in which France would be the ally of Piedmont: the betrothal of Prince Napoleon and the Princess Clotilde, daughter of King Victor Emmanuel.

CHAPTER II

THE MARRIAGE OF PRINCE NAPOLEON

THE *Moniteur* of January 14 announced that Prince Napoleon had set off for Turin the previous day and that his absence would be short. The object of this journey was already known in Europe. The same day, the Marquis de Banneville, *chargé d'affaires* of France at Vienna, wrote to Count Walewski: "Count Buol (Austrian Minister of Foreign Affairs) offered me his congratulations on the subject of the marriage of Prince Napoleon with the Princess Clotilde of Savoy, with a very good grace and without the slightest constraint. He spoke of the family ties which this union would establish between the imperial houses of France and Austria. 'I desire sincerely,' he added, smiling, 'that this alliance may prove more profitable to you than our own very numerous ones with the house of Savoy have been to us.'"

The betrothal was officially announced by the *Moniteur* of January 24. The government organ expressed itself as follows: "The intimate relations which have long existed between the Emperor and King Victor Emmanuel, and the reciprocal interests of France and Savoy, have induced the two sovereigns to draw still more close the ties uniting them by a family alliance. For more than a year the preliminaries have been under discussion, but the youth of the Princess has delayed until now the date of the marriage." At the close of this communication, and to prevent the public from considering it as a symptom of war, the *Moniteur* wrote: "The *Union* journal has not been afraid to reproduce the following lines from the *Indépendance Belge:* 'It is affirmed that King Victor Emmanuel gave his consent to the marriage of the Princess Clotilde only on condition of an offensive and defensive alliance between France and Sardinia. It is added that the treaty between France and Sardinia was signed the day before yesterday.' We regret having to repeat and contradict in the French press an assertion not less false than it is insulting to the dignity of the sovereigns. The Emperor must desire that his family alliances should be in accord with the traditional policy of France, but he will never make the great interests of the country depend upon a family alliance."

Prince Napoleon landed at Genoa in the morning of January 16. He was received there by Count Nigra, minister of the household of the King, by General Cialdini, aide-de-camp of His Majesty, and by Prince de La Tour d'Auvergne, minister of France. He left the same day for Turin, where he arrived at three o'clock.

The next day, the minister of France wrote to

Count Walewski: "On the road from Genoa to Turin, and particularly at Alessandria, the Prince received the most flattering and cordial welcome; but nothing can give an idea of the immense throng of people, and the ardent demonstrations of sympathy, which awaited His Imperial Highness at Turin. All the streets from the railway to the palace were filled by a crowd, who were anxious to behold the Emperor's cousin, and who respectfully lifted their hats as he passed by. Numerous cries of 'Long live Napoleon!' were heard. The King received his august visitor in the most cordial way. After the dinner, at which the ministers of the King, the court agents, and the personnel of the legation were the only guests, the King, accompanied by His Imperial Highness and Prince de Carignan, went to the Reggio theatre, brilliantly illuminated for the occasion. The house was full, and His Majesty as well as His Imperial Highness were saluted by hearty applause."

In the evening of January 17, after a family dinner at the court, Prince Napoleon went to Count Cavour's reception, where the assembly was very large, all displaying the best sentiments for the cousin of the Emperor.

January 18.— Another despatch from the Prince de La Tour d'Auvergne to Count Walewski: "Prince Napoleon's arrival at Turin has produced a general and profound sensation. It seems to me that the prevailing sentiment is one of entire confidence in the Emperor's sympathies for Piedmont, and the assistance of his government in escaping honorably from a situation whose dangers are evident to all and begin to disquiet gravely even the most ardent partisans of the policy of Count Cavour. The projected union between H. I. H. Prince Napoleon and H. R. H. Madame the Princess Clotilde, now known to everybody and very favorably received by public opinion, with some exceptions, which are, however, much less numerous than was thought at first, comes to confirm these expectations. It is to be hoped, and such, Count, is the desire of all prudent minds, that these motives of confidence will react in the direction of calmness and patience on the attitude and the projects of the cabinet of Turin. . . . In reality, there exists at present among the representatives of foreign governments resident at Turin a sort of uncertainty, I might even say of anxiety, concerning the future and likewise our intentions. I feel it my duty to notify Your Excellency of this sentiment, which it might be well to bear in mind to some extent."

January 22. — Another despatch from the Prince de La Tour d'Auvergne: "The most cordial relations have been established between the King and His Imperial Highness. The young Princess seems equally satisfied with the fate in store for her. The partisans of Italian independence hail the marriage with joy. They consider it an assured pledge of support to be given their cause by the Emperor in a near future. Impressions are different and less favorable among the upper classes. The skilfully fostered dread lest a war which Piedmont alone would not dare to maintain against Austria may be the foreseen result of the new ties by which the houses of France and Savoy are to be united, is very keen. . . . The Chamber will certainly not refuse the means necessary to protect the country from an attack by Austria, but public opinion plainly fears rash and headlong enterprises more than ever, and Count Cavour will act wisely if he profits by the occasion to reassure it as far as lies in his power."

January 23. — General Niel officially requested the King to give the hand of Princess Clotilde to Prince Napoleon. This request was received by the sovereign in the most cordial manner. During the day, deputations from the Senate and Chamber of Deputies came to the palace with the response to the speech from the throne. His Majesty acquainted them with the approaching marriage of his daughter.

January 24. — Prince Napoleon dines at the French legation, going afterwards to a splendid court ball. The Princess Clotilde, who dances with him several times, is the object of general attention. Everybody notices the easy grace displayed by the young Princess throughout the evening. Already she seems much attached to her future husband. The Prince had just done something which had deeply affected her. He went to see Prince Otho, third son of the King, at the castle of Moncalieri, where His Royal Highness lives. The young prince, whom an infirmity of infancy had always kept away from court, was deeply moved by this visit. "Perhaps I shall never know my brother-in-law," he had mournfully remarked a few minutes before the Prince arrived.

January 25. — In concert with Count Nigra, minister of the royal household, the French minister signs the matrimonial agreement. By Article III., the King, conformably to the law of the country, assures the Princess a dowry of 500,000 francs. Article IV. mentions that the King presents the Princess with a sum of 100,000 francs specially intended to provide her trousseau, independently of rings and jewels valued at about 245,000 francs.

January 28. — A deputation from the municipal and communal councils of Turin present the Princess with a beautifully chased silver chandelier which had been admired at the last exhibition as a masterpiece of Piedmontese industry.

January 29. — The marriage contract is signed at the palace, in presence of the ministers and the whole court. Count Cavour acts as notary of the crown. He reads the act by which the Princess renounces all right to inherit from the royal family, and the contract is signed by all present. In the evening, the city is brilliantly illuminated.

Sunday, January 30. — The marriage is celebrated

at ten o'clock in the morning in the palace chapel. Assisted by the Bishops of Diella, Pignerol, Casal, and Savona, the Archbishop of Vercelli gives the nuptial benediction.

At half-past one the married pair, the King, Prince de Carignan, the entire court, the French minister, and all the members of his legation, set off for Genoa. The national guard and the troops in garrison at Turin are under arms. The whole population awaits anxiously the coming of the royal procession. Victor Emmanuel, in a fine open carriage drawn by six horses, has the Princess Clotilde on his right. Opposite the Princess is Prince Napoleon. Prince de Carignan sits opposite the King. The sovereign and the husband and wife are touched by the emotion of the crowd. There is a general acclamation; blessings, cheers, wishes for her happiness, are incessantly addressed to the young Princess, who replies by saluting with as much grace as affability. The railway platform is decorated with flowers. The ovation does not end until the piercing whistle of the locomotive is heard.

All along the road, from Turin to Genoa, the country people hasten to greet the King, his daughter, and his son-in-law. The train stops at Moncalieri, and again at Asti, where five hundred Piedmontese decorated with the Saint Helena medal are assembled, and where the municipality offers the Princess a bouquet and a box of candy; again at Alessandria, where the crowd is immense, and at

Novi, where there are also a great many Saint Helena medallists. Everywhere Victor Emmanuel receives the homage of the local authorities with his usual kindliness, and everywhere the noble attitude and gracious physiognomy of the Princess excite deep sympathy.

They arrive at Genoa. On its way to the palace the royal cortege is preceded by students. Eighty-five deputies and twenty senators are in the city. The King and the newly married pair are present in the evening at the Carlo Felice theatre, where the audience receive them with transports of enthusiasm. Brilliantly illuminated, Genoa the Proud, with her marble palaces and her splendid roadstead, presents an enchanting spectacle.

January 31.— The King and Their Imperial Highnesses go aboard the French vessels sent to Genoa to escort the spouses as far as Marseilles. The ensemble and the manœuvres of these vessels are highly appreciated. In the evening, a grand ball reunites the élite of Genoese society and the diplomatic corps which has followed the court to Genoa.

February 1. — Victor Emmanuel is touched when parting from his cherished daughter; he asks himself what will become of her in France, a land disturbed by so many revolutions, and so often fatal to its princes and princesses. It wants a quarter to eleven o'clock. The spouses go aboard the *Reine Hortense*. With the Princess goes her governess, the Marquise de Villamarina del Campo, who is to remain with her for a month. The King would not bid his daughter farewell until the *Reine Hortense* had left the harbor. He returned to Genoa in a launch, and his manly face betrayed his emotion.

CHAPTER III

THE PRINCESS CLOTILDE

THE Princess who lands at Marseilles on February 2, 1859, will be sixteen on the second of March.

Daughter of King Victor Emmanuel (born March 14, 1820) and of the Austrian Archduchess Adelaide (born June 3, 1822, died January 20, 1855), she has profited well by an excellent education. In her attitude, language, and her entire person, there is a blending of simplicity and nobility, of modesty and dignity, which is full of charm. No sooner does she touch the soil of France than this daughter of kings, this descendant of saints and heroes, is saluted with veneration. She inspires all French people with profound respect, even those who are not in favor of a war for Italy. Is it the fault of this gentle creature if her marriage is linked with warlike negotiations? Can she in whose veins the blood of the Hapsburgs flows with that of Savoy be reproached for a struggle which will be a sort of family war between two rival houses? What is there in common between the horrors of the battlefield and the good Princess who, true to the precepts of the Gospel, would desire that all peoples might dwell in fraternal and Christian unity? The crowd feels a vague presentiment that the young Princess will not be happy. A trace of sadness and premature melancholy is already perceptible on her youthful features.

February 2. — On arriving at Marseilles, Prince Napoleon and the Princess find there the Emperor's aide-de-camp, General Fleury, and also Countess de Rayneval and Madame de Saulcy, ladies of the palace of the Empress, commissioned to congratulate them on their arrival in France. Their Imperial Highnesses, after receiving the authorities, breakfast at the prefecture and start for Paris at half-past three. They stop at Fontainebleau for a few hours' rest in the morning, and are received there by the Princess Mathilde, who embraces her new sister-in-law.

At three o'clock they arrive in Paris, where they are met at the Lyons station by Marshal Magnan, General de Lowoëstine, the prefect of the Seine, the prefect of police, the officers of the household of Prince Napoleon, and the members of the Sardinian legation. A regiment of the line is drawn up at the entrance of the station; a squadron of cuirassiers forms the escort. The streets through which the cortege is to pass are hung with French and Sardinian flags. The spouses and their suite get into court carriages. That occupied by the Prince and Princess attracts all eyes. The General Prince de La Moskowa, aide-de-camp of the Emperor, rides beside the right-hand door, the commander of the escort of cuirassiers at the left. The procession passes through the rue de Lyon, the rue de Rivoli, Place Saint-Germain-l'Auxerrois, the court of the Louvre, and the Place of the Carrousel. The national guard and the light infantry of the imperial guard form the line from the entrance of the Louvre to the triumphal arch of the Carrousel; the first regiment of cuirassiers of the guard and a regiment of dragoons are in line of battle on this place. The line is bordered in the court of the Tuileries by a battalion of light infantry of the guard.

The Emperor comes to the foot of the grand staircase to receive Their Imperial Highnesses. The Empress awaits them at the top. She embraces the Princess. The presentations then take place in the white salon, situated between the hall of the Marshals and that of Apollo. A few moments later, Their Highnesses go with the same cortege to the Palais-Royal. King Jerome, surrounded by the officers of his household, receives the Princess as she leaves the carriage, and, after embracing her, leads her to the apartments she is to occupy. In the evening, the pair dine at the table of the former King of Westphalia.

February 5. — Grand dinner at the Tuileries, in the hall of the Marshals, in honor of the bride. Among the guests of the Emperor and Empress are the princes and princesses of the Imperial family, the Princess Marie of Baden, the Duchess of Hamilton, the ministers and great dignitaries of State, the foreign ambassadors and ministers plenipotentiary and their wives, the entire Sardinian legation, the great officers of the crown, and the principal officers of the households of Their Majesties and the princes. After dinner a play is performed in the gallery of Diana.

The Princess Clotilde is at once appreciated at Court. In spite of her extreme simplicity she has a very noble bearing. Her reserve, her modesty and tact, gain the good opinion of all. At the time of her installation at the Palais-Royal, the sad associations which might make that residence a gloomy one are carefully avoided. Paris seems a magnificent city to the young Princess, and one enjoying extraordinary prosperity. It is still hoped that current differences may find a peaceful diplomatic solution. The Austrian ambassador, reflecting that the wife of Prince Napoleon is the daughter of an archduchess, shows her the greatest deference, and is present at all entertainments given in her honor. Speaking of the marriage so much commented on, Count de Buol assures Marquis de Banneville that for his part he is "not one of those who have found a *hidden significance* in it, the motives of this union having always appeared to him such as the Emperor Napoleon states them, natural and suitable."

Certain Viennese journals, notably the *Presse*, having reproduced some unseemly remarks concerning the marriage, attributing them to Piedmontese sources, what course is taken by the royal and imperial government? It publishes in the official journal, the

Correspondance Autrichienne, an article whose result might be the suppression of the *Presse*, which had already received two warnings. Concerning this, the Marquis de Banneville writes to Count Walewski, February 2: "Count Buol has told me that he merely acted in accordance with a due sense of propriety in instigating the suppression of such sallies; and that without ascribing any merit to himself for an act of simple decorum, he at least wished to show his spontaneous readiness to stigmatize and repress such unnamable attacks." The French government appreciates the kindly procedure of that of Austria, and expresses its gratitude.

The Princess Clotilde will be always and everywhere respected. During the eleven and a half years which she will spend in France, she will set there the example of all the virtues. At official festivities she will appear with the noble bearing of a woman born on the steps of the throne, but in the palace she will lead the austere life of the cloister. She will suffer without ever speaking of her sufferings; she will humbly offer them to God. Politicians of all parties will pay homage to this pious and charitable princess who will not be less honored in misfortune than in days of prosperity, and who, compelling the admiration of all by her resignation, tranquillity, and courage, will depart from France with as much dignity as she entered it.

CHAPTER IV

THE ANONYMOUS BROCHURE

VICTOR EMMANUEL, after witnessing at Genoa the departure of his daughter for France, had gone back to Turin to assent to a project for borrowing fifty millions submitted to him by M. Lanza, his Minister of Finance. It was a veritable war loan, the intent of which nobody sought to disguise. The minister concluded his statement of its motives by these words: "You know that there are supreme moments in the life of peoples when sacrifice is a sacred duty, an inexorable necessity." Every one anxiously wondered what part Napoleon III. would play in the great crises which were in preparation.

February 3, the very day of the Princess Clotilde's arrival in Paris, the Emperor announced to his amazed ministers the appearance of a brochure which would reflect his ideas upon the Italian question. Some hours later, this pamphlet was in the windows of all the bookshops. It contained sixty-four pages, and was unsigned. Its title was: *The Emperor Napoleon III. and Italy.*

In his *Souvenirs du Second Empire*, M. A. Granier de Cassagnac has said of the Emperor: "His throne turned his attention from his books; but those who have read them know that neither France nor any other country has ever had a sovereign fitted to reign by a higher intellectual cultivation. That is why he had so correct an idea of the action of the press on modern society, and why he was so anxious to direct that action. The Emperor, who was all his life a journalist, was very fond of the press. As a prisoner at Ham he practised journalism in the *Progrès du Pas-de-Calais;* he did the same at the Élysée with M. de La Guéronnière; at the Tuileries with M. Duvernois and M. Vitu; from 1850 he did so everywhere with me, even at Wilhelmshöhe and at Camden Place, where, a few months before his death, he corrected the proofs of a brochure we wrote together, which was published by Amyot."

The crowned journalist rated the press above diplomacy; he preferred a good article to a good despatch. Quite naturally, his ministers regarded his passion for publicity with disfavor, and were annoyed at finding themselves often less well informed concerning their master's intentions than certain journalists. Napoleon III. sometimes governed against his own government. He had not said a single word to Count Walewski, his Minister of Foreign Affairs, concerning the brochure which he was preparing so mysteriously with the Viscount de La Guéronnière, and which was, in fact, absolutely opposed to the official policy pursued at the quai d'Orsay.

The anonymous author of the brochure, *The Emperor Napoleon III. and Italy*, was a very charming man who united real talent as a writer to exquisite manners. A legitimist by origin, he had become the favorite disciple of M. de Lamartine, on whose style he modelled his own. In 1848 he was writing in the *Pays* newspaper, which supported the illustrious poet as a candidate for the presidency. In 1851 he published a series of *Political Portraits*, among which figured those of the Count de Chambord and Louis Napoleon. This publication had a great success. The Prince-President was greatly struck by it and sought to win the author. Elected deputy from Cantal in 1852, La Guéronnière resigned his seat to enter the Council of State, and was publicly known to be the auxiliary and close confidant of the Emperor.

The brochure inspired by the sovereign was an ardent and enthusiastic defence of the Italian cause. In a style truly Lamartinian, it said: "Italy is more than a sister to other nations, she is a mother. Her genius, her power, her institutions, conquests, masterpieces, and, later, her misfortunes, her ruins, her troubles, in a word, everything in ancient as in modern times, her consuls, her tribunes, her historians, emperors, popes, and martyrs, have contributed to give her in some sort a generative character. In politics, in war, in civil and penal legislation, in the arts, in eloquence and poetry as in religion, she has been the common country of all civilized States. Hence, it may be said that her influence over the world has never ceased. After subduing she has enlightened it; when her material domination was overcome, her moral domination began. Forgetfulness on the part of Europe would be ingratitude; on that of Italy, self-abnegation. Can we demand this sacrifice from those to whom nothing remains of their past greatness but the pride of having justified it, and the hope of one day recovering some of its fragments? And if we should demand it from Italy, would she not have the right to answer us by this thought of Tacitus in the *Life of Agricola*, 'We should have lost memory as well as speech could we forget as well as keep silence.'"

In a masterly work entitled *Napoleon III., His International Design*, M. Émile Ollivier has very judiciously remarked that a wrong has been done the second Emperor in isolating him from the general ideas amidst which his mind was formed, and of which he was later a reflection; he ought to have been connected with the movement of his times rather than considered as a solitary individuality deriving from himself alone. "Take the democratic theses," adds M. Ollivier, "as Lamennais, Armand Carrel, and finally Lamartine, our thinkers and popular poets, have formulated them; blend with these certain ideas of the great poet and thinker of Saint Helena; re-read the agitating speeches made by Thiers before 1848 in favor of Italy under the sword of Charles-Albert and the pastoral staff of Pius IX., and that of Cavaignac, May 23, 1849, calling on the ministry to safeguard the independence and liberty of peoples. . . . Combine these writings, words, and actions, deduce a rule of conduct from them, and without losing yourself in conjectures, dissertations, bewilderments, you will have an accurate definition of the whole policy of Napoleon III. It may be summed up in a simple formula: that of nationalities."

On the rock of Saint Helena, Napoleon had said: "The first sovereign who, in the midst of the great affray, will in good faith embrace the cause of peoples will find himself at the head of Europe, and he may venture whatever he chooses." This thought, inscribed in the *Memoir*, was evidently the inspiration of the brochure, *The Emperor Napoleon III. and Italy*. Its fundamental idea is that peoples have the right to dispose of their destiny.

What the brochure recommended for Italy was not unity but a federal union with the Pope as president. "Instead of governing a stationary people, he extends his hand over all Italy to bless and lead it; he is the irresponsible and revered chief of a confederation of twenty-six millions of Christians who, classified in different States, tend towards one centre where the activity and greatness of Italy are recapitulated."

Under a dispassionate form and conciliatory aspects, the brochure developed ideas that were in the most startling opposition to every tradition of ancient European diplomacy. It declared that "the absolutely clerical character of the government of the

Roman States is a misconception, an active cause of discontent, and consequently an element of weakness for the Pope himself, and a permanent risk of revolution." Not contented with demanding reforms in the peninsula, it made a clean sweep of the treaties. "The treaties which unite governments," it said, "are the international laws of peoples, and could be invariable only if the world were stationary. If treaties which should protect the security of Europe endanger it, it is because they do not respond to the needs by which they were dictated. In that case political prudence counsels their substitution by something else. A power which should intrench itself behind treaties to resist modifications universally demanded by public opinion, would doubtless have written law on its side, but against it would be arrayed the moral law and the conscience of the world."

The brochure concluded as follows: "What is to be done, then? Shall appeal be made to force? May Providence shield us from such an extremity! An appeal must be made to public opinion. . . . Without doubt, God would reserve to those who should bear the brunt of the struggle a noble share of human glory. We are not tempted by that glory; we have had enough of it in days that are historic as well as in contemporary events to keep us from desiring more. Hence we ardently wish that diplomacy may do before a battle what it would do the day after a victory. Let Europe unite energetically in this cause of peace and justice! It should be with us, because we shall always be with it in defence of its honor, equilibrium, and security."

To sum up, the brochure was pacific in appearance, bellicose in reality. What it asked for, namely, the abolition of treaties and the enfranchisement of Milan and Venice, could not be obtained except by war. It recognized as much, for, after having enumerated the military forces of Austria and its formidable strategic positions in the north of Italy, it adds: "From these facts there results for every military man the incontestable truth that Italian nationality will never be the result of a revolution, and that it cannot succeed without foreign assistance." This foreign assistance was that of Napoleon III. and the French army.

For the first time, a sovereign was seen to lay his personal programme before public opinion, and transform himself, so to say, into a journalist who publishes a notable article without signing it.

CHAPTER V

THE SPEECH FROM THE THRONE

NOWADAYS it would be difficult to form a just notion of the importance of the speeches from the throne under the Second Empire. Napoleon III. drew them up himself with the greatest care; he corrected the proofs, and he delivered them in a strong and sonorous voice which made itself distinctly heard by all who were present. The Emperor had the privilege of power to raise or lower the funds in every exchange throughout the world by a single phrase, by a mere allusion. Telegraphed immediately to all civilized countries, the imperial harangues were everywhere the subject of innumerable commentaries. Each of their phrases received minute attention, and contradictory conclusions were frequently deduced from them.

Never had a throne speech been more impatiently awaited than that by which Napoleon III. was to open the session of the Senate and the Corps Législatif, February 7, 1859. The brochure of Viscount de La Guéronnière had appeared three days earlier, and all were anxious to know whether the ideas formulated in it would be reproduced, wholly or in part, by the sovereign. The public were not of one mind on the subject. Some regarded it as a serious event, others as a simple feeler whose importance they sought to diminish. In the business world, as in that of diplomacy, there was uncertainty as to the real intentions of the Emperor, and it was hoped that the speech from the throne would dispel anxieties and put an end to equivocations.

The ceremony took place in the new hall of the Louvre intended for the opening of the legislative sessions, and called the hall of the States. The throne was placed on a platform at the back of the hall. On the right of the throne was the tribune of the Empress. Half an hour before the Emperor's arrival, the great bodies of State, the deputations, and invited guests occupied the places reserved for them. On the steps of the throne, to right and left, were placed the cardinals, ministers, marshals and admirals, a deputation from the grand crosses of the Legion of Honor, and the members of the Council of State. Opposite the throne, on the right, the senators, on the left, the deputies. In the upper right-hand gallery were the members of the diplomatic body and their wives. The corresponding gallery on the left was occupied by other ladies who had been invited.

At one o'clock the Empress, preceded and followed by great officials, officials and ladies of her household, entered the hall to renewed shouts of "Long live the Empress!" Her Majesty was accompanied by the Princess Clotilde, the Princess Mathilde, the Princess-Duchess of Hamilton, the princesses Lucien, Joachim, and Anna Murat.

As soon as the Empress had taken her place in her tribune, the cannon of the Invalides announced the Emperor's departure from the Tuileries. Preceded and followed by great officers of his household, the sovereign repaired to the session through the great picture gallery of the Louvre. He took his seat on the throne, with King Jerome on his right, and Prince Napoleon on his left. Then he delivered his speech in a firm and emphatic tone. The first part of it seemed very pacific. "One has a right to be surprised," he said, "by the excitement lately produced when no imminent dangers were in sight, because it shows at once too much distrust and too much alarm. On one hand, the moderation of which I have given so many proofs seems to have been doubted; and on the other, the real power of France. Happily the mass of the people is far from experiencing such impressions." Next, the Emperor recalled the declaration of Bordeaux: "*The Empire is peace*," meaning by that, he added, "that if the heir of the Emperor Napoleon remounted the throne, he would not renew an era of conquests, but inaugurate a system of peace which could be disturbed by nothing but the defence of great national interests." This last phrase began to disseminate anxiety. Would not Napoleon III. actually regard a war for Italy as the defence of great national interests for France?

The Emperor afterwards dilated on his disagreements with Austria concerning the Danubian Principalities, and added, apropos of this, that France was interested wherever there was question of making a just and civilizing cause prevail. In fact, he talked like a sibyl. When he said: "I shall remain immovable in the path of right, of justice, and of national honor, and my government will not permit itself either to be persuaded or intimidated, because my policy will never be either provocative or pusillanimous," no one knew whether the sovereign desired peace or war.

While the Emperor was speaking, the attitude of his audience was a curious thing to see. Senators and deputies at first emphasized by their approbation all that seemed calculated to reassure and give pledges of peace; then, when the imperial language became enigmatic and obscure, they abstained from all demonstration and gave none of the customary applause until the close of the discourse, which terminated as follows: "When, sustained by popular sentiment and desire, one ascends the steps of a throne, he rises, by the gravest of responsibilities, above that meanest of regions where vulgar interests are at war, and has for his initial motives as well as for his final judges, God, his conscience, and posterity."

The discourse when read produced a more bellicose impression than when listened to. In reading between the lines, in pondering the phrases on just and civilizing causes which must be made to prevail, on the abnormal situation of Italy, on the community of interests between Piedmont and France, perspicacious minds found the preliminary tokens of an approaching war in words apparently very moderate. This was the general impression at Turin, and Victor Emmanuel, like Count Cavour, found encouragement and a promise in the imperial speech. At Vienna, on the other hand, people gave, or pretended to give, a more pacific meaning to it.

We read in the official organ, the *Correspondance Autrichienne*, February 8: "The speech delivered by the Emperor Napoleon at the opening of the legislative session, is calculated to dispel the fears of war which have lately been felt in Europe. . . . The Emperor will appeal to the military forces of the nation he governs only in defence of the great national interests of the country, and as these great interests are not menaced from any quarter, nobody dreaming of endangering the position and authority of so great an empire as France, we believe that we have every reason to share the confidence of Europe; peace will not be disturbed."

February 11, the Marquis de Banneville wrote to Count Walewski: "As the chief interest of the speech of February 7 lay in the reference it would make to the state of the relations of France with Austria, it was awaited with more impatient anxiety at Vienna than elsewhere. The sensation has been profound. The authority and prestige of the Emperor's words have never produced a more powerful impression. But, as it was easy to foresee, the first effects were contradictory, and according to his personal disposition each sought in it the confirmation of his fears or the justification of his hopes. . . . As to the government, it has not hesitated to declare that it is satisfied, having interpreted the Emperor Napoleon's speech in a conciliatory sense. This declaration has reacted successfully against the contrary impressions, and notably against those experienced at first by German diplomacy, always too much inclined to suspect France."

The *chargé d'affaires*, himself ardently desirous that peace should be maintained, added in the same despatch: "Count Buol has spoken to me about the speech with admiration, praising without reserve its elevation, cleverness, calmness, and candor. 'The Emperor Napoleon,' he said to me, 'in believing himself obliged to remind France of *his force and his moderation*, has renewed to her his promise to persevere in his *firm but conciliatory* policy. It now depends on Austria, at present prudent, moderate, conciliatory, to bind the Emperor to Europe by the same pledge.'" The Marquis de Banneville concluded thus, "I think people feel the necessity of all this here, and that they desire it."

To sum up, the Austrian government, by indicating immediately through an official journal the impression it had itself adopted, sought to banish apprehension and direct public opinion. European diplomacy, about to undertake the work of maintaining treaties and preventing war, pretended to take the pacific words of Napoleon III. seriously, and to repeat with him: " Far from us be false alarms, unjust suspicions, selfish weaknesses! Peace, we hope, will not be disturbed." The optimistic note remained dominant for some time longer. The Emperor took good care to conceal his ulterior designs, and prudently avoided any too direct thrust at public opinion which, in France as elsewhere, Piedmont excepted, was strongly opposed to war. Hence it was possible for some weeks longer to believe that ideas of peace and conciliation would finally prevail.

CHAPTER VI

THE PARTISANS OF PEACE

AT the beginning of the year 1859, I went almost every evening to imperialist salons. There was a good deal of talk about foreign politics, and the conversations were interesting. I was able to ascertain how greatly peace was desired and how adversely warlike tendencies were criticised, not merely in the ministries, the embassies, at the presidency of the Senate and that of the Corps Législatif, but even at the Tuileries. With the exception of certain military men, eager for adventures and glory, advancement and decorations, I met nobody who avowed himself in favor of a war in co-operation with Italy. When the prefects came to Paris the ministers personally advised them not to conceal from the Emperor that their constituents earnestly wished for peace. In the official world this might have been called the order of the day.

A few of the Emperor's closest intimates were the only ones who shared his longing for war, and they were extremely careful not to own it; for, if he drew the sword, Napoleon III. wished people to think his hand had been forced by Austria. His entire policy had a tendency to so conduct matters that the Emperor Francis Joseph should appear to be the aggressor. Hence he avoided all that might be regarded as a provocation, and discouraged none of those who pleaded with him the cause of peace.

Nearly all the members of the Corps Législatif said that, with the exception of a few advanced liberals and revolutionaries, their constituents protested against warlike tendencies with the utmost energy. Nothing but the universal obsequiousness prevented the Chamber from displaying its sentiments in a striking manner, and at the houses even of those who protested their devotion to the Emperor most noisily, one could already discern the germs of a secret opposition to the ideas of which the speech from the throne had been the first symptom. The deputies contrived a small manifestation, friendly enough, but significant. Called upon to appoint presidents and secretaries of boards, they did not select a single one of their colleagues who had either a military rank or a position at Court.

Count de Morny, president of the Corps Législatif, was one of the greatest advocates of peace. Nor did he conceal it in the speech he made at the opening of the session, February 8. When he said that "religion, philosophy, civilization, credit, industry, have made peace the first essential of modern societies," his words called forth unanimous applause. "The blood of peoples," he added, "is no longer shed lightly. War is the last resort of disregarded rights or offended honor. Most difficulties are smoothed away by diplomacy, or settled by friendly arbitration. Rapid international communications and publicity have created a new European power with which all governments are forced to reckon, and this power is public opinion. It may be uncertain or ignored for a moment, but in the end it ranges itself on the side of justice, right, and humanity." In speaking thus, Count de Morny expressed the sentiments of the entire Chamber.

In the business world, a similar disposition was everywhere manifested. Financiers, speculators, brokers, manufacturers, merchants, expressed the same views as the peasants, the farmers, and the city and country people. The wish for peace was universal.

The journals, even those which professed the keenest sympathy with Piedmont and the greatest admiration for Count Cavour, declared against war. M. Eugène Forcade, who edited at the time the chronicle of the fortnight in the *Revue des Deux Mondes*, wrote in it March 31: "War nowadays must seem an inevitable necessity in order to be accepted by the conscience of peoples. Nothing which the French public has been able to ascertain thus far gives this character of irresistible necessity to the war with which we are threatened. This war could only arise out of the Italian question. Possibly war may seem necessary to the Italians themselves, who are burning to free their country from all foreign domination. Personally, we feel a sincere sympathy for the Italian patriots, and we recognize their right to determine the moment when they should try to conquer their independence by a resort to arms, but on one condition, namely, that they alone shall be bound by their resolve, and that they shall recognize that Frenchmen have neither the same rights, the same duties, nor the same interests as Italians, when it is a question for them to decide whether there is any reason why they should co-operate in the independence of Italy by an immediate war."

In 1852, at the time when Count Cavour had just been appointed Prime Minister by King Victor Emmanuel, M. Thiers, then in Piedmont, wrote: "I have seen a wise country, an excellent government, and an admirable army. Piedmont, if it continues to act well, and if France does not drag it along by plunging herself into a career of *mad adventures*, will some day become the foundation on which an Italy may be constructed; but that would require many years of peace and good behavior. War would ruin it." In 1859, such was still the opinion, not merely of M. Thiers, but of almost all French diplomatists.

M. de Persigny, M. Drouyn de Lhuys, M. de Morny, were partisans, the first of the English alliance, the second of the Austrian, the third of the Russian; but on one point, namely, in their opposition to the principle of nationalities, they were all of one mind. M. de Morny thought this principle was chiefly supported by revolutionists, and he said, "Revolutionists are never very sure friends; they make use of the sympathies which they excite in order to attain their ends, but they have neither gratitude nor moderation."

Count Walewski, Minister of Foreign Affairs in 1859, belonged, like his predecessor, M. Drouyn de Lhuys, to the school of the past. Essentially a conservative, a convinced defender of the temporal power of the Pope, a personal friend of the King of Naples and the Grand Duke of Tuscany, he considered treaties as a sacred ark, and always and everywhere showed his opposition to revolution. The French diplomatists nearly all shared the opinions of their chief. They regarded an auxiliary like Garibaldi as dangerous, and, in spite of the *Memorial from Saint-Helena*, they were opposed to the system of great national agglomerations. To them, the unity of France was what constituted its strength, and it was not its interest to labor to give its neighbors a force of which it had the monopoly. They thought that France was great in proportion as its neighboring States were small, and consequently declared themselves in favor of particularism in Germany as well as in Italy. Such were notably the opinions of the Duc de Montebello, ambassador at Saint Petersburg, of the Duc de Gramont, ambassador at Rome, of the Marquis de Moustier, the Prince de La Tour d'Auvergne, the Marquis de Ferrière le Vayer, one minister of France at Berlin, the other at Turin, the third at Florence. Hence the imperial diplomacy was in absolute opposition with the Emperor's programme. He knew it very well, and far from complaining of it, far from disavowing his agents, he maintained all of them at their posts and made use of them the better to conceal his ulterior designs and mental reservations.

None the less, it was a curious spectacle to behold a sovereign conspire in his foreign policy, not merely against the Chambers, but against his ministers, diplomats, prefects, in a word, against his entire government.

Had Napoleon III. at least the moral or material support of England to sustain him in his projects in favor of the Italian cause? Not at all. We are about to prove by means of incontestable documents that, far from favoring the programme of King Victor Emmanuel and Count Cavour, Queen Victoria and the British government declared themselves most energetically for the maintenance of treaties, and, consequently, for that of the Austrian domination at Milan and Venice.

CHAPTER VII

ENGLAND AND PIEDMONT

FEBRUARY 3, 1859, Queen Victoria opened the Parliament. "I receive from all the foreign powers," said she in her speech from the throne, "assurances of good and friendly sentiments. To cultivate and consolidate these sentiments, to maintain intact the faith of public treaties, and to contribute as far as my influence may extend to the preservation of universal peace, such are the objects of my incessant solicitude." The speech was discussed the same day by both Houses. The Tories, then at the head of affairs, Lord Derby being Prime Minister and Lord Malmesbury chief of the Foreign Office, were entirely of one mind with the Whigs on the Italian question.

In the House of Lords the Prime Minister expressed himself as follows: "Actuated by the most sincere friendship for Sardinia, we have, nevertheless, been made uneasy by the attitude which for some time past she seems disposed to take. This attitude is wholly opposed to her own interests, to her duties towards European society, and to the duration of the sympathy which her previous conduct had acquired for her in the civilized world. . . . The remarks made by King Victor Emmanuel at the opening of the Chambers were very ominous; but I am sure that Sardinia will follow better counsels."

Lord Granville, the Whig leader, declared that in virtue of treaties, Austria possessed rights over her Italian provinces of which no one could despoil her by any right or under any pretext, and he added that the Italians must forget the lessons of history if they supposed Italy could be delivered by calling on one foreign nation to expel another.

Lord Brougham said that having recently arrived from France, he was able to affirm that in all ranks and classes of society public opinion was unanimously opposed to war. "Everything inclines me to believe," he added, " that France will take no share in the *Sardinian Speculation*, as it is called, and that this speculation will fail completely."

In the House of Lords all the speakers expressed themselves like those of the House of Commons, in favor of peace and absolute respect for treaties. Even Lord Palmerston, who, in 1847, had sent Lord Minto to the peninsula to encourage to the utmost the boldest aspirations of Charles-Albert, and who wrote, October 29, 1848, to the English ambassador at Vienna " that there was not the slightest chance of Austria's being able to retain upper Italy in a useful and permanent manner, since all its inhabitants were profoundly imbued with an invincible hatred against the Austrian army," now made no further objection to Austrian domination in Venetia and Lombardy. "The treaties must be respected," said he. "If the stipulations of a treaty might be set aside in the name of some theoretic preference, all the affairs of Europe might go to rack and ruin, and no one could predict the possible consequences of such a principle."

It had been announced that Lord John Russell would champion the cause of Italian nationality in Parliament. He did nothing of the sort. "I have always," said the Liberal orator, "had a profound sympathy for the independence and liberty of Italy, but I find it impossible to believe that this cause could ever be served by such a war as that with which we are menaced. . . . The treaty which gives Venetia and Lombardy to Austria is part of the public law, and nobody could dream of disturbing this territorial arrangement by force without committing an offence against Europe."

Finally, Mr. Disraeli said: "I cannot believe that a ruler so prudent as the Emperor of the French is going out of pure good-will to disturb the peace of the world and destroy forever the confidence he has so justly inspired in Europe by the thorough wisdom and moderation of his previous conduct."

The Court was not less uneasy than the ministers and the Parliament. Prince Albert, always a German at heart, shared, like his uncle the King of the Belgians, all the suspicions of Germany concerning Napoleon III., and was convinced that a war in Italy would be the prelude to a war on the Rhine. He believed that Belgium was threatened, and that the Emperor wished to restore her natural frontiers to France. In this respect, Queen Victoria shared the apprehensions of her husband. She thought it necessary to intervene personally in the question, and on February 4 she wrote a letter to Napoleon III. which was simply an ardent plea in favor of peace. "Seldom," said the Queen, "has it been given a man to exercise a personal influence so powerful as that of Your Majesty over the tranquillity and well-being of Europe." In conclusion, the Queen explicitly informed the Emperor that if he entered into a warlike career, it would be utterly impossible for England to associate itself with him in such a policy.

February 14, Napoleon III. replied at length to Her British Majesty's letter. He attempted to vindicate himself from the accusations brought against him, and maintained that he had made no preparations for war. He admitted that treaties could not be altered but by general consent, but he added this significant remark: "However, treaties could not militate against my duty, which is to pursue everywhere the policy most in harmony with the honor and interests of my country." The only result of this reply was to increase the anxieties felt by Queen Victoria, her husband, and her government. It was all over with the cordial alliance.

The cabinet of London gave a further proof of its pacific sentiments by sending Lord Cowley, English ambassador at Paris, to Vienna with an official commission to establish there, if possible, the bases of an agreement between France and Austria. This diplomat reached Vienna February 7, and was most cordially received by the Emperor Francis Joseph. He declared in favor of the evacuation of the Roman States by the Austrian troops as well as by the French, and asked for the concession of reforms in Italy, but he did not say a single word about Milan and Venice, where it seemed to him that the rights of Austria should be considered inviolable. England not merely did not encourage the designs of Victor Emmanuel, but it asked him to lay down his arms. Lord Cowley left Vienna March 10. Before going he gave an account of his mission in a despatch addressed to Lord Malmesbury, in which he expressed the hope that he had arranged a peaceful solution of the difference. It concluded thus: "As long as Piedmont is allowed to remain under arms, I doubt Austria's willingness to enter into negotiations, because she considers the Piedmontese army as the vanguard of that of France, intended to give the latter time to arm itself, and she will have no confidence in the pacific intentions of her neighbors so long as this vanguard remains. Hence, in the Austrian view, the disarmament of Piedmont is the pledge of the sincerity of France."

To sum up, the chief aim of English diplomacy was the absolute maintenance of the territorial *status quo* in Italy. If Lord Cowley had succeeded in his mission, the whole scaffolding of the plans of Victor Emmanuel and Count Cavour would have tumbled like a house of cards. In spite of his pro-English sympathies, the Piedmontese statesman was perfectly aware that he had nothing to expect from England, and that apart from the armed concurrence of France the policy of nationalities in Italy had not the slightest chance of success. The Italians should be loyal enough to recognize this at present. But for Napoleon III., Milan and Venice would still be under Austrian domination.

CHAPTER VIII

PRUSSIA AND THE GERMANIC CONFEDERATION

PIEDMONT had nothing to hope from England. As to Prussia and the Germanic Confederation, the most it could expect was that they should not take up arms against it. All the suspicion, rancor, wrath, of 1813 had just revived against imperial France. In Germany everybody was saying that all that Napoleon III. began war in Italy for was to end it on the banks of the Rhine, and that the only object of his policy was to reconquer what, in his view, constituted the natural frontiers of his empire. His efforts to dispel such alarms were multiplied in vain. He did not succeed in this, even by making himself the precursor and champion of Germanic unity.

The brochure *The Emperor Napoleon III. and Italy* contained some very curious passages. For instance: "The Germanic Confederation has not obtained a single one of the guarantees of unity and freedom of action which it sought; subjected to the influence of two great powers, it possibly has no hope but in their necessary rivalry. . . . Prussia, which tends to become the head of the Germanic body, has an immense interest in curbing Austria. In becoming her ally she would make herself an accomplice in her own abasement, and thus disavow the work of Frederic the Great. . . . The solution of the Italian question, were that possible, would be a new strength for the German nationality. . . . Germany has nothing to fear from us on the banks of the Rhine."

It was not only in the celebrated brochure, but in the *Moniteur* that the sovereign sought to reassure the Germans. The official journal thus expressed itself, March 15: " A part of Germany responds to the tranquil attitude of the French government by the most groundless alarms. On a mere presumption which nothing justifies and everything repels, prejudices rekindle, suspicions spread, passions are unleashed, a sort of crusade against France is begun in the Chambers and the press of several States of the Confederation. She is accused of entertaining ambitions she has disavowed, of making ready for conquests which she does not need, and by these calumnies it is sought to alarm Europe, concerning imaginary aggressions of which she does not even think. Men who mislead German patriotism in this fashion are behind their time. Of such as they it may well be said that they have forgotten nothing and learned nothing. They went to sleep in 1813, and they wake up after a slumber of half a century, with sentiments and passions which history has buried, and which are utterly absurd in relation to modern times; they are visionaries who are absolutely bent upon defending what no one dreams of attacking."

The article in the *Moniteur* terminated with this justification of Napoleon III.: "The Emperor, who has been able to overcome all prejudices, probably expects that they will be rekindled against him. What would have happened if, in ascending the throne, he had taken thither the narrow sentiments and revengeful feelings now attributed to him by those who seek to make him suspected? Instead of becoming the closest ally of England, and thus obeying the interests of civilization, he would have become its rival, as the ancient rivalries of the two peoples might seem to have required. Instead of welcoming men of all parties, he would have mistrusted and repelled adherents of the elder dynasties. Instead of reassuring and calming Europe, he would have disturbed it by atoning for the memories of 1814 and 1815 at the cost of its security and independence."

The *Moniteur* was preaching in the desert. The Germans would not allow themselves to be convinced. It is curious to note that in 1859 the only German who shared the views of Napoleon III. was possibly Herr Bismarck. If the celebrated Prussian statesman had been at the head of affairs, he would probably have concluded arrangements with the Emperor by which Piedmont and Prussia would have simultaneously aggrandized themselves at the expense of Austria. During a visit he made to Paris in September, 1855, at the time of the universal Exposition, he had been presented to Napoleon III. and most cordially received. In April, 1857, he was sent on a mission to Paris to assist the Prussian minister in the conferences just opened concerning the Neuchâtel affair, and it was due to the Emperor's efforts that King Frederic William IV. was enabled to settle his difference with Switzerland honorably and without resort to arms.

Napoleon III. had a special liking for Bismarck. He believed in the star of the Prussian statesman, and fancied that he might find in him an auxiliary who would aid him to destroy the treaties of 1815, to complete the enfranchisement of Italy, and to establish the principle of nationalities. On his part, Herr Bismarck, at the beginning of the Second Empire, professed a great admiration for Napoleon III. In a memoir intended for Frederic William IV., and dated June 2, 1857, he undertook to combat one by one the prejudices entertained by that prince against a close union with imperial France. He said in it: "The Napoleonic dynasty is reproached with its illegitimate origin; but the majority of thrones are not more legitimate: a fact which does not prevent the Court of Prussia from contracting political or family alliances with these dynasties. . . . Louis Napoleon did not arrive at the throne by means of an insurrection against the established authorities, and should he resign his power to-day, he would probably embarrass Europe, which would entreat him to retain it. And since Prussia has recognized the Emperor Napoleon, how could it be contrary to its honor to contract engagements with him which would command events?"

In 1859, Herr Bismarck, who then bore the title of Count, was at Frankfort, where he had represented Prussia since 1854 as its minister to the Germanic Confederation. There he opposed the influence of Austria, the rival power, with all the vehemence and obstinacy of his character. Had his government listened to him then, we believe that Prussia would not have hesitated to overthrow the old federal edifice, and to conclude an alliance of ambition with Napoleon III.

Since October 9, 1858, King Frederic William IV., on account of the poor condition of his health, had confided the regency to his brother, the future Emperor of Germany. The Prince Regent cherished very vast designs but did not as yet avow them, and none but his intimate friends knew how he brooded over the dream of expelling the Hapsburgs from Germany in order to install the Hohenzollerns in their place. But this audacious policy was still in a state of latency, and at that time the Prince did not think of embroiling himself with Austria, still less of contracting an alliance with Piedmont. He considered that Count Bismarck was going too fast, and changed his post from Frankfort to Saint Petersburg, February 29, 1859. The Prussian diplomat had desired to continue his opposition to Austria in the German Diet. He left Frankfort with regret, and not without criticising adversely the hostility displayed by the Confederation to the policy of Victor Emmanuel and Napoleon III.

February 5, Count Buol, Austrian Minister of Foreign Affairs, had addressed a circular to the Austrian agents accredited to German Courts, in which he expressed the satisfaction experienced by the cabinet of Vienna in consequence of the friendly manifestations which its cause had excited in Germany. It was especially in the south, at Munich, Stuttgart, Darmstadt, and Carlsruhe, that the Austrian Court had been encouraged to resort to violent measures against Piedmont.

The Emperor Francis Joseph sent as his envoy to the Prince Regent of Prussia the Archduke Albert, son of the Archduke Charles, the celebrated rival of Napoleon. The Archduke Albert arrived at Berlin April 14, and announced that at the earliest possible moment Austria would send an ultimatum to the Court of Turin, the rejection of which would at once entail the occupation of Piedmontese territory by the imperial troops. Austria was then under very grave illusions. Considering the war of Italy a secondary matter, she was chiefly occupied with the war on the Rhine which seemed to her inevitable, and the brunt of which she proposed to bear with two hundred and sixty thousand men. This army would have been placed under the command of the Archduke Albert, simultaneously invested with the command of several federal corps in the south.

In face of the possible complications which might be entailed by the outbreak of war, M. d'Usedon, who had succeeded Count Bismarck as Prussian minister at Frankfort, laid the following motion, April 23, before the Diet: "The Diet resolves that it will invite the Confederated States to put their principal contingents in *marching order;* it enjoins the necessary measures for the arming of the federal fortresses." In support of this motion the cabinet of Berlin declared to its confederates that it believed it urgent to give Germany a defensive organization in harmony with the military dispositions taken by neighboring States.

The Austrian government rejoiced in all these demonstrations. Count Buol said to Lord Loftus, English ambassador at Vienna: "If the Emperor wanted to feel the pulse of the German nation, it has given him a salutary warning."

So then, in order to defend the Italian cause, Napoleon had not merely to fight with Austria. He ran the risk of finding all Germany combined against him, without having the least assurance that it would be restrained by Russia. Seldom has any sovereign incurred risks so great and embarked in so dangerous an enterprise.

CHAPTER IX

RUSSIA

THE war of Italy was possible only because the relations of Napoleon III. with Alexander were very cordial in 1859. Had they been as cold at that period as they were in 1870, France would not have dared to incur the risk of meeting the ill-will of Russia as well as the declared hostility of Austria and all Germany.

At the beginning of 1859, the two sovereigns mutually displayed a very lively sympathy. The Marquis de Chateaurenard, *chargé d'affaires* of France at Saint Petersburg in the absence of the ambassador, the Duc de Montebello, wrote to Count Walewski, January 13: —

"The Emperor held a diplomatic reunion on the occasion of the new year. His Majesty honored me with a particularly cordial reception, and said to me: 'Each day brings me additional proof of the confidence which presides over the relations between the Emperor Napoleon's government and mine, and of the friendly sentiments which animate France in reference to Russia. There is more than confidence between the two Courts, there is the most intimate cordiality, and I am very glad of it. I wish the Emperor Napoleon to know that he may count on me as I do upon him. Be so kind as to convey to him this assurance.' I cannot too greatly insist, *Monsieur le Comte*, on the accent of profound conviction with which the language of His Majesty was impressed. The bystanders could not hear the words addressed to me, but they all noticed the air of satisfaction and sympathy with which the Emperor approached the *chargé d'affaires* of France."

In the mind of Napoleon III. the chief object of the Stuttgart interview had been to insure the moral support of Russia, if not its armed assistance, in the event of a war against Austria. Had Alexander II. condemned this war, it is indisputable that the different German States would have risen as one man to prevent it, and that Sardinia, with all the great powers against her except France, would have found it very difficult to continue the policy of defiance against her redoubtable neighbor. But the attitude of the cabinet of Saint Petersburg allayed the Germanic effervescence and permitted Napoleon III. to carry out his plans.

The Marquis de Chateaurenard wrote to Count Walewski, January 24: " Prince Gortchakoff told Sir John Crampton, the English minister, that Russia doubtless desired the maintenance of peace as much as any other power, but that she would not interfere in the course of events which may occur, even if they were such as might lead to war. She would confine herself to a policy of expectancy which, she believed, became her better than any other for the present. These words seem to me to express with fidelity the mind of the Russian government. The resentment inspired by the conduct of Austria during the Crimean War is as acute as ever it was, although it no longer translates itself on every occasion by the most violent language; it suffices to explain that the cabinet of Saint Petersburg, agreeing herein with the unanimous sentiments of the army and the country, is unwilling to lend its good offices to assist in defending a situation which the press signalizes as likely to create serious dangers for a power which is regarded here as guilty of treason and ingratitude towards Russia."

Alexander II. had not consented to peace with the Western powers until after the Austrian ultimatum, and he was convinced that it was the Emperor Francis Joseph — saved in 1849 by the Emperor Nicholas, at the time of the Hungarian insurrection — who had prevented the testament of Peter the Great from being carried out. Let us add that since the treaty of Paris Russian policy and Austrian policy had been continually at war in the Balkan peninsula. That is why the Czar wanted to give a lesson to Austria, and why the embarrassment into which that power might be plunged gave such lively satisfaction to all classes of Russian society. The war of Italy was, in fact, a consequence of the Crimean War. Without being obliged to draw the sword, Russia was about to take her revenge on Austria.

Sir John Crampton, the English minister, solicited peace in vain, Prince Gortchakoff greeting each new representation with mingled pride and bitterness. True, he would express some faint desire for peace, but he always took care to add: "As to weighing France and Austria in the same scales, we will not do it. Our relations with France are cordial, with Austria they are not so, nor are they tending to grow better. Russia was formerly in the habit of offering her friendly advice to the European cabinets. In following that policy she has been the dupe of her own disinterestedness. At present we have no advice to give. Our solicitude is directed just now to our internal improvements to the exclusion of everything else, and that anxiety is great enough to absorb our attention. However, it does not do so to such an extent that we are willing to promise neutrality. We do not say we will keep out of the fight. We reserve our liberty of action in the future as well as in the present." (Despatch of Sir John Crampton to Lord Malmesbury, January 26, 1859.)

M. de La Gorce was right in saying: "The Czar's complaisance was the source from which Napoleon III. obtained the boldness to dare everything." The support given by Russia to France was, however, very limited. It was Platonic in its character, for the government of the Czar confined itself to advising Germany to be prudent, and had not the least intention of making war against her in case this

MARSHAL MAC MAHON

advice were not accepted. In a despatch addressed to Count Walewski, February 4, the Marquis de Chateaurenard expressed himself as follows: " Prince Gortchakoff has told me that in speaking with the minister of Prussia he had especially insisted on the point that the cabinet of Berlin would efficaciously contribute to the peaceful solution of the existing situation by firmly declaring its intention to abstain from taking part in a dispute which had no direct bearing on the interests of Prussia. 'By so doing,' said the Prince, 'I thought I could comply with the request of the Emperor Napoleon's government that I should assist him in enlightening public opinion in Germany on the principles by which his policy is directed; you may assure Count Walewski that I will do what lies in my power to meet his wishes on this subject.'"

On the other hand, in spite of his ill-will towards Austria, Alexander II. had no desire whatever for the unification of Italy under the sceptre of Victor Emmanuel, although such a combination entailed no danger to an empire so vast and so remote as that of the Czars. But the essentially conservative ideas of the Russian government, its respect for the treaties of 1815, its dread of the triumph in Italy of revolutionary principles which might have their rebound in Poland, rendered it naturally hostile to the intrigues of the Mazzinians and of Garibaldi. Let us add that Alexander II., like his father, always showed an especial sympathy for the King of Naples who had resisted the revolution so energetically, and whose reactionary system pleased the cabinet of Saint Petersburg. But in 1859 the government of the Czar fancied that territorial changes would be confined to the north of Italy, and that in any case the Kingdom of the Two Sicilies could not incur any danger.

The ideas of Russia were in flat contradiction with those of the partisans of Italian unity, and, to recapitulate, all that was needful to make the war of Italy materially impossible would have been for Alexander II. privately to encourage Prussia to defend Austria. We shall see later on that the cabinets of Berlin and Saint Petersburg remained on good terms with each other, and that at the time when the German Confederation seemed determined to march to the assistance of Austria, after the battle of Solferino, Alexander II. did not disguise from Napoleon III. that he would not take up arms to support him.

Nor should it be forgotten that before the war the power that proposed a conference in the hope of arriving at a peaceful solution, was Russia. For the present we will not consider further the efforts she made in this direction, but turn our attention to the situation in Paris during the three months that elapsed before the breaking out of hostilities.

CHAPTER X

THE CARNIVAL

IT was not politics but pleasure that was the great affair in Paris during the carnival of 1859. Never were salons more brilliant nor entertainments more numerous and splendid. The chronicler of the *Illustration* wrote on February 12: "God be praised! A beam from on high has dispelled the last clouds which weighed upon the situation. *It seemed like a north wind, but now it is only a zephyr*. The carnival which is beginning already seems like one that is ending. It is a week full of bustle, lights, and enchantments; nobody walks nowadays except in cadence between flowery thickets and diamond necklaces." On the 19th, M. Busoni added: "So then, in spite of the alarmists, there will be a real carnival in Paris. People are abandoning the war, or rather the phantasmagoria of one, to the conjectures of the idle and to some belated journalists. . . . The situation of Italy, the obduracy of Austria in its regard, the great powers in alarm and even in arms, must all be provisionally forgotten. Here are memorable fêtes and dazzling spectacles. Beauty keeps vigil six nights in the week and does not sleep on Sundays."

The official world, the aristocratic society of the faubourg Saint-Germain, and the moneyed society of the Chaussée-d'Antin vie with each other in luxury and elegance. Soirées and balls go on with untiring emulation. Fashionable men and women seem to have the gift of ubiquity. Some of them make their appearance at the theatre and at three or four salons during the same evening.

Everybody is tranquil. Pius IX. is under a benevolent illusion, and fancies that his temporal power may be preserved without recourse to either French or Austrian troops. The Duc de Gramont, ambassador of France at Rome, writes to Count Walewski, February 12: "That passage of the Emperor's speech which relates to Italy has given rise on the part of Cardinal Antonelli, and even of His Holiness, to certain observations which display greater clearness and precision than I have met before in the language of the Secretary of State. The Pope, says His Eminence, had regretted to see His Majesty declare that order could not be maintained in the Roman States except by foreign troops, and that his government, by that very fact, constituted a permanent source of anxiety for diplomacy. . . . The Pope has, at present, sixteen thousand six hundred men under his standards, and within a few weeks the figures will be seventeen thousand, a number deemed sufficient for internal service and the security of the Pontifical States. . . . So far as the Pope is concerned, he is quite willing to allay the uneasiness for which he is held responsible, and if, as is said, the occupation of his States by foreign troops is an obstacle to the repose of Italy and the peace of the world, he is ready to come to an arrangement with France and Austria for their simultaneous evacuation of his territory."

February 22, the Duc de Gramont sent the following telegraphic despatch to Count Walewski: "Cardinal Antonelli, by order of His Holiness, has to-day made a demand of the ambassadors of France and Austria for the evacuation of the Pontifical States by the armies of occupation within a very near fixed time. The Pope having been apprised by General de Goyon of the speedy arrival of nine hundred and seventy soldiers, has requested me to ask by telegraph that they shall not be sent."

The Holy Father had reckoned without the machinations and the incessant propaganda of the Sardinian government. In a memorandum addressed to England, March 1, M. Cavour recapitulates the grievances of the Italian peoples and the remedies which he considers necessary. In his view, these remedies are an autonomous government for Lombardy, Venetia, and the Pontifical provinces east of the Apennines; a large régime of administrative reforms throughout central Italy; and finally the cancelling of the military conventions of Austria with the Grand Duchy of Tuscany, and the duchies of Parma and Modena. Evidently Count Cavour had enlarged his programme so as to shut the door against every policy of conciliation. From one end of the kingdom to the other the journals spoke of war as if it had already been declared. A law was passed to increase the regimental staffs of the national guard. Committees were formed for recruiting and arming volunteers. Napoleon III. was still unwilling that people should be alarmed. He thought the time had come to reassure the public.

The *Moniteur* of March 5 published a long note, in which it said: "The Emperor has nothing to conceal or disavow, either in his preoccupations or his alliances. French interests predominate in his policy and they justify his vigilance. In face of the anxieties, ill founded as we like to believe, by which people have been disturbed in Piedmont, the Emperor has promised the King of Sardinia to defend him against any aggressive act on the part of Austria; he has promised nothing more, and people know that he will keep his word. Is there any hint of war in that? Since when has it become contrary to prudence to foresee more or less proximate difficulties and to calculate all their consequences? We have just pointed out what there is of reality in the thoughts, duties, and disposition of the Emperor; all that has been added to this by the exaggerations of the press is pure imagination, falsehood, and frenzy. They say that France has made considerable preparations for war. That is a purely gratuitous accusation. . . . Is it not time to inquire when an end will be put to these vague and absurd rumors, spread from one end of Europe to the other by the press, and everywhere pointing out the Emperor of the French to public credulity as inciting to war, and throwing upon him the sole responsibility for the disquietudes and the warlike preparations of Europe? Who has the right to mislead public opinion so outrageously, to alarm vested interests so gratuitously?"

The conclusion of the *Moniteur's* note reads thus: "To study questions is not to create them; nor will turning attention from them be to summarize or settle them. For that matter, the examination of these questions has passed into the region of diplomacy, and no one is authorized to believe that the result will be unfavorable to the consolidation of the public peace."

The note of March 5 reassured the alarmists. At the Bourse stocks rose in a way to which people were no longer accustomed.

March 7, the Emperor transmits a decree by which Prince Napoleon is relieved of his ministerial functions. The Prince turns over to M. Rouher his portfolio of the ministry of Algeria and the Colonies. The advocates of peace consider this demission as a disgrace and rejoice over it, for by his marriage as well as by his personal sentiments the Prince passes as the chief supporter of the Italian cause near the Emperor.

The carnival is about to close in the most brilliant fashion. All Paris seems to be exclaiming: "Time enough to-morrow for serious matters! All parties and all classes amuse themselves." Listen once more to the chronicler whom we have already cited: "The violins make more noise than politics; it is only fair to say so, and the programme of Strauss or of Pilado is more successful than that of diplomacy. The carnival scatters fire and flames: balls, banquets, masquerades, — one escapes from one enchantment only to fall into a hundred others. . . . This carnival has miraculous effects; it throws politics into oblivion and imposes silence upon it, however little part it seeks to take in conversation. Shall we have war? The care of replying to this question is left to the grave newsmongers who are reduced to putting it for their own pleasure."

The tremblers, the mar-sports, meet a poor reception. If war must come, let it come! No Frenchman will be afraid of it. But let the orchestras keep up their joyous noise while we are waiting for that of bombs and cannon balls. Perhaps people are dancing over a volcano! What of it? provided they keep on dancing. Private persons, ministers, the Emperor himself, rush into the fashionable whirl. The balls given by the Baroness de Pontalba, the Duchess d'Istria, the Marchiones de Pommereu, the Duchess de Riario-Sforza, sister of M. Berryer, the Countess Duchâtel, the Countess Lehon, the Duchess d'Uzès, are superb. But nothing can equal the grand official fêtes. The government says the last word in matters of luxury, splendor, and magnificence. The ministries are palaces. The Tuileries appears in the glow of an apotheosis.

Napoleon loves pomp and considers it necessary to the prestige of a sovereign. He is unwilling that any court in Europe should be more brilliant than his own.

CHAPTER XI

LENT

PARIS is quite as lively in Lent as during the carnival. Political preoccupations do not interfere with the theatres nor with mundane vanities. There is no dancing in official circles, but there are balls in many salons. The aristocratic routs of the faubourg Saint-Germain are numerous and brilliant. At the Tuileries there are receptions and concerts. Diplomatic affairs, warmly discussed on 'Change, create movements in stocks which excite the gamblers. Large sums are gained and lost, but the market is full of animation. Well-to-do persons who are not fond of war resign their places to others, and people say that should war break out it would not interfere with civil careers. The number of riders, men and women, and of elegant carriages that go round the lake at the Bois de Boulogne daily is not diminished. The toilettes are as costly, the equipages as fine, the theatres as well filled, and the evening parties as frequented. Paris has not lost a jot of its brilliance and gaiety.

Count Walewski at the Ministry of Foreign Affairs, and Count de Morny at the Presidency of the Corps

Législatif, resume their Wednesday evening receptions on March 16. These are very elegant reunions where certain Legitimists and Orleanists, personal friends of the two statesmen, both very much in vogue, occasionally show themselves. During his embassy in Russia Count de Morny had noticed among the demoiselles of honor of the Empress, Mlle. Sophie, Princess Troubetzkoy, a descendant of one of the companions of Rurik. He fell in love with and married her, and on her arrival in Paris she excited universal attention. Fair, with dark eyes, slender and distinguished in appearance, the Countess de Morny had delicate features and a sculpturesque head. The splendid salons of the Presidency were a frame worthy of her. Those of the mansion on quai d'Orsay — a real palace — were not less magnificent. Count Walewski, a typical great noble, and the Countess Walewska received with exquisite courtesy. Every member of the foreign diplomatic corps was present at all the soirées at the Ministry of Foreign Affairs.

March 17. — The Piedmontese government, which, on March 9, had recalled to active service all soldiers dismissed or maintained in their homes from the class of 1832 to that of 1828, publishes a decree authorizing the creation of free companies.

March 20. — The Emperor reviews the imperial guard on the Champ-de-Mars. The advocates of peace had feared that the ceremony might give rise to warlike demonstrations. Nothing of the kind occurs. Napoleon III. is received by the troops with applause, but the cry of "Long live Italy!" is not raised by either the army or the people. The principal object of this military fête seems to have been the presentation of the Prince Imperial to the troops, his name appearing on the muster-rolls of the 1st grenadiers of the guards. The child, who is in an open carriage with the Empress, wears the regimental uniform. The Emperor, leaving the place he had occupied during the march past, and going towards the Jena bridge, orders the sentries to let the crowd come nearer. He is immediately surrounded by an immense multitude, who fling themselves almost under the feet of the horses while shouting "Long live the Emperor!" There is a moment of great excitement in the cortege, but no accident happens. The review is favored with splendid weather.

March 22. — The following note, which produces a great effect, is published in the *Moniteur:* "Russia has proposed a congress with a view of preventing complications which might arise from the condition of Italy, and which would be likely to disturb the peace of Europe. This congress, composed of plenipotentiaries from France, Austria, England, Prussia, and Russia, would assemble in a neutral city. The government of the Emperor has signified its adhesion to the proposition of the cabinet of Saint Petersburg. The cabinets of London, Vienna, and Berlin have not yet replied officially."

March 24. — The *Moniteur* announces the adhesion

of the cabinets of London and Berlin to the proposal of a congress.

March 25.— The *Moniteur* says: "The cabinet of Vienna has adhered to Russia's proposal concerning a congress. Count Cavour has left Turin for Paris at the invitation of the Emperor."

The first item of news has a reassuring tendency, but the second is disquieting. The public at large likes to believe in the efficacy of a congress as a peaceful remedy. Men who know more about diplomatic matters see nothing in it but a preliminary to war. It is at this moment that M. Thiers writes in a private letter: "The Emperor has a fixed idea: to bring about war while talking of peace."

What are the two associates of Plombières, Napoleon III. and M. de Cavour, going to say to each other? Everybody is anxiously pondering this question.

March 26.— The Piedmontese statesman arrives at Paris. He goes to the Hôtel de Londres, rue Castiglione, No. 5, and during the day has an interview with the Emperor, not a word of which reaches the public.

For the next two days he is not received by the sovereign, who is either indisposed or pretending to be so. To the anxious questions asked by financiers the Piedmontese minister contents himself by replying: "There are chances for peace and there are chances for war." As Baron James Rothschild insists, Cavour smilingly replies: "Hold on, I will make you a proposition: let us buy together; bull the market; I will hand in my resignation; there will be a rise of three francs." "You are too modest, Count," replies the banker; "you would fetch at least six francs."

March 29. — Count Cavour has a final interview with the Emperor in presence of Count Walewski. In spite of the strong representations of the latter, he declares that Piedmont will not disarm, and he leaves the Tuileries dissatisfied with the Minister of Foreign Affairs if not with the sovereign. That evening he writes to General de La Marmora: " The Italian question has been broached as awkwardly as possible, but war is inevitable; it will be delayed for two months at least; it will be fought on the Po and on the Rhine."

March 30. — Just before leaving Paris, Cavour writes a letter to Napoleon III., in which he reminds the sovereign of his former sympathy, his encouragements and promises, and entreats him to turn a deaf ear to the advice of Count Walewski, and oppose a retrograde policy which would transform Italy into a deadly enemy of France, and force Victor Emmanuel to abdicate.

April 1. — Count Cavour returns to Turin, where he is met at the railway station by a large group of friends who make him a clamorous ovation. On the same day, at Paris, the great Italian tragedienne, Mme. Ristori, appears in Paris in *Fedra*, a translation of the *Phèdre* of Racine.

April 3.— The Emperor reviews the troops of the army of Paris, and of the 1st military division on the Champ-de-Mars. The Empress, attended on either side by the Princess Mathilde and the Princess Clotilde, and holding the Prince Imperial in front of her, witnesses the review from the balcony of the Military School.

April 10.— The *Moniteur* publishes an article which is a vindication of the imperial policy: "One does not fear the light when one seeks nothing but justice," says the official journal. "The French government has nothing to conceal, because it is sure of having nothing to disavow. Far from authorizing the suspicions of the Germanic spirit, the attitude it has taken on the Italian question should inspire it with the greatest security. France could not attack in Germany what she wishes to protect in Italy. Her policy, disowning all ambition to make conquests, pursues nothing but the satisfactions and guarantees demanded by international law, the welfare of nations, and the interest of Europe. . . . To represent France as hostile to the German nationality is not, therefore, an error, but a misapprehension. The example of a national Germany which should reconcile its federative organization with the unitary tendencies the principle of which has already been laid down in the great commercial union of the *Zollverein* would not alarm us. All that develops in neighboring countries the relations created by commerce, industry, and progress is profitable to civilization, and all that increases civilization elevates France."

Such was the doctrine of which Napoleon III. was to be the apostle and the martyr. Alas! what a cruel awakening from this lofty dream of nationalities was reserved for the generous and unfortunate sovereign! Was not the Germanic unity to which he looked forward so complacently to be the cause of his final disasters and the ruin of his dynasty?

Lent closed amidst complicated and barren negotiations, characterized by incessant fluctuations, to which even the powers engaged in the discussion attached slight importance. The congress was only a sort of diplomatic phantasmagoria which took seriously neither Napoleon III. nor Victor Emmanuel, both of whom desired war, nor Francis Joseph, resolved on yielding nothing to his enemies. Agreement was impossible. Austria demanded the disarmament of Sardinia, and Sardinia refused to disarm. If a congress was to be held, Sardinia was bound to take her place in it at any cost, and Austria would not allow her plenipotentiaries to sit beside Sardinian plenipotentiaries. It was the intention of Napoleon III. and Victor Emmanuel to wrest Milan and Venice from Austrian domination. That of Francis Joseph was to maintain that domination against all attacks. It was plain to all perspicacious minds that such questions could be settled only by the sword.

CHAPTER XII

HOLY WEEK

WHEN Holy Week began people were still hoping for peace. The churches were filled on Palm Sunday, April 17. Those whose ideas were bellicose could meditate on these words of Christ in the Gospel of the Passion: "He that taketh the sword shall perish by the sword."

During the day there was a religious concert at the Conservatory which the Empress had resolved to attend. They executed the *Stabat Mater* of Rossini, who sat in Auber's box. After the *Inflammatus*, sung by Mme. Gueymard-Lauters, all the spectators turned towards the author of *William Tell*, and saluted him with long and loud applause. The master, affected even to tears, rose to thank the audience, who likewise rose. Men clapped their hands, women waved their handkerchiefs, the musicians struck their instruments with their bows. The enthusiasm of the Empress was marked and undisguised.

Monday, April 18.—It seemed possible to arrive at a peaceful solution. Count Walewski despatched the following telegram to Marshal Pélissier, ambassador of France, at London: "Kindly inform Lord

Malmesbury without delay that if England promises to insist with us on the admission of the Italian plenipotentiaries to the congress, I will immediately pledge Piedmont, by telegraph, to adhere to the principle of disarmament, the execution of which will be regulated, if there is time for it, even before the assembly of the congress. If you answer *yes*, my telegram will be sent at once."

The English government instantly gave an affirmative response. The telegram imperatively advising disarmament leaves Paris for Turin. It is communicated to Count Cavour in the night of April 18-19.

Tuesday, April 19. — M. de Cavour despairingly submits. The acceptance of the Sardinian government is immediately notified to Paris and London. But the Piedmontese statesman does not abandon a vague hope that some unexpected circumstance may extricate him from the promise he has unwillingly made.

He is not mistaken. That very day the Austrian Court adopts *ab irato* a resolution which is the most serious of faults. It sends two officers to Paris with an ultimatum against which the great powers protest.

Nothing of the sort is as yet suspected at Paris. In the morning, the *Moniteur* had published a note on the diplomatic negotiations which concluded thus: " Everything seems to authorize the belief that if all the difficulties have not yet been smoothed away, a definitive understanding will soon be arrived at, and that there will be no further opposition to the assembling of the congress."

During the night of April 20-21, it is learned at the Tuileries that Austria has determined to send to Turin the ultimatum which will make war inevitable.

Holy Thursday, April 21.— In the morning people read in the *Moniteur* a note which is considered pacific. It is worded as follows: "The government of Her Britannic Majesty has made the subjoined propositions to the four powers: (1) That a general and simultaneous disarmament shall first be effected; (2) that this disarmament shall be regulated by a military or civil commission independent of the congress; this commission to be composed of six commissioners, one from each of the five powers, and the sixth from Sardinia; (3) that as soon as this commission shall have assembled and begun its task, the congress shall assemble in its turn and proceed to the discussion of the political questions; (4) that the representatives of the Italian States shall be invited by the congress, as soon as it assembles, to sit with the representatives of the five great powers, absolutely in the same manner as at the congress of Laybach in 1821. France, Russia, and Prussia have adhered to the propositions of the government of H. M. Britannic."

Thus, at the very moment when all the chanceries knew the storm was about to break, Paris still deluded itself for a few moments with hopes of peace.

The Empress knew the truth. She got into a hack and went incognito to pray in five churches. She was recognized under her veil. At Saint-Roch she got entangled in a heavy drapery of black cloth from which a stranger politely assisted to extricate her.

In the evening, Rossini's *Stabat* was sung in the chapel of the Tuileries. Afterwards there was a reception in the salons of the Empress. The news of the Austrian ultimatum had been confirmed. The Countess Stéphanie Tascher de La Pagerie, who was present, thus describes it: "It meant war," she says. "Everybody got that impression. . . . I read it in the thoughtful countenances of the ministers grouping together to discuss it; I saw it in the confident glances of the officers present, who carried their heads high; I divined it still more in the anxious faces of their wives, who wept in spite of themselves, and who hid themselves to weep. . . . I sought at the same time to read in the eyes of the Emperor what he experienced in presence of so serious an event, and I wondered whether, at such a moment, he would not depart from his habitual and impenetrable calmness. I admit that no alteration in his impassible countenance was visible. At most he seemed somewhat preoccupied, but content, and he chatted with his ministers and showed them the latest despatches which he had just received."

Good Friday, April 22. — The *Moniteur* published the following note: "Austria has not given her adhesion to the proposition made by England, and accepted by France, Russia, and Prussia. Moreover, it would appear that the cabinet of Vienna has resolved to address a direct communication to the cabinet of Turin to obtain the disarmament of Sardinia. In presence of these facts, the Emperor has ordered the concentration of several divisions on the frontier of Piedmont."

Holy Saturday, April 23. — In the afternoon, the two Austrian officers bearing the Austrian ultimatum, Baron von Kellersberg and Count Ceschi de Santa-Croce, arrived at Turin. At that hour the proposed law which in the event of war remitted to the King, during the continuance of hostilities, the plenitude of civil and military powers, was under discussion in the Chamber of Deputies. The law being passed, Count Cavour left the Chamber. "It is," said he, "the last session of the Piedmontese parliament which has just ended; next year we will open the first Italian parliament." He had no sooner returned home than he was apprised of the presence of the two Austrian messengers. He took from their hands the ultimatum of Count Buol, which concluded thus: "I have the honor to beg Your Excellency to tell me, *yes* or *no*, whether the royal government consents to put its army on a peace footing without delay, and to disband the Italian volunteers. The bearer of this, to whom you will, M. le Comte, kindly remit your reply, has orders to hold himself at your disposition for that purpose during three days. If, at the expiration of this term, he receives no reply, or should that reply be not entirely satisfactory, the responsibility for the serious consequences which this refusal will entail, will rest exclusively upon the government of His Sardinian Majesty. After having exhausted in vain all conciliatory means of procuring for his peoples the guaranties of peace on which the Emperor has a right to insist, His Majesty, to his very great regret, will be obliged to resort to arms to obtain them."

Count Cavour, after reading this ultimatum slowly, dismissed the messengers politely, and took good care not to notify them at once of the refusal of his government. He needed every moment of delay, as much for completing his military preparations as in order to leave time for the arrival of the French army.

The same day, in Paris, people read in the *Moniteur:* "The Austrian government has thought itself obliged to address a direct communication to the Sardinian government for the purpose of requesting it to place its army on a peace footing and to disband its volunteers. This communication was to be transmitted to Turin by an aide-de-camp of General Giulay, commander-in-chief of the Austrian army in Lombardy. This officer was to be charged to declare that he would await a reply for three days, and that any dilatory reply would be considered a refusal. England and Russia have not hesitated to protest against the conduct of Austria in this circumstance."

The same issue of the *Moniteur* announced that the great military commands had been distributed in the following manner, — Army of Paris, Marshal Magnan; army of Lyons, Marshal Count de Castellane; army of observation at Nancy, Marshal Pélissier, Duc de Malakoff; 1st corps, army of the Alps, Marshal Count Baraguey d'Hilliers; 2d corps, General Count de MacMahon; 3d corps, Marshal Canrobert; 4th corps, General Niel. Prince Napoleon was to have the command of a separate corps. Marshal Randon was appointed general of the army of the Alps.

In the course of the same day there reached the Tuileries an official request from the Sardinian government for the support, already assured, of France. In the evening, M. Berlioz gave a concert at the *Opéra Comique*. Fragments from his fine work, the *Damnation of Faust*, were successfully executed. The audience was scanty. As the musical chronicler of the *Illustration* said: "Political events begin to give the public terrible distractions; flutes, hautboys, sopranos, and tenors, who can listen to you when the voice of cannon serves as your accompaniment?"

Holy Week, which had opened with hopes of peace, was closing amidst warlike preoccupations. The precepts of the Gospel had not been attended to. Three Catholic nations were about to cut each other's throats in spite of the great saying: Glory to God in the highest, and on earth peace to men of good will!

CHAPTER XIII

EASTER WEEK

EASTER SUNDAY, April 24.—The day of the greatest of religious joys is, this time, profoundly troubled. The churches are more crowded than ever with the faithful. But the *alleluia* does not ring out with its habitual gladness. "The disciples being assembled, Jesus appeared in the midst of them, and said: Peace be with you!" This saying does not apply to France. France is not in peace. At the very hour when the divine office is celebrated, soldiers are making their preparations to depart with feverish activity. Crowds swarm towards the barracks and the quarters. They hear the trumpets and the rolling of the drums. Here come regiments in campaign uniform on their way to the Lyons station, followed by an enthusiastic populace, and who take route for Italy.

Monday, April 25.—The entire garrison of Paris has departed. Only the imperial guard remains, and that, too, is preparing to start. Garrison duty, and that of the staff, is performed by the Paris guard, and there is such a shortage of men that at the Bourse cavalrymen have to take the duty of foot-soldiers.

Tuesday, April 26. — The grenadiers of the imperial guard, before beginning their campaign, go to receive their flag at the Tuileries. The Empress and the Prince Imperial come down to the court, and the sovereign embraces the flag with emotion. It is on this day that the delay accorded to Piedmont by the Austrian ultimatum expires. This ultimatum had assumed the form of a despatch addressed by Count Buol to Count Cavour, and delivered to the latter by Baron Kellersberg, April 23, at half-past five in the afternoon. The reply is contained in a despatch addressed, on the 26th, by Count Cavour to Count Buol. It ran as follows: "Your Excellency has requested me to reply by a *yes* or a *no* to the invitation given us to reduce the army to a peace footing and disband the Italian volunteers, adding that if, at the end of three days, Your Excellency receives no response, or if the response is not completely satisfactory, His Majesty the Emperor of Austria has decided to have recourse to arms to impose on us by force the measures indicated by his communication.

"The question of the disarmament of Sardinia has been the object of numerous negotiations between the great powers and the government of His Majesty. These negotiations have resulted in a proposition formulated by England, to which France, Prussia, and Russia have adhered. Sardinia, in a spirit of conciliation, has accepted it without reserve. . . .

"The conduct of Sardinia in this circumstance has been appreciated by Europe. Whatever consequences it may entail, the King, my august master, is convinced that the responsibility will rest upon those who first resorted to arms, who have rejected the propositions formulated by one great power and recognized by the others as just and reasonable, and who now substitute in place of it a menacing summons."

It is half-past five in the evening. Baron Kellersberg is introduced into the apartments of Count Cavour, who hands him the despatch, expresses a hope of seeing him in happier days, and sends him away with Colonel Govone, who is to accompany him to the frontier. The familiars of the Piedmontese minister are waiting in the anteroom of his cabinet; he comes out to them and exclaims: "The die is cast. *Alea jacta est.*"

On that same day, April 26, a summary of the situation, drawn up by Count Walewski in accordance with the Emperor's orders, is read at Paris to the Senate and the Corps Législatif. This document represents the action of the imperial diplomacy as having been invariably correct, moderate, conciliatory. It says among other things: "If the reiterated efforts of the four powers to preserve peace have encountered obstacles, these obstacles did not proceed from France. If war must be the result of existing complications, the government of His Majesty will be profoundly convinced that it has done all in its power to avert this extremity. If in presence of this state of things Sardinia is menaced, if, as everything gives occasion to presume, its territory is invaded, France cannot hesitate to respond to the appeal of an allied nation to which it is united by common interests and traditional sympathies renewed by a recent confraternity of arms and the union contracted between the two reigning families. Thus, gentlemen, the government of the Emperor, strong in the constant moderation and the spirit of conciliation with which it has never ceased to be inspired, calmly awaits the course of events, confident that its conduct in the different vicissitudes which have just occurred will meet the unanimous approbation of France and of Europe."

This document is several times applauded, not with long-sustained cheering, but sufficiently to give the idea of approbation. The president of the Council of State then offers two bills, one of which raises from one hundred thousand to one hundred and forty thousand men the contingent of the forthcoming levy of troops, while the other authorizes a loan of five millions.

The president of the Corps Législatif, Count Morny, who has always been an ardent advocate of peace, rises to speak. "If war is inevitable," he says, "there is at least a reasonable certainty that it will be localized and limited, especially if the other Germanic powers have the wisdom to comprehend that nothing is concerned but a purely Italian question which does not cloak any scheme of conquest, and which cannot produce any revolution. As to you, gentlemen, at the opening of this question, you displayed a pacific spirit inspired by your solicitude for the great interests of the country; that was your right and your duty, and it gives additional value and weight to the support you will lend the Emperor. Make it evident to-day, so that none may misunderstand it, either at home or abroad, that when confronting foreigners, we are all united in a single thought, — the success and glory of our arms."

In the course of the same day the advance guard of the French army is disembarked in Italy. The squadron with General Bazaine's division on board, coming from Toulon, arrives in the port of Genoa. The landing of the troops is effected to the music of the military bands. An immense concourse of spectators greets the French soldiers with frenzied applause.

Wednesday, April 27. — The Emperor and the Empress are present at the representation of *Herculanum* at the Opéra. The audience rises spontaneously and cheers them as they enter.

The day goes by without the appearance of any Austrian troops on the right bank of the Tessin. It was generally supposed that Austria would profit by her opportunities, and that she had hastened the rupture merely that she might also push on the attack. Her troops, however, remain immovable during the 27th and 29th, and it is not until the afternoon of the 29th that they decide to cross the Tessin, which act is the commencement of hostilities. This inexplicable delay is as great a blunder as the ultimatum had been.

Saturday, April 30. — The Corps Législatif holds an interesting session in which it discusses the bill authorizing the five hundred million loan. The speech of M. Jules Favre is a violent accusation of Austria and an enthusiastic defence of Piedmont. The orator says that Austria has ruled Italy during forty years by violence, proscriptions, confiscations, and terror; but that violence, thank God, is always transient and can never establish a durable government. Piedmont has the prestige of a good and holy cause, and the moral support of all generous hearts. It is ruled by a young sovereign, the pride of his people, a sovereign who longs to avenge the death of his noble, illustrious, and unfortunate father. . . . The policy of the French government has been the traditional policy of France; for the orator is convinced that France will be powerful only when Italy shall be regenerated and free. Let us break the chains of the enslaved; that is the mission of France.

Jules Favre expounds the thesis of the Left. The Viscount Anatole Lemercier expresses the anxieties of the men of the Right, the advocates of the Papacy. Before voting the loan, he asks permission to put a question to the government commissioners. According to him, Catholic consciences are disturbed by the events which are preparing in Italy. To be completely reassured, he would like to hear the government of the Emperor declare that it has taken every necessary precaution to guarantee the security of the Holy Father. The orator is firmly persuaded that it will never be threatened so long as our soldiers shall reside in Rome. He knows that the visible head of the Christian religion possesses forces superior to those of all armies, the veneration of the world on one hand, and on the other his own weakness; but it is none the less a glorious spectacle for a Catholic Frenchman to see the honor of being the auxiliaries of that veneration and that weakness reserved to our own troops. The orator demands that this rôle, so clearly assigned to France, the eldest daughter of the Church, shall not be abandoned.

M. Baroche, president of the Council of State, remarks that the previous speaker has just replied to his own question by invoking souvenirs which the government of the Emperor will take good care not to forget. There is no room for doubt. The government will take all measures necessary to ensure the security and independence of the Holy Father amidst the disturbances of which Italy will be the scene.

Another Catholic orator, the Viscount de La Tour, succeeds the Viscount Anatole Lemercier. He says that France ought to disavow in the most explicit manner all alliance with the Revolution. He does not admit that the fine and noble sword of France may be coupled with that of General Garibaldi. He does not see allies for our country in these undisciplined bands, but enemies of European order. He is unwilling that we should incur, in the eyes of Europe, the suspicion of setting means at work the employment of which may become the germ of new revolutions for Italy.

Still more characteristic is the speech of M. Plichon. It is a sort of prologue to the violent and excited debates of the future. The deputy from the North says aloud what many of his colleagues are saying in a whisper. He states with precision and summarizes the criticisms passed upon the Italian policy of Napoleon III. M. Plichon has voted for the augmentation of the contingent, because our troops have crossed the frontier and, the honor of the flag being involved, there is no room for deliberation. But if the question had been intact, and if one could have examined the matter to find out what interest France had in going to war, he would have said no. He has voted in the affirmative, but sadly and with pain, and above all with the profound conviction that the government had unnecessarily involved the country in a hazardous and dangerous war for results that were at least uncertain. According to M. Plichon, it does not appear from any of the governmental communications that the policy of Austria in these latter times has assailed either the honor or the security of France, or even the equilibrium of Europe. The orator wants to know why war is made and what war it is. Is it to be a revolutionary or a political war? will it be the negation or the consecration of the Roman expedition, the expulsion of the Austrians, the independence, the unity, or the federation of Italy? He wants to know where we are going and where we are to stop. He does not see what guarantees one can have against the unknown. It is impossible to be revolutionary in Italy and remain conservative in France and in Rome. The revolutionary spirit cannot be over-excited on one point without being roused upon all others. It is easy to see what France can lose by a war, but it is not easy to see what she can gain.

Nevertheless the five hundred million loan is unanimously voted. Yet the speech of the deputy of the North, delivered in a milieu ordinarily so docile, so submissive to every indication of the sovereign's will, so receptive of all his ideas, has given rise to serious reflections in the Corps Législatif. The Emperor, in fact, had always desired the war, but it had never been desired by an overwhelming majority of that body. All the prestige of victory would be needed to efface this impression.

CHAPTER XIV

THE OPENING OF THE WAR

ONE noticeably curious thing about all wars is that until the very hour when they are declared, optimists may be found who are still predicting peace. Certain ingenuous souls, when they learned that on April 27 and 28 the Austrian troops had not yet crossed the Tessin, still insisted on believing that the swords would remain in their scabbards. There was a good deal of talk about a pacific article in the *Morning Herald* and a speech by Lord Derby hinting the possibility of a resumption of negotiations. This final gleam of hope was extinguished in Paris on May 1. It was learned that the Austrians had crossed the Tessin on April 29. Therefore the war had begun.

Criticisms and recriminations ceased at once. The French nation felt its ancient warlike instincts revive. The journals of all parties thought of nothing any longer but the honor of the flag. There was not one discordant note. Even those publicists who had blamed the war before it was declared, spoke now in patriotic tones. In the *Revue des Deux Mondes*, the chronicler of the fortnight, M. Eugène

Forcade, wrote: "We have got through with the complex duties of the discussion it was necessary to maintain so long as France seemed free to choose between peace and war. Necessity has spoken. No more recriminations over the irreparable and the irresolvable; the era of simple duty has begun. France is engaged in a war against Austria for the independence of Italy; henceforward we have but one opinion and one will: France must triumph and Italy must be independent. Our hearts contain now but a single wish, and it is that the conscientious objections we were obliged to express during the phase of public deliberation may be radically and gloriously refuted by the bravery and success of France."

The French troops had penetrated into Piedmont even before hostilities began, some by way of the Alps, some by sea. Marshal Canrobert and General Niel arrived at Suze during the night of April 28. They were at Turin the following day, and in company with King Victor Emmanuel inspected the positions of the Boire. General Baraguey d'Hilliers landed at Genoa the same day, and was soon rejoined there by General MacMahon and General Regnaud de Saint-Jean d'Angely. Genoa put on a festive air. Frenchmen and Italians seemed to form but one family. As the city was not provided with barracks enough for so many troops, soldiers were lodged with private persons, who gave them every attention. The sumptuous palaces of the city opened their doors to offer hospitality to the soldiers of France.

Part of the cavalry entered Italy by the Corniche road. Listen to an officer of the guides, the Marquis de Massa: "Having come from Melun to Marseilles by rail, we were at once sent forward by day stations to Genoa, by way of Brignoles, Cannes, and the bridge of Var. Being the first regiments of cavalry to cross the frontier like this, we got the cream of the Nicene ovations, passing over a flower-strewn road where all the vehicles of the country, hired by its usual tourists, were waiting to meet us in a line that stretched far beyond the limits of the octroi. And among them, bolt upright on their coursers, were fair *ladies* who flung roses at us; brown Italians who distributed bags of bonbons; beautiful Americans, recognizable by their carnation tints, who clapped their little hands as hard as they could. I recollect one old English lady from whom I received a packet tied up with a string, on which was written: 'Safe return with promotion.' It contained six cakes of chocolate. In the evening, the municipality treated us to a full-dress performance with a ballet, singing, and a sending up of pigeons."

At Paris things were taking a more decidedly warlike turn. "Great hopes are entertained," wrote the *Illustration*, "that the sun of May, propitious to our arms, may light up a new day of Marengo. This holy confidence of patriotism, the Bourse, and those who live by it, cannot greatly disturb by their discouraged attitude. Whenever '*Malbrook goes to war*,' money takes the alarm. But that is a kind of panic which always subsides when the cannon announce the first victory. The Bourse waits for the report to adore the echo."

May 3, M. Achille Fould, Minister of State, read the following communication to the Senate: "So long ago as the 26th of last month, His Majesty's *chargé d'affaires* at Vienna notified the Austrian government that if its troops crossed the frontier of Piedmont, France would be obliged to consider this invasion of an allied country as a declaration of war. The Court of Austria having persisted in employing force, the Emperor has ordered me to bring this fact, which constitutes Austria in a state of war with France, to the knowledge of the Senate."

Shouts of "Long live the Emperor!" resounded.

The president of the Senate, M. Troplong, then spoke as follows: "If it is permissible for me to translate into a few words the meaning of the acclamations we have just heard, I will say that while my illustrious colleagues who have been given commands are sustaining the glory of the French name in face of the enemy, the senators who remain here will not recoil from any act of civil courage and devotion to the Emperor. We shall rival each other in patriotism, because this is a just war, it is merely a response to a defiance and an aggression. It is a consequence of that time-honored policy which is as much excited by Italian crises as if they were French emergencies."

M. Troplong contrived to praise Napoleon III. and Pius IX. in a single sentence. "The Emperor," he added, "cannot allow Turin, which is the key of the Alps, nor Rome, which holds the keys of the Church by the hands of a saintly and venerated Pontiff, to fall under the usurping yoke of an influence hostile to France. Therefore its nationality will be restored to Italy. It will not be revolutionized but enfranchised, and that beautiful land will find a liberator."

On the same day appeared the Emperor's proclamation to the French people. Dated from the palace of the Tuileries, May 3, 1859, this document bears to the utmost degree the peculiar stamp of the style and ideas of the sovereign: "Frenchmen!" says Napoleon III., "Austria, by sending her army upon the territory of the King of Sardinia, our ally, declares war upon us. Thus she violates justice and the treaties, and threatens our frontiers. All the great powers have protested against this aggression. Piedmont having accepted conditions which ought to ensure peace, people ask what can be the reason of this sudden invasion: the reason is that Austria has brought things to an extremity where either she must dominate as far as the Alps, or Italy must be free as far as the Adriatic; for, in that country, every piece of ground that remains independent is a danger for her power."

The Emperor declares that the natural allies of France have always been those who desire the amelioration of humanity, and that when she draws the sword it is not to domineer, but to enfranchise: "The object of this war," he adds, "is to restore Italy to herself, not to change her master, and we shall have a nation on our frontiers which owes to us its independence. We are not going to Italy to foment disorder nor to unsettle the power of the Holy Father, whom we have replaced on his throne; but to withdraw it from that foreign pressure which crushes the entire peninsula, and to assist in basing order there on satisfied legitimate interests. We are going, in fact, to recover the traces left by our fathers upon that classic land, made illustrious by so many victories. God grant we may be worthy of them!"

The sovereign terminates his proclamation by these pathetic words, calculated to affect the masses: "I shall soon go to place myself at the head of the army. I leave in France the Empress and my son. Seconded by the experience and intelligence of the last brother of the Emperor, she will be able to prove herself equal to her mission. I confide them to the valor of the army which remains in France to guard our frontiers as well as to protect the domestic hearth; I confide them, in fine, to the whole people, who will surround them with that love and devotion of which I daily receive so many proofs.

"Courage, therefore, and union! Our country is going once more to demonstrate to the world that it has not degenerated. Providence will bless our efforts; for the cause which relies on justice, humanity, the love of country and of independence, is holy in the sight of God."

Napoleon III. has attained his object. He has found means to frustrate all the efforts of European diplomacy, which desired peace, and to make the Emperor Francis Joseph imprudently assume the part of the aggressor. He has succeeded in inclining the sympathies of the people to a war which is censured by the ruling classes. He has cleverly prepared public opinion. He has made the national fibre vibrate. Now he can depart.

CHAPTER XV

THE DEPARTURE OF THE EMPEROR

THE Emperor had witnessed already the departure of his entire guard. Preceded by a band, each regiment defiled on the Place du Carrousel, where it halted, surrounded by an immense crowd. An officer left the ranks and went to the palace of the Tuileries for the flag which had been left there. As soon as the officer had returned to his regiment, the Emperor appeared at one of the windows of the Marsan pavilion with the Empress and the Prince Imperial. The soldiers presented arms; the band played the air of Queen Hortense: *Partant pour la Syrie;* shouts resounded.

While a regiment of grenadiers was marching through the rue de Rivoli, on its way to the Lyons station, its vivandière inquired the number of the house in that street where the secretary of the Empress lived. It was pointed out to her. She went in, taking with her a little girl of six years, and said to the secretary: "I am obliged to go with my regiment. I beg Madame the Empress to take charge of my child. I have no fear about her; I know she will bring her up well until I return." Then she vanished, leaving the little girl behind her. On being informed of this, the Empress willingly complied with the desire of the valiant mother.

The Emperor's preparations for departure were finished. Marshal Randon, who had at first been selected as major-general of the army of Italy, had just replaced Marshal Vaillant as Minister of War, the latter becoming a major-general. The Emperor took with him all his military household, which was made up as follows: —

Aides-de-camp: Generals, Count Roguet, de Cotte, Count de Montebello, de Béville, Prince de La Moskowa, Fleury; Colonels, de Waubert, de Genlis, Marquis de Toulongeon, Count Lepic, Count Reille, Favé.

Orderly officers: Colonel Baron de Menneval; Chief of squadron Schmitz; Captains, Brady, Count d'Andlau, Klein de Kleinenberg, Viscount Friant, de Tascher de La Pagerie, Prince de La Tour d'Auvergne, Eynard de Clermont-Tonnerre, Darguesse; Lieutenant Prince Joachim Murat, and the Viscount de Champagny Cadore, lieutenant of a man-of-war; Baron Nicholas Clary, officer of the national guard.

Besides these, the Emperor was also attended by two equerries: Baron de Bourgoing and M. Davillier; a chaplain, the Abbé Laîne; a physician, Doctor Conneau; a surgeon, Baron Larrey; and two secretaries.

On Sunday, May 8, two days before the departure, a soirée at the Tuileries brought together the great officers of the Crown, the ministers, and all those who formed part of the households of Their Majesties. It is thus described by the Countess Stéphanie de Tascher de La Pagerie, who was present: "The attitude of the Empress was truly admirable. One felt that she had undertaken to conceal her emotion and impart courage to all present. She was affable to all; instead of remaining seated in the chimney corner, surrounded by a small group of privileged persons, she went from one to another, talking seriously with the men, affectionately with the women. My eyes followed her with satisfaction, for I love her when she is like this. One feels that she is thoroughly impressed by the mission entrusted to her, and that she is bent on proving herself worthy of it. The Emperor talked with all the ladies, promising to look after their husbands, brothers, or sons. Nobody wept; but hearts shed inwardly those tears which are not seen, but which are only the sadder and more bitter on that account."

Tuesday, May 10. — A Mass of adieu is celebrated in the chapel of the Tuileries. The Cardinal Archbishop of Paris officiates. Pale and lost in meditation, the Empress in prayer resembles a beautiful statue of marble.

The Minister of Worship and of Public Instruction has addressed a circular to all the archbishops and bishops of the Empire, which is thus worded: "Monseigneur, the Emperor is about to place himself at the head of the army of Italy. His Majesty desires that public prayers shall be ordered in all the churches of the Empire to ask God to ensure the success of our arms and protect France. I pray Your Grandeur to be so good as to take the necessary measures to comply with these pious intentions."

The hour of departure is at hand; the members of the privy council, the ministers, grand officers of the Crown, ladies and officers of the households of the Emperor and the Empress, are waiting in the salons of the Tuileries. The Princess Mathilde, the Princess Marie of Baden and her husband the Duke of Hamilton take leave there of the sovereign.

It is half-past five in the evening. Their Majesties are about to enter the carriage. Napoleon III. may count on an ovation. Journals which favor the Italian cause have been educating opinion. It is the liberal tradition to hasten to the support of oppressed peoples. The principle of nationalities, much disputed by the aristocracy and the middle classes, combines the sympathies of the workingmen and the proletariat. It is an essentially democratic doctrine. All the men on the Left benches and many of those on the Right have been preaching it continually throughout the entire reign of Louis Philippe and the period of the Second Republic. The Emperor is taking the line of the Liberals of the monarchy and the Republicans of 1848. He is certain to be applauded by the crowd.

The procession moves. Large groups of the common people mingle with it. Preceded and followed by detachments of the hundred-guards, the Emperor is in an open carriage with the Empress. Five carriages follow them. The cortege starts from the court of the Tuileries, passes beneath the arch of triumph of the Carrousel, crosses the Louvre court, and debouches on the rue de Rivoli, which is completely hung with flags. The windows of every story in the houses are filled with spectators who wave their hats and handkerchiefs. No troop had been detailed for the service; it is the population which forms the line along the route to be taken by the Emperor. At times, the crowd is so compact, so close to the sovereign's carriage, that the horses can scarcely advance. The enthusiasm continually increases. In the democratic quarters, the faubourg Saint-Antoine, the Place of the Bastile, the rue de Lyon, it amounts to frenzy.

Men who are generally under police surveillance are among those who shout *Long live the Emperor!* most loudly. There are workingmen who address him remarks like this: "Be easy, we will watch over your wife and your son until you come back," and women who throw rosary beads and medals of Our Lady of Victories into the carriage. In spite of his imperturbable phlegm, Napoleon III. is a man who hungers for emotions. He loves adventures and delights in dangers. His temperament, that of a political gamester, prefers the greatest risks. The more hazardous an enterprise, the more attractive he finds it. The ovation of which he is the recipient at the moment of his departure fills him with a joy which betrays itself on his ordinarily impassive countenance. This spontaneity of acclamations as he passes, this community of ideas between him and the democracy, this popular suffrage, flatters him more than the approbation of all the European chanceries would have power to do.

The passage has lasted about three-quarters of an hour. Their Majesties alight from the carriage and find King Jerome and the Princess Clotilde at the station. Prince Napoleon does not leave his old father and his young wife without emotion. There are tears in the eyes of the Princess, but remembering the fearlessness of her race, she murmurs, "That is enough," and ceases to weep.

It is a quarter past six. The imperial train starts, as quick as lightning. The Empress is going as far as Montereau with the Emperor. They stop there for a few moments, and a dinner of forty covers is served. Here the last farewells are spoken. The Empress gives a medal to each officer of the Emperor's household. Him she embraces tenderly and sets off for Paris, while he continues his route to Marseilles. The inhabitants of towns and country places, hastening with torches to all the way stations, greet with acclamations the passing train which carries Cæsar and his fortunes.

May 11. — Quarter past eleven in the morning. The train arrives at Marseilles. Napoleon III. goes directly from the railroad to the old port where the imperial yacht, *La Reine Hortense*, is waiting to carry him to Genoa. All the streets are draped with flags. The enthusiasm is as noisy as that of Paris. About two o'clock, the imperial yacht, followed by the *Vauban*, gains the open, passing between bedecked vessels and the numerous boats of all descriptions which fill the harbor. One hundred and one discharges of cannon salute the departure. The sky is clear. A glorious sun shines down upon waves as smooth as a looking-glass, and the two vessels soon vanish on the horizon.

CHAPTER XVI

GENOA AND ALEXANDRIA

THE city of Genoa is preparing to receive Napoleon III. May 11, a proclamation of the syndic celebrates the "champion of justice and of civilization, the avenger of oppressed peoples, the heir of the name and the glory of Napoleon the Great," he who "not content with having sent instantly a formidable army into Italy, comes himself, accompanied by the good wishes of all France, to take command of it." "Citizens," adds the syndic, "the Emperor of the French could not give us a stronger proof of sympathy, nor a surer pledge of victory. Let us then, with full hearts, express our profound sentiments of admiration and gratitude for the august chief of the great nation which extends a kindred hand to Italy, that she may effectually assist her to conquer at last the independence she has coveted so long."

Genoa has been in holiday trim since morning. All the city is afoot. A special train brings Count Cavour, who is bound to be among the first to greet Napoleon III. The Genoese national guard and a regiment of the grenadiers of the imperial guard are drawn up in battle array to pay the usual honors to the sovereign. Two steamers of the State, lying at either side of the passage into the harbor, serve as reserved tribunes for the higher classes of society. All the places are filled by eleven o'clock, and the ladies are not afraid of exposing themselves to the rays of a hot sun. The Bourse closes. The shops are shut. An enormous crowd gathers on the commercial port, invades the vessels, and even climbs into the yards.

Half-past twelve.—A discharge of cannon from the batteries of the *Lantérne* announces that the imperial yacht, *La Reine Hortense*, is in sight. At this signal, Prince de Carignan, Count Cavour, Count Nigra, minister of the household of King Victor Emmanuel, the Marquis de Brême, grand master of ceremonies, the Prince de La Tour d'Auvergne, minister of France, and all the members of the legation, the French generals, Herbillon, military commander of Genoa, Lebœuf, commander of the artillery of the army, and Frossard, commander of engineers, go aboard the little steamboat *Amphion*, and advance to meet the Emperor. More than a thousand small vessels, all decked with flags, join with this advice-boat to go and bid the sovereign liberator welcome.

Standing on the main deck of his vessel, Napoleon III. contemplates a splendid horizon; Genoa the *Superb*, the *noble* and *royal city*, made famous by Tasso and Alfieri, Genoa, with its marble palaces, rising above each other like the seats of a vast amphitheatre, its chain of lofty hills, its harbor forming a semicircle nearly half a league in length, and separated from the sea by two immense moles.

Two o'clock. — The cannons roar, the bells ring, the drums beat the general, the troops present arms, a loud shout issues from all throats. The imperial yacht enters the basin and advances rapidly to the quay. On reaching the landing-place, where he is received by General Regnaud de Saint-Jean d'Angély, commander-in-chief of his guard, and by the principal Genoese authorities, the Emperor goes down the side into a yawl hung with the Sardinian and French colors and almost concealed from view by flowers, and sails slowly in the direction of the Palais-Royal between the boats thronging the harbor. Hats and handkerchiefs are waved. Frenzied acclamations resound.

The Palais-Royal is an admirable residence bought by King Charles-Felix from the Durazzo family. It rises facing the sea, with which it communicates by a gallery issuing in the arsenal of the port. A marble staircase, usually reserved to the King alone, dips its lowest steps in the waters of the military basin. Here the Emperor is to lodge. From here he addresses his first order of the day to the army of Italy : —

"Soldiers! I come to place myself at your head to lead you to the combat. We are about to second the struggle of a people to revindicate its independence and withdraw it from foreign oppression. It is a sacred cause which has the sympathies of the civilized world. I do not need to stimulate your ardor, each station will remind you of a victory. In the Sacred Way of old Rome the marble was crowded with inscriptions recalling to the people its lofty deeds; so, to-day, in passing by Mondovi, Marengo, Lodi, Castiglione, Arcola, Rivoli, you will be marching in another sacred way, amidst its glorious memories.

"Preserve that severe discipline which is the honor of the French army. Do not forget that here there are no enemies but those who fight against you. In battle remain compact, and do not abandon your ranks to rush forward. Mistrust too great enthusiasm, it is the only thing I dread. The new weapons of precision are only dangerous from a distance. They do not prevent the bayonet from being, as of old, the terrible weapon of the French infantry.

"Soldiers! let us all do our duty and put our entire confidence in God. The country expects much from you. Already these words of good omen are heard from one end of France to the other, 'The new army of Italy will be worthy of her elder sister.'"

In the evening, the Emperor goes to the Carlo Felice theatre, where a gala representation is given in his honor. All along the streets through which he passes — rue Balbi, Place de l'Annunziata, via Nuovissima — the houses are draped and illuminated.

When he enters the theatre there is a real frenzy. Three times, after having saluted the crowd, he attempts to sit down, and three times the renewal of applause keeps him standing in his box. He finally takes his seat, with Prince de Carignan on his right and Prince Napoleon on his left. Count Cavour, Count Nigra, and M. Morro, syndic of Genoa, remain standing behind him. His friend, Count Arese, one of the most fervent partisans of Italian independence, is one of those who come to meet him. "My dear Arese," the Emperor says to him, "we ought to thank God for having permitted the Emperor of Austria to cross the Tessin, for otherwise how could I be here?"

The next day, May 13, at six o'clock in the morning, Victor Emmanuel arrives incognito at Genoa to shake hands with his ally. The King places himself under the orders of the Emperor, who is in command of the French and Sardinian armies. The two sovereigns embrace each other warmly. Some hours later Victor Emmanuel returns to his own headquarters at Occimiano, between Casale and Valenza.

In the course of the day the Emperor, accompanied by two officers only, makes a long excursion, sometimes on foot and again in a carriage, on the Alexandria roads, the faubourgs of Rivarole, rue San Antonio, etc. He is received with remarkable enthusiasm on his unexpected visit to these quarters, for the most part poor ones.

May 14. — At two o'clock Napoleon III. leaves Genoa to go by rail to Alexandria, where he is to establish his headquarters. The train crosses the Bormida River, leaving to the left the celebrated plain where the battle of Marengo was fought, and enters the station of Alexandria at four o'clock. The Emperor mounts a horse as soon as he leaves the train, and goes to the Palais-Royal, escorted by several squadrons of cavalry, and amidst a tumultuous ovation. At the exit of the station, on two columns, is an inscription reproducing the imperial words: "The object of this war is to restore Italy to herself, and not to make her change masters; we shall have on our frontiers a friendly people which will owe to us its independence. Let France arm and resolutely say: I want no conquests, but I proudly avow my sympathy for a people whose history is blended with my own." On the *Piazzetta* there is a bust of Napoleon I., and at the entrance of the *Strada della Pierra* a triumphal arch with this inscription: "To the heir of the victor of Marengo; to the ally of Victor Emmanuel." The *Piazza Larga*, where the Palais-Royal, the dwelling of Napoleon III., is situated, is thronged with people who keep up an incessant shouting. In the theatre that evening, an actor recites the following ode which the audience oblige him to repeat: "Hymn to Napoleon III. Sovereign of the greatest of peoples, valorous warrior sent by God, sublime soul, noble heart, generous and pious, O great man, O powerful monarch, we behold thee at last among us. Thanks to thee the right of peoples to independence is already recognized, and by us the unjust treaties by which men are divided into oppressors and oppressed will be destroyed. Thanks to thee, the sun of liberty will rise on Italy. Here, where the genius who gave his laws to the world, and whose name is the pride and glory of our time began to shine, within these walls whence the eagle took his radiant flight, France and Italy come to unite with each other in a single thought."

Sunday, May 13. — The Emperor, accompanied by Marshal Vaillant, Marshal Canrobert, and some officers of his household, walks to Saint Peter's Cathedral. The national guard forms the line along his route. He is received by the clergy at the door of the church, and the Mass is celebrated by his chaplain, the Abbé Laîne. On his exit, as on his entrance, the sovereign is cheered by an enthusiastic crowd.

CHAPTER XVII

MONTEBELLO

WAR had been declared April 26, and as yet not a shot had been fired. The first fighting took place, May 20, at Montebello.

The allied army already occupied the entire line of the Po, without giving the least indication as to where it would probably cross the stream. The 1st and 2d French corps were established at the two extremes. General Forey, whose division formed the vanguard, had been expecting an early combat since the 6th of May. On that day he had addressed to his troops the following order of the day from Gavi: "Soldiers of the 1st division of the 1st corps, to-morrow we shall find ourselves in the first line, and it is probable that we shall have the honor of the first engagements with the enemy. Remember that your fathers have always beaten this enemy, and you will do as they did."

May 20, at half-past twelve, General Forey, being apprised that a strong column of Austrians, with cannon, had occupied Casteggio and driven back from Montebello the outguards of the Piedmontese cavalry, went immediately to the outposts on the

Montebello road with two battalions of the 74th. Meanwhile the rest of the division got under arms. An artillery battery marched at the head.

The village of Montebello is built on the first eminence seen by one going from Tortona to Plaisance. This hill has always been disputed in the fights which have taken place on the plains of Alexandria. In the days of antiquity it gained its name — mount of war (*mons belli*) — from the combats delivered there. It was the scene of the rencontre between the Numidian cavalry of Hannibal and the advance guard of Scipio which preluded the battle of Trebbia. It was there, June 9, 1800, that General Lannes, going to the rendezvous of Marengo, forced the passage defended by the Austrians, and merited by his valor the title of Duc de Montebello, afterwards given him. With its natural defences, the solid masonry of its houses, its fortified cemetery, this famous village is a very strong position. The tall crops, the trees and vines, concealed the movements of the enemy, and had allowed him to advance without being seen.

The Forey division was composed of four regiments of infantry, the 74th, 84th, 91st, and 98th, and a battalion of light infantry, the 17th, to which were joined six squadrons of Sardinian light cavalry, commanded by Colonel Maurice de Sonnaz. All vied with each other in courage and high spirits. In spite of broken ground, cut up by ravines, obstructed by vineyards, and very difficult of access by cavalry, the Sardinian light-horsemen made a heroic charge. On a sign from General Forey, the clarions sounded; the cry "Forward!" came from every throat; the French battalions sprang towards the heights and soon attained their summits. The village of Montebello had next to be attacked. It was not an easy task. The Austrians, ambushed behind the crenellated walls, rained a shower of balls upon the assailants. Every window had its sharpshooters, every house was a citadel to be taken. Dismounting, General Forey placed himself, sword in hand, at the head of his troops. He was always seen in the most dangerous places; balls whistled around him; one might have thought the very grape-shot was daunted by such audacity. Even when the village had been surrounded, prodigies of valor were required to make a successful advance. An incessant series of hand-to-hand combats went on in the streets, the gardens, the very houses. It was at this moment that General Beuret received a glorious death. Forced to give way before the ardor and impetuosity of the French troops, whose bayonets were irresistible, the Austrians fell back into the cemetery where they made a fierce resistance. But this last position being finally wrested from them, they beat a retreat. It was half-past six o'clock.

General Forey thought it imprudent to push the day's success further. He halted his troops behind the undulation of ground on which the cemetery is situated, protecting its crest by four pieces of artillery and numerous sharpshooters, who forced the hindmost Austrian columns into Casteggio. Soon afterwards they saw them evacuate the place, leaving a rear-guard, and withdrawing by the Casatisma road.

At the close of the day, when the victorious general passed in front of his troops, he was received with unanimous cheers. Every man wanted to touch the hand of the intrepid leader who had given so noble an example.

In his report to Marshal Baraguey d'Hilliers, commander-in-chief of the 1st corps, the general wrote: "I cannot praise too highly, M. le Maréchal, the enthusiasm of our troops. . . . Nor can I forget the officers of my staff who seconded me perfectly. . . . I do not know the exact figure of our losses; they were numerous, especially in superior officers, who exposed themselves greatly. I reckon them approximately at between six and seven hundred men killed or wounded. Those of the enemy must have been considerable, judging from the number of dead found, especially in the village of Montebello. We have made about two hundred prisoners, among whom are a colonel and several officers. A number of military wagons have also fallen into our hands. For myself, M. le Maréchal, I am glad that my division was the first to have an engagement with the enemy. This glorious baptism, which revives one of the great names of the Empire, will mark, I hope, one of the halting-places referred to in the order of the Emperor."

General Forey added in a postscript: "From what I learn from all quarters, the forces of the enemy could not have been less than from fifteen to eighteen thousand men; and, if the prisoners are to be believed, they went beyond that figure." To contend against such forces, General Forey had had only his division, composed of five thousand nine hundred men, and six squadrons of Sardinian light-cavalry. Great joy was caused by this admirable feat of arms throughout Italy and France. This first success was a good omen.

CHAPTER XVIII

PALESTRO

THE war began well. At the time when the battle of Montebello was going on, Garibaldi and his redshirted volunteers were distinguishing themselves in the neighborhood of Lake Majeur. They entered Como May 29, and the city placed itself under the government of King Victor Emmanuel.

May 30, the King crossed the Sesia with four Sardinian divisions. The Durando division went in the direction of Vinzaglio, the Fanto and Castelborgo divisions towards Casalino and from there towards Confienza. The Cialdini division, which had established itself on the left bank the previous day, was charged with the principal attack, that on Palestro. This village was difficult of access. Cut into by canals and obstructed by temporary breastworks of trees, the road thither presented obstacles of every description. The ground on either side was laid out in rice-fields and divided by innumerable ditches, which rendered the attack very difficult. In front of Palestro, the river, with its banks covered with tall weeds, poplars, and willows; to right and left of the river, wide, marshy meadows; every declivity surrounding and dominating the road up to the entrance of the village supplied with troops; Tyrolese chasseurs, chosen sharpshooters, stationed at regular intervals, hidden behind trees, crouching in the weeds; the bridge occupied by numerous tirailleurs; the heights forming on either side of the village two sorts of natural bastions at an elevation of about fifteen yards; the first houses crenellated in order to make attack more difficult and permit the Austrians to send a plunging fire down upon the assailants,— such were the obstacles of every kind encountered by the Sardinian column detailed for the taking of Palestro. Led by Victor Emmanuel in person, it triumphed over all of them and seized the village. The other divisions simultaneously carried Vinzaglio and occupied Casalino and Confienza without resistance. The next day, the Austrians were to return the attack and in considerable force.

When the Emperor had sent to Victor Emmanuel, May 29, the order containing merely these words: "The army of the King will take up its position in front of Palestro," he foresaw that the Sardinian sovereign would be forced to give several successive battles, and he placed at his disposal the 3d regiment of zouaves, momentarily detached from the 5th corps. This regiment camped at Torrione, May 30. At six in the morning of May 31, it received orders from the King to move on Palestro.

At nine o'clock it established its bivouac to the right of the village, in a plain covered with ripe grain and groups of trees, with the Calcina canal in front. Towards ten o'clock the Austrians debouched by the Robbio and Rozasco roads. The zouaves immediately took up their arms and moved some five hundred yards to their own right, where brisk firing had begun. They had taken down their tents and laid aside their knapsacks, and they concealed their approach in the first place by hiding in the grain and under a screen of poplars. Then, making a sudden rush from the brushwood, they sprang upon the enemy.

Nothing stopped them, neither ditches nor the acacia thickets which scratched their faces, neither the marshy ground in which they sank to their knees nor the canal where they found the water up to their belts and sometimes up to their shoulders. Suddenly from the midst of the grain where the Tyrolese chasseurs were ambuscaded came an almost pointblank fusillade; to the grape-shot, which threw their first ranks into disorder, the zouaves replied by yells, and without resorting to their weapons, climbed the hill covered with thick mud.

"There is only a step between them and the mouth of the cannons," says the historic Journal of the 3d zouaves; "the Austrian artillerymen, stupefied by such audacity, have not even time to fire. In vain they try to rake them down, the terrible bayonets of the zouaves pin down in their places those who seek to defend themselves. The routed infantry disperse in all directions. Five pieces of cannon are in our power."

The zouaves next attack the road; some rush to the right, others escalade the cliffs to the left, and find themselves at once in a field of ploughed ground facing several Austrian battalions whom they attack with the bayonet. Just then they see King Victor Emmanuel galloping up, sabre in hand. The intrepid monarch, followed by Sardinian battalions worthy of such a leader, plunges into the thickest of the fight. Near him, General de La Marmora has a horse grievously wounded. The fiery ardor of the sovereign electrifies the zouaves; they hurrah for him.

The Austrians, hotly pursued, are driven as far as the Bridda River, traversed by a narrow bridge, the entrance of which they bar with two pieces of artillery. Some of the reserves are massed behind this bridge, and line the steep acclivities of the bank. The zouaves fling themselves on the bridge and seize the two pieces. A terrible hand-to-hand fight ensues. Many combatants are thrown into the stream. Some are drowned, others dashed to pieces in their fall. A number of Austrians save themselves by swimming. The zouaves, who pity them, are seen descending the steep banks and holding out their carbines like fish-poles to draw them from the water. At the same time General Cialdini, who has been valiantly defending the village of Palestro, forces the enemy to retreat. They are repulsed at Confienza likewise, and fall back on Robbio. The victory is complete.

Napoleon III., leaving his headquarters at Verceil, had followed in all haste the sound of the firing at Palestro. Victor Emmanuel acquaints him with the day's success. The zouaves get into line of battle on both sides of the bridge which has been the scene of a heroic struggle. The two monarchs pass through the ranks of intrepid soldiers who, still animated by the heat of combat, wave with powder-blackened hands their reeking carbines and shout: "Long live the Emperor! Long live the King!"

Finding two mortally wounded Italian volunteers on the battlefield, Victor Emmanuel addressed them in affectionate terms. One of them answered, "Sire, I regret to die in the first battle," and the other, "Sire, deliver this poor Italy." In the evening this fine proclamation was issued by the King: "Soldiers, to-day a new and striking feat of arms has been signalized by a new victory. The enemy attacked us vigorously at Palestro, bringing powerful forces to bear upon our right; the intention was to prevent our soldiers from joining those of Marshal Canrobert. The moment was supreme. Numerically our force was greatly inferior to that of the adversary, but the latter was confronted by the brave troops of the 4th division, under General Cialdini, and the incomparable 3d regiment of zouaves which, fighting to-day with the Sardinian army, has powerfully contributed to the victory. . . . His Majesty the Emperor, on visiting the field of battle, has expressed his most cordial felicitations, and he appreciates the immense advantage of this victory. Soldiers! persevere in your sublime conduct, and I assure you that heaven will crown the work you have so courageously begun."

A singular incident occurred the following day. We quote the description of it from a remarkable history of the campaign by Baron de Bazancourt, who had been summoned to the army of Italy by order of the Emperor: "A young officer of Sardinian cavalry, commissioned to escort the prisoners, presented himself before Colonel de Chabron to receive those taken by the regiment of zouaves. Astonished to hear this Piedmontese officer expressing himself in French, with not the slightest trace of a foreign accent, the colonel questioned him concerning his nationality. 'I am a Frenchman,' replied the sublieutenant of Sardinian cavalry. 'Your name?' 'De Chartres, colonel.' And, as the colonel looked at him attentively on hearing that name, he added simply, 'I am the son of the Duke of Orléans.' And bowing to the colonel, whose orders he had received, he withdrew. Colonel de Chabron, moved by this chance encounter, and the touching simplicity of the young man, already an orphan, and stricken by many great misfortunes, followed him with his eyes until he disappeared amidst the surrounding tents."

The same day Victor Emmanuel addressed this

FRANCIS JOSEPH I.

letter to Colonel de Chabron: "From the principal headquarters, Torrione, June 1, 1859: Colonel, the Emperor, in placing the 3d regiment of zouaves at my orders has shown me a precious testimony of friendship. It seemed to me that I could not give a better reception to this choice troop than by affording it an immediate occasion to add a new exploit to those which rendered the name of zouaves so formidable to the enemy on the battlefields of Africa and the Crimea. The irresistible vehemence with which your regiment marched to the attack yesterday excited my utmost admiration. To fall upon the enemy at the point of the bayonet, to seize a battery in the face of grape-shot, was the affair of a few minutes. You should be proud of commanding such soldiers, and they ought to be happy to obey a leader like you. I keenly appreciate the idea of your zouaves in bringing to my headquarters the pieces of artillery taken from the Austrians, and I beg you to convey my thanks to them. I shall make haste to despatch this fine trophy to H. M. the Emperor, whom I have already acquainted with the matchless bravery with which your regiment fought yesterday at Palestro and sustained my extreme right. I shall always be well satisfied to see the 3d regiment of zouaves fighting beside my soldiers and winning new laurels on the battlefields which still await us. Kindly acquaint your zouaves, colonel, with these sentiments.

"VICTOR EMMANUEL."

The dynasty of Savoy is a race of heroes. In 1823, during the Spanish War, the bravery of Charles-Albert, who was serving in the French army, excited the enthusiasm of the soldiers to such a point at the attack of Trocadero that they conferred upon him the epaulettes of a grenadier. When the battle of Palestro was over, his son, Victor Emmanuel, was proclaimed a corporal of zouaves by acclamation.

CHAPTER XIX

TURBIGO

THE effect of the two combats of Palestro was to disguise the reverse movement of the French army towards Novara, and its result to oblige the Austrian army to fall back on the Tessin and evacuate the territory of Piedmont. The allied army pursued them and made ready to cross the Tessin.

June 2, the Emperor ordered General MacMahon to send the Espinasse division to occupy Trecata, on the Milan road, and General Camou, commander of the light infantry division of the guard, to march towards Robbio, on the left bank of the Tessin, to force the passage opposite Turbigo, and protect the establishment of a bridge of boats by which the 2d corps could be transported to the other bank the following day. June 3, at eight o'clock in the morning, the 2d corps quitted Novara for Turbigo, a Lombard village nine kilometres from Buffalora, to cross the Tessin on this bridge.

General MacMahon preceded his army corps with the officers of his staff, in order to reconnoitre the ground on which he might be called to operate. He reached the encampments of the light infantry of the guard detached to defend the approaches to the bridge at three o'clock; then, after passing through Turbigo, he went to the village of Robechetto, two kilometres east of Turbigo, on the left bank of the Tessin. No enemies had yet been perceived when he arrived. Let us leave the tale to his chief of staff, General Lebrun, who says; "At Robechetto he found out that it was difficult to get a good view of the ground, on account of the neighborhood of the village being covered with vines and trees. He went up to the top of the church steeple." MacMahon, on the platform of the steeple, had spread out a map of the country, and was looking at the horizon, when an Austrian column, apparently coming from Buffalora, advanced upon the village. It was not more than a few hundred yards away.

General Lebrun adds: "We rushed to the stairway of the steeple, and went down four steps at a time. Those who were behind shouted to those ahead of them, 'Go faster!' We were soon in the saddle when once we got out of the church. It was time; two or three minutes more and the Austrians would have made a fine haul — a commander of a French army corps, his chief-of-staff, a general of division, General Camou, and the officers who accompanied them."

To prevent the enemy from installing themselves at Robechetto was indispensable, both to protect the bivouacs and to ensure the execution of the subsequent movement of the 2d corps on Buffalora and Magenta. Not a minute was to be lost.

MacMahon set off at full gallop and regained Turbigo, where he ordered a regiment of Algerian sharpshooters — the only one at his disposal for the moment — to march as quickly as possible on Robechetto, to repulse the enemy and occupy the village.

At the same instant, the Emperor, who had just been visiting the great bridge of San Martino, arrived at Turbigo, and in one of the houses crowning the plateau to the north of the road, gave General Camou orders to march the light infantry of the guard to the outlets of the canal, south of Turbigo, so as to reinforce the troops of General MacMahon.

The Algerian sharpshooters — the Turcos, as they are called — are about to be launched into the fire. General de La Motterouge passes in front of their three battalions, and addresses them in a few energetic words which, immediately translated into Arabic by Colonel Laure, electrify them. The general himself heads the centre battalion, and gives the signal of departure with his lifted sword. The point of direction is the church steeple of Robechetto. Nothing could be more impetuous than this attack made on the double-quick. Uttering their war-cries in their sharp and guttural voices, the Algerian sharpshooters advance to the music of the regimental air, "When the Turcos march to combat." In an instant they envelop Robechetto. In ten minutes the enemy, dislodged from the village, beat a retreat along the road by which they came. Nevertheless, they keep on using their artillery as they go, sending back a dozen volleys of grape which do not abate in the least the furious ardor of the Turcos. General Auger comes up with four pieces of artillery, and vigorously returns their fire. Thinking they see an Austrian piece among the wheat, which seems to have some difficulty in following the retreat, they rush at it on the gallop, seize it and sabre the artillerymen.

The head of an Austrian cavalry column, coming from Castano, simultaneously presents itself on the left. A battalion of the 65th goes at once to meet it with two pieces of cannon, and drives it back the way it came.

The fighting was over at five o'clock. General MacMahon addressed his report to the Emperor the same day. "The enemy," said he, "has experienced considerable losses. The battlefield is covered with their dead, and a considerable quantity of effects of all descriptions which they have left in our hands: camp equipages, full knapsacks thrown down on the scene of combat in order to flee with greater agility. We have picked up weapons, carbines, and muskets. We have made few prisoners, a fact explained by the nature of the ground on which the engagement took place. . . .

"I cannot as yet give precise details concerning this affair which has once more since the campaign begun shown all that Your Majesty may expect from your brave soldiers. . . . All have done their duty worthily; but I will at once mention General de La

Motterouge to Your Majesty as having manifested irresistible impetuosity; General Auger who, by the terms of our military legislation, merits a citation to the general order of the army; Colonel Laveaucoupet who, in a hand-to-hand fight with the Austrian sharpshooters, received a bayonet wound in the head; Colonel Laure, of the Algerian sharpshooters, for the intelligent impetus with which he led his battalions at the enemy."

General Lebrun saw an affecting sight after the combat in the street which runs through the village of Robechetto. The Abbé Bragier, chaplain of the 2d corps, was on his knees amongst the wounded, attending to the duties of his ministry; among these were soldiers of the 45th of the Line, Austrian chasseurs and Turcos, all of whom were stretching their hands out to him and kissing his. The compassionate Abbé lavished consolations upon all, without regard to religion or nationality. Raffet had promised the general to take this scene as the subject of one of his works, but death carried him off too soon.

The battle of Robechetto, which afterwards took the name of the neighboring locality and was called the battle of Turbigo, had done great honor to General de La Motterouge and the two regiments of his division, the Algerian tirailleurs and the 45th of the line, which had taken part in it. It inaugurated gloriously the operations which were to make the 2d army corps illustrious in the sequel of the campaign.

CHAPTER XX

THE BATTLE OF MAGENTA

THE 4th of June had been decided on by Napoleon III. as the day for taking definitive possession of the left bank of the Tessin. General MacMahon's corps, the 2d, reinforced by the light infantry division of the guard, and followed by the entire army of the King of Sardinia, was to move from Turbigo on Buffalora and Magenta, the division of grenadiers of the guard seizing meanwhile the head of the bridge of San Martino on the left bank, and the 3d corps, under Marshal Canrobert, advancing along the right bank so as to cross the Tessin at the same point. The 4th corps, commanded by General Niel, was also to make its way towards the Tessin. The 1st corps, that of Marshal Baraguey d'Hilliers, was held in reserve.

However, on the morning of June 4, no one in the French army anticipated a great battle on that day. The Emperor, who was at Novara, breakfasted there at his usual hour. After breakfast, he went to San Martino where the grenadiers and zouaves of his guard, who were to open the fight, were stationed.

At ten in the morning, the 2d corps, commanded by General MacMahon and composed of two divisions, that of General de La Motterouge and that of General Espinasse, to which was joined the light infantry division of the guard, under command of General Camou, started from Turbigo for Magenta. The La Motterouge division and the Espinasse division took different routes. The first collided with several Austrian detachments at Casata and repulsed them. The Emperor heard the firing from the bridge of San Martino, and at once ordered his guard to attack the banks of the grand canal, the *Naviglio Grande.*

The division of the guard, which was about to accomplish prodigies of valor, included three regiments of grenadiers and a regiment of zouaves. Commanded by General Mellinet, with two brigadier generals, De Wimpffen and Cler, under him, it comprised but five thousand men. During five hours these were to resist the attack of about forty thousand Austrians.

Now let us glance at the scene of this heroic resistance.

An army going from Piedmont into Lombardy finds two redoubtable obstacles in its way, the Tessin and the *Naviglio Grande.*

The Tessin is a large river whose abundant waters, swift as those of a torrent, are intercepted by wooded islands.

The *Naviglio Grande* is a very deep canal, about

sixteen yards in width and situated some two or three kilometers from Tessin, whose banks are lined with acacia hedges. It is protected by high embankments.

On the left bank of the Tessin there is a little village containing but few houses. It is called San Martino. Here is the bridge which must be crossed in going to Buffalora.

Buffalora is a village of sixteen hundred inhabitants, situated on the Naviglio Grande, twenty-seven kilometers from Milan. The two parts of the village are united by a bridge. On the right are two villages, or rather, two groups of houses, one of which is known as Ponte Nuova di Magenta, and the other as Ponte Vecchio di Magenta, with two bridges across the Naviglio Grande. These three bridges, the railway station, the houses and the hills, are occupied by Austrians with more than one hundred thousand men to defend these formidable positions. Their commander-in-chief confidently expected to cut off the French army from the bridge of San Martino, to isolate in this way all who had crossed the Tessin and to compel the 2d corps and the King's army to fall back precipitately on Turbigo in order to renew communication with the remainder of the army. Such was the plan which the intrepidity of the French troops was to bring to naught.

General Regnaud de Saint-Jean d'Angély, commander-in-chief of the guard, carries the Emperor's orders into execution. He sends the Wimpffen brigade against Buffalora. The Cler brigade follows the movement. They promptly carry Buffalora and the heights bordering the Naviglio Grande. But then they find themselves facing considerable masses which they cannot break through and which impede their progress. Chiefs and soldiers rival each other in heroism. General Cler, one of the most distinguished officers of the army, meets a glorious death in leading the zouaves of the guard to the charge. General Mellinet has two horses killed under him. General de Wimpffen is wounded in the face in conducting the attack of the right.

Notwithstanding the sublime efforts of the guard, it will end by being destroyed if reinforcements do not arrive. The day does not promise well for the French army. The march of the 3d and 4th corps is hindered by the obstacles presented by ground intersected by irrigating canals and covered by mulberry trees, poplars, and willows. Their columns, forced to stretch out indefinitely on the causeways, the marshy state of the soil often rendering the side paths impracticable, advance with difficulty. The army of King Victor Emmanuel is delayed in its passage of the Tessin, and only one of its divisions is able to follow at a distance the corps of General MacMahon.

The Emperor, still at the bridge of San Martino, experiences unutterable anguish. He no longer hears the cannon of the 2d corps in the distance. Can General MacMahon have been repulsed, and is the division of the guard to bear the whole brunt of the enemy's attack?

Colonel Raoult, chief of staff of the imperial guard, comes to tell the Emperor, on behalf of General Regnaud de Saint-Jean d'Angély, that the forces of the enemy are momently increasing and that he cannot hold out unless he receives reinforcements. "I have none to send him," replies Napoleon III., with calmness; "tell him to hold on with the few he has left."

"It was essential to the success of the day," the commander-in-chief of the guard will say in his report to the Emperor, " to protect the access to the bridge over the Naviglio so as to permit the army corps of General Niel and of Marshal Canrobert to fall upon the enemy as soon as they should arrive. Your Majesty directed an energetic defence to be made while awaiting the approaching reinforcements. The orders of Your Majesty were executed; the zouaves and grenadiers of the 3d as well as those of the 1st regiment, who had come to their assistance, resisted all attacks in the posts confided to them." What heroism in this simple and temperate language!

What had happened to General MacMahon, and why were the guns of the 2d corps still silent? At the village of Cuggione, General Lebrun, chief of staff, having ascended the church steeple, observed that considerable movements of Austrian troops were going on between Buffalora and Magenta. He went down very quickly and said to General MacMahon:

"There is a great battle in preparation just now. Unless we wish to risk being thrown into the Tessin by troops much superior to any we can oppose to them, there is only time enough to concentrate the two divisions of your army corps and the light infantry division of the guard." General MacMahon replied: "I am going to look for the Espinasse division myself." And he darted off like an arrow, followed by only a few horsemen. At breakneck speed he crossed vineyards, fields, and ditches, barely escaped being taken prisoner by the enemies, thanks to the speed of his horse, and at last reached General Espinasse. "Make haste," said he, and the regiment took the road from Buffalora to Cuggione. It rejoined those of General de La Motterouge and General Camou. The concentration was effected, and the three divisions advanced upon Magenta.

"The 2d army corps," General Lebrun has said, "in marching resolutely but alone upon Magenta, was exposing itself to the greatest dangers. For, towards four o'clock in the afternoon, the division of grenadiers of the imperial guard, which the Emperor was near, had not yet been able, in spite of its glorious and frequently renewed attacks, to force the passage of the canal (the Naviglio Grande) neither before the tunnel of the railway, nor before the Ponte Nuova di Magenta. The Austrian forces defending the crossings of the canal were sufficiently numerous and strongly established to keep up their resistance for a good while longer."

While General MacMahon was marching on Magenta with no forces but his four divisions, some troops had finally come to the assistance of the division of the guard. At last the dark uniforms of the light infantry and the red pantaloons of the line came into sight along the railway embankment. It was one of the brigades of the 3d corps, the Picard, which was coming in haste with Marshal Canrobert. In company with the zouaves and the grenadiers it performed prodigies of valor. The village of Ponte di Magenta, after being taken and retaken three times, had still to be defended against the return of the Austrians. General Picard, Colonel Bellecourt of the 85th, and many other officers, setting an example of pluck and tenacity to the troops, made them retake it once more. Marshal Canrobert has written in his report to the Emperor: "The enemy realized the importance of this point, which, had it remained in their power, would have brought them on the very flank of our line of communication with the bridge of Tessin. This explains their tenacity in the successive attacks, and the irresistible vehemence of ours in the renewed attempts to take the position."

The Marshal adds: "The Jannin brigade, led by General Renault, was finally able to debouch and move quickly on the Austrian line, resting on Ponte di Magenta, in that part of the village which is on the left bank of the Naviglio Grande canal. Several times taken and retaken, this portion of the village, isolated by the Naviglio bridge, which the enemy had blown up, remains in possession of General Renault, who has definitively established himself there."

Now let us return to General MacMahon. His troops begin to march about four o'clock, with the church steeple of Magenta as their point of direction. It is on this march that the 3d zouaves seize an Austrian flag, a feat which earns for this regiment the pleasure of seeing their own flag decorated with the cross of the Legion of Honor a few days later. The moment is solemn; the fate of the battle is about to be determined. Just then General Lebrun says to MacMahon: "The trees and vines prevent our battalions from seeing each other; but if they hear the drums beating and the trumpets sounding to right and left of them, they will understand that they are shoulder to shoulder, and then they will have no anxiety; they will go on marching with entire confidence." MacMahon takes the advice of his chief of staff. The drums beat, the trumpets blow their warlike flourish. When the three divisions, La Motterouge, Espinasse, and Camou, are within three or four hundred yards of Magenta, they are a compact mass able to defy the Austrian forces who occupy the railway station, the approaches and the interior of the city.

On the left, the Espinasse division rushes upon the street at the entry of Magenta, known as the rue de Marcallo.

On the right, the La Motterouge division attacks

the principal entrance by which the highway of Buffalora and Magenta passes into the town.

In the centre, the Camou division attacks the approaches to the station.

All the houses at the entrances of Magenta and the station are occupied by Austrian forces who bravely resist the assailants.

The intrepid General Espinasse, trying to force the entrance of rue de Marcallo, in front of him, wishes to set an example to his troops. He places himself at the head of the 2d zouaves and fights like a private soldier. His horse stumbles in stamping on corpses in a pool of blood. "One can't keep up on this shifting soil," says he, and alights, imitated by his orderly officer, Lieutenant de Froidefond, and his fanion-bearer, Count Horace de Choiseul. M. de Froidefond has scarcely left his horse when he falls, mortally wounded.

The most deadly firing comes from a large house of several stories at the left corner of the street. It is occupied by three hundred Tyrolese whose aim is wonderfully correct. "Whatever it costs us, that house must be taken," shouts General Espinasse. "Come on, zouaves, break in the door!" The zouaves make a rush, presenting themselves as targets to the rifles of the Tyrolese, who fire point-blank. The door the zouaves are trying to break resists their efforts. Thereupon the General strikes the blind of a window on the ground floor with the pommel of his sword, and cries: "Go in through there!" At that very instant there comes through the window against which he is leaning a rifle shot which lays him dead on the ground.

Roaring like lions, the zouaves rush at the window and shiver it into pieces. At last they are masters of the house. General de Castagny takes the place of General Espinasse, and, under a rain of fire, leads the zouaves to the public square. There the Castagny brigade (2d zouaves, 1st and 2d foreign regiments) is rejoined by the Gault brigade (11th battalion of chasseurs, 71st and 72d of the line), which had made its attack on the opposite side by the road from Buffalora to Milan.

While the two brigades of the Espinasse have been penetrating into Magenta, the La Motterouge division has carried the part of the town in front of it with no less vigor. Arriving by a sunken road, enfiladed by two pieces of Austrian artillery, the 65th of the line, under Colonel Drouhot, debouches in front of the railway station. The sharpest sort of firing from the crenellated buildings occupied by thousands of Austrian sharpshooters does not arrest its impetuous march. Within a few minutes it has seized the station and the two cannon intended for its defence. Not contented with this first success, Colonel Drouhot makes a rush for the city, followed by his flag, which is floating in the front ranks. The firing is redoubled. The brave colonel falls mortally wounded. The flag is riddled with balls and grape-shot; the handle is broken into four pieces.

L

Two French cannon arrive at this moment; under their protection, the 65th is at last able to make its way into the streets opening before them.

The 70th of the line, sent to the right of Magenta, after crossing the railroad finds itself confronted by formidable obstacles. A number of Austrian battalions are intrenched in the church, the neighboring houses, and behind thick, crenellated walls. Two battalions of the regiment *Roi des Belges* occupy the middle of the cemetery, whence they receive the French attacks in flank. The soldiers are fighting hand to hand in the courts and inside the houses; and the presbytery, the church, and the cemetery are not taken until after a bitter contest, which is prolonged until night.

The 45th of the line and the Algerian tirailleurs, reaching the edge of the deep ditch beside the railroad, have rallied the 52d, crossed the obstacle, and, mingling with the 65th and the 70th, assisted gloriously in the taking of the station, the church, and the neighboring houses. The division of voltigeurs of the guard has also lent powerful assistance.

It is eight o'clock in the evening. Some Austrian detachments, intrenched and barricaded in the houses, still keep up a vigorous defence. But they are soon forced to lay down their arms. Thousands of prisoners and several cannon are the trophies of the 2d corps.

The success is not less decisive at Ponte Vecchio, at the other extremity of the battlefield. At the head of the 86th of the line, General Vinoy has seized this village, situated on the left bank of the Naviglio Grande.

General Auger's artillery, established along the railway tracks, decimates the Austrian columns, which, unable to rally, beat a hasty retreat towards Castellano and Corbetto.

The victory is complete. The enemy, whose losses are estimated at twenty thousand men killed or wounded, has left four cannon, two flags, and seven thousand prisoners in the hands of the victors. The great battles of the First Empire had not been more glorious.

CHAPTER XXI

THE MORROW OF MAGENTA

THROUGHOUT the battle, Napoleon III. had kept within reach of his guard, hurrying up the reinforcements, and directing them in proportion to their arrival at the points most severely menaced. He did not hear until late in the evening of the taking of Magenta and the complete victory of his troops; he then established his headquarters at San Martino, that little group of houses which scarcely deserves the name of a village. He lodged in a wretched inn, where, after a long talk with Marshal Canrobert, he threw himself, all dressed, on a carter's bed for a few minutes of repose. But he soon got up again. The officers of his military household, who had lain down in the open air, some on bundles of hay, some on sacks of maize, could see him by the light of the solitary candle burning in his chamber, sometimes walking up and down, sometimes leaning his elbows on the wooden table to read the reports which he received, and addressing to the Empress the bulletin of victory.

The victor of Magenta — he deserves that title, since he was the commander-in-chief — triumphed modestly, more like a philosopher than a warrior. Until then, all he had known of war was its epic narratives. Now, he saw its horrors close at hand, and his sensitive, compassionate soul suffered. On one hand, he considered the cause for which he had taken up arms as just and civilizing. But on the other hand, he could not escape the knowledge that he was largely responsible for the torrents of blood which had been shed. This reflection disturbed in him the friend of the people, the humanitarian sovereign, and on the morrow of his triumph his countenance retained the impress of his habitual melancholy, deepened by the bitter remembrance of the perplexities and wretchedness of the battle. He knew, moreover, that the war was barely yet begun, and the existing hecatombs made him forebode those which were to come. He thought of all those whose death would be made known at the same time as the victory; of General Espinasse, his aide-de-camp, and friend, and confidant; his Minister of the Interior and of Public Security on the morrow of the Orsini attempt; of General Cler, concerning whom Marshal Canrobert said: "Cler has everything,—intelligence, audacity, activity, a body of iron, an indefatigable soul, the temperament, the knowledge, and the aptitudes of the profession"; of two accomplished superior officers, Colonel de Senneville, Canrobert's chief of staff, and Lieutenant-Colonel de La Bonninière de Beaumont, deputy chief of staff to MacMahon; of Colonels Drouhot of the 65th of the line, Charlier of the 90th, de Chabrière of the 2d foreign regiment, all of whom had been gloriously slain at the head of their troops. He thought of many promising officers mowed down in the flower of youth. Possibly, since he loved the poor and the humble, he thought still more about the private soldiers, most of them absolutely without prospect of advancement, who had sacrificed their lives like heroes without other recompense than the satisfaction of duty fulfilled. Occasionally a cruel doubt presented itself, and the crowned thinker asked himself whether war, which Joseph de Maistre considered a divine thing, is not in reality an infernal one.

At San Martino the ambulances were near the Emperor's headquarters, and next door to the inn where he lodged was a large house which served as a depot for prisoners. At dawn on June 5, the troops had ceased defiling upon the bridge. Nothing was in sight but mule ambulances and carts transporting the wounded.

During the morning Napoleon III. was called on by Victor Emmanuel, who regretted extremely that his troops had arrived too late. He afterwards examined the banks of the Tessin in person so as to supervise the establishment of the boat-bridges himself. The commander-in-chief of the imperial guard had his headquarters on the left bank of the river. As soon as the Emperor caught sight of him he hastened to meet him, and, shaking his hand with evident emotion, he said: "General, yesterday you and the imperial guard deserved well of France."

June 6.—Napoleon III. transferred his headquarters from San Martino to Magenta. At seven o'clock in the morning he mounted his horse and went over the whole of the battlefield, followed by his entire staff. The story is told by the Marquis de Massa, an eyewitness: "It was easy to read on the countenance of Napoleon III. the painful impression he received from so dearly bought a victory. And so full of abnegation were these chosen souls that I have heard the wounded themselves, when he was expressing his interest in them, seek to reassure him by saying: 'It won't amount to anything, we shall be better! We shall come back all the same to go at it again.'

"There was a moment when the litter-bearers had to stand aside to allow a vehicle to pass in which were two dead bodies. Coming near it, the Emperor at once took off his hat with signs of deep distress. He had recognized the corpse of General Espinasse, side by side with his orderly officer, Ensign Froidefond. As he contemplated the inanimate countenance of the valiant general whom he had intended to make a marshal of France, the loyal adherent who had served him so well in Paris on the day of the *coup d'État*, and on African, Crimean, and Italian battlefields, he murmured, 'poor Espinasse,' and his eyes filled with tears."

Just as he reached the Naviglio Grande canal, on either bank of which his troops had performed prodigies of valor, the sovereign perceived General MacMahon who was coming to meet him, and gave him the most flattering reception. He congratulated him warmly on the taking of Magenta, which had decided the final success of the day, and kept him at his side all the rest of the way. When they had entered in this manner the town which had been the scene of such bloody combats two days before, Napoleon III. said to MacMahon: "I make you Marshal of France and Duke of Magenta." Very much affected, the new marshal was overwhelmed by gratitude.

General Fleury and the other aides-de-camp of the Emperor greatly regretted that he should have done nothing for General Regnaud de Saint-Jean d'Angély, the commander-in-chief of his guard. Fleury says: "When we were installed at Magenta, His Majesty was fatigued and suffering a little, and sent us word that he would not come to table with us. We had been sitting for some minutes in complete silence, every one thinking to himself what no one dared to say aloud. Convinced that I must take the initiative on this occasion as on so many others, and tell my sovereign the truth, I left the table without a word and went upstairs to the Emperor's room: — 'I hope Your Majesty will forgive me for disturbing your repose, but I think I shall be doing my duty by laying before you certain reflections suggested by the double distinction just accorded to General MacMahon. Sire, it was not he who gained the battle. You are the victor of Magenta; you were in command. It was the imperial guard, your own guard, which decided the fate of the army by its indomitable bravery.

... Not to recompense the superior officer of the guard would be to allow Europe to suppose that the imperial guard did not even see the battle.'"

When General Fleury stopped talking, the Emperor replied: "You are right. I had not thought of the question in that light. Go tell General Regnaud de Saint-Jean d'Angély that I appoint him Marshal of France. And at the same time tell General de Wimpffen that I make him general of division."

A moment later, General Fleury said to an equerry of the Emperor, son-in-law of the new marshal: "Davillier, come with me to tell your father-in-law the good news," And they both set off at full gallop.

Napoleon III. had divested himself of his own victory to attribute the chief merit of it to MacMahon.

CHAPTER XXII

THE ENTRY INTO MILAN

FROM Magenta, when the weather is fine, one can see the bell-towers and steeples of the Milan cathedral, the Duomo, that mass of marble white as mountain snows. Throughout the battle of the 4th of June, the Milanese population had listened with anxiety to the noise of the cannonading. They knew that the independence of Italy was then at stake. Their emotion was full of anguish. Night came and they were still uncertain as to the decree of destiny, and the crowd thronging the streets and squares awaited news with feverish impatience. At a very late hour a horseman made his appearance at the Vercellina gate and flung the mere words, "The Austrians are beaten," into the different groups. Perhaps the news was false. People hesitated to believe it.

There was no room for doubt by daybreak. The Austrians, encamped on the Castle Square, were folding their tents and making ready to depart. During the day they vanished. At once Italian and French flags floated from the house windows, and the whole population prepared to give their liberators an enthusiastic welcome.

In the evening of June 6, Marshal MacMahon received the following order: "The 2d corps will have the honor of entering Milan to-morrow at the head of the French army. The Emperor himself will lead this army corps. In execution of this order, the troops of the 2d corps will quit their barracks at San Pietro l'Olmo and march towards Milan. They will set off early on June 7. Between nine and ten o'clock in the morning they will unite before Milan, their head of column established at the foot of the arch of triumph erected at the entrance of the capital of the kingdom of Italy in honor of Napoleon I., and to the glory of his armies."

Listen to the chief of staff of the 2d corps, General Lebrun: "The monument is grandiose; the sculptures decorating it are magnificent. After the arch of triumph in the Place de l'Etoile at Paris, an edifice resplendent with all the glories of the First Empire, there is not a more imposing arch of triumph in the world than that of Milan.

"On arriving at the foot of the monument, Marshal MacMahon got off his horse and threw himself down on the ground to rest and wait for the Emperor. It would not be easy to enumerate the ovations given him by the inhabitants from San Pietro l'Olmo to Milan. When the Milanese saw him lying down and looking at their glorious arch of triumph, they began and kept up an incessant round of applause."

Meanwhile, the marshal ordered his chief of staff,

General Lebrun, to go into the city and settle upon the sites where the troops should establish their bivouacs in the evening. At the moment when the general was passing through the largest of the streets, an innumerable crowd which was waiting for the Emperor took him for Napoleon III. and threw down an avalanche of flowers upon him from the balconies. "I saw women of the people," said he, "and great ladies also, who were on the pavements, spring towards me, and, at the risk of being crushed under the feet of my horse, seize my hands to press them; some went so far, must I say it, as to cover my boots with their kisses."

Towards eleven o'clock in the morning, the Emperor apprised Marshal MacMahon that as Victor Emmanuel had not yet arrived, he would not make his entry until the next day, with the King beside him.

June 8. — The imperial guard, which camped at Cava Piobetta, four kilometres from Milan, received orders to march towards the Lombard capital and wait for the Emperor before the outer gate, called the *Porta Vercellina*. It was believed that the two sovereigns would not arrive until eleven o'clock. They came three hours sooner.

"The imperial guard, under command of Marshal Regnaud de Saint-Jean d'Angély," says the Marquis de Massa, "is massed upon the grand place of arms. From every window lorgnettes are bent upon the grenadiers whose high bearskin caps, long cloaks, white belts crossed on the breast, recall their predecessors of the First Empire whose traditions they have just revived. The new ones have held their own at Magenta as the old ones did at Friedland. In front of them the silhouette of their chief of division, General Mellinet, who has had two horses killed under him in the hottest of the fight, defines itself. A hot sunbeam striking across his masculine profile brings his cheekbone into high relief, and underneath it a deep cavity marks the trace of the ball which ploughed his cheek at the siege of Sebastopol. General Camou's light infantry division rests on his left. Opposite this infantry deploys our brigade, guides, and chasseurs."

The cortege approaches. At the head the detachment of the hundred guards; next Napoleon III. with Victor Emmanuel on his left; at some distance behind them, their two staffs; closing the march a mixed escort composed of a squadron of guides and a squadron of light horsemen from Novara; in front of the latter the Duke of Chartres, General La Marmora's orderly officer.

The cortege arrives opposite the triumphal arch of Milan which is usually surrounded by enormous iron chains connected by high stone pillars. Never had any troop whatever passed underneath the arch, this interdiction having been decided upon by the municipality at the time of its erection. But this time the authorities have made an exception to the rule, the iron chains have been removed; the Emperor and the King are going to pass under the arch of triumph.

The two sovereigns cross the city amidst the universal enthusiasm. Napoleon III. goes to the Bonaparte villa which is to serve as his residence, from there he issues the following proclamation:—

"Italians! the fortune of war leads me to-day into the capital of Lombardy. I am going to tell you why I am here.

"When Austria unjustly attacked Piedmont, I resolved to support my ally, the King of Sardinia: the honor and the interests of France made this my duty. Your enemies, who are also mine, have sought to diminish the existing sympathy in Europe for your cause by seeking to make it believed that I am going to war through motives of personal ambition.

"If there are men who do not comprehend their epoch, I am not one of them. In the enlightened state of public opinion, one is greater to-day by the moral influence he exerts than by barren conquests, and I proudly seek this moral influence in endeavoring to free one of the most beautiful portions of Europe. Your welcome has already proved that you have not misapprehended me.

"I do not come here with a preconceived system for dispossessing sovereigns, nor to impose my will upon you; my army will concern itself with two things only: with combating your enemies and maintaining internal order; it will put no obstacle to the free manifestation of your legitimate desires.

"Providence sometimes favors peoples as well as individuals by giving them an opportunity to grow greater suddenly; but on condition that they are able to profit by it. Profit then by the chance presented to you. Your desire for independence, disappointed for so long, will be realized if you show yourselves worthy of it.

"Unite, then, in a single aim: the enfranchisement of your country. Organize yourselves in military fashion. Make haste to enroll yourselves under the standards of King Victor Emmanuel who has so nobly pointed out to you the road to honor. Remember that there can be no army without discipline, and, animated by the sacred ardor of patriotism, be nothing now but soldiers; to-morrow you will be free citizens of a great country.

"Done at the imperial headquarters of Milan, June 8, 1859. — NAPOLEON."

The Emperor was not without anxieties in the midst of his triumph. He had just learned that at Melegnano, fifteen kilometers from Milan, the Austrians were fortifying themselves and possibly intended to make an offensive return against the Lombard capital. Consequently he had ordered the 1st and 2d corps to move as fast as possible upon Melegnano. He had scarcely arrived at the Bonaparte villa when he mounted a horse and went to assure himself that Marshal MacMahon and his troops had begun to march. He reached the exterior ramparts without being recognized, for the passers-by could not suppose that this unescorted horseman might be the Emperor. But, on his return, the crowd had learned that it was he, and gave him an indescribable ovation.

In the course of the same day, Napoleon III. addressed this proclamation to his army: "Soldiers, a month ago, relying on the efforts of diplomacy, I was still hoping for peace, when the sudden invasion of Piedmont by Austrian troops summoned us to arms. We were not ready; men, horses, material, provisions, were lacking, and, to assist our allies, we were forced to march in haste and by small instalments beyond the Alps, to meet a redoubtable enemy long in readiness. The danger was great, the energy of the nation and your courage made up for everything. France has found again her ancient virtues, and, united in a single aim as in a single sentiment, she has displayed the abundance of her resources and the strength of her patriotism. Here it is, but ten days since operations began, and Piedmontese territory is already freed from its invaders. The allied army has given four successful battles and gained a decisive victory which has opened to it the capital of Lombardy. You have disabled more than thirty-five thousand Austrians, taken seventeen cannon, two flags, and eight thousand prisoners, but all is not yet ended; we shall still have combats to maintain, obstacles to overcome. I rely on you, brave soldiers of the army of Italy! From the heights of heaven your fathers look down on you with pride."

At that very moment when this proclamation appeared, the troops of Marshal Baraguey d'Hilliers, united to those of Marshal MacMahon, were fighting at Melegnano.

CHAPTER XXIII

MELEGNANO

MARSHAL Baraguey d'Hilliers regretted deeply that the 1st army corps, of which he was the chief, had not had the honor of taking part in the battle of Magenta. He made up for it, June 8, in fighting that of Melegnano.

Melegnano (Marignan) is a little village of three thousand souls, situated fifteen kilometers southeast of Milan. It was there that in 1515, François Premier gained a memorable victory over the Swiss which is known as the battle of giants.

When Napoleon III. learned that the Austrians were retiring towards Lodi but still occupied Melegnano, he resolved to dislodge them, and gave the job to the 1st and 2d. corps. The operations were to be directed by Marshal Baraguey d'Hilliers, with Marshal MacMahon under him.

The 1st corps left its bivouac at San Pietro l'Olmo very early in the morning of June 8, to go to Melegnano, twenty-eight kilometers distant. The 1st division was commanded by General Forey, the 2d by General de Ladmirault, the 3d by General

Bazaine. They began marching, the first at four o'clock, the 2d at five, the 3d at six.

All three went first to Milan, which they crossed in all haste, amidst an enthusiastic crowd who deluged them with flowers and wreaths. They left the city by the *Porta Romana* and turned towards Melegnano. Each went by a different road. It was the 3d — the Bazaine division — which went by the highroad, a causeway twenty meters in width, bordered by ditches full of water, from eight to ten meters wide, across which stone bridges with parapets give at intervals access into the fields.

To right and left the ground is cut up by a large number of ditches and irrigating canals. Meadows, wheatfields, thick hedges, and a great many trees covered its surface.

The Bazaine division, to which was reserved the honor of being first to attack the positions of Melegnano, was far ahead of the other two divisions, which were often halted by ditches, or retarded by the windings of side roads. It reached San Giuliano at five in the evening, and at a quarter of six was in sight of Melegnano, about a kilometer away.

Prudence would have counselled a halt until the Forey and Ladmirault divisions should come up, and a combined movement with the troops of the 2d corps which, at no great distance, was making ready to manœuvre on the rear of the enemy. But Marshal Baraguey d'Hilliers was impatient to make the powder talk.

It is nearly six o'clock, and the Bazaine division has been marching for twelve hours. The marshal orders the attack to be begun. At once a company of zouaves, acting as a vanguard, deploys on either side of the road as tirailleurs.

The Austrians have only the Roden and the Boer brigades to defend the city, but they occupy excellent positions; their artillery enfilades the road by which the French are coming. Remnants of ancient fortifications, hedges, gardens, and farms give them secure shelter. The majority of the houses looking down on the principal avenues are barricaded and supplied with defenders. Braving the grape-shot, the 1st zouaves, followed by the 33d and 34th of the line, attack with extreme impetuosity. The Austrians have furnished the houses at the entrance of the city, the cutting of the road, and the cemetery with a swarm of sharpshooters, but all in vain; in vain they make a valiant resistance in the streets, at the castle, behind the hedges and the garden walls; they cannot withstand the dash of the intrepid General Bazaine and his admirable division.

General Goze, commandant of the 1st brigade, and Colonel Paulze d'Ivoy, at the head of his regiment, the 1st zouaves, precede and launch the assaulting columns. All the officers, with lifted swords, march in front of their soldiers. It is at the old castle that the Austrians have concentrated their principal efforts, for it is there that their movement of retreat upon Lodi and Pavia might be intercepted by the

French troops. All along the walls they have made loopholes through which they rain a plunging fire.

Here come the 1st zouaves debouching on the open place of the old castle. A rolling fire of musketry from the windows does not daunt their ardor. While some rush into the castle, chasing out the Austrians and taking their places, others, led on by Colonel Paulze d'Ivoy, go through the gate leading to the Carpiano suburb. At this moment the brave colonel, who has not ceased to animate his zouaves by word, gesture, and example, and whose horse has just been killed under him, falls, mortally wounded by a bullet in the head, close to a church which stands in a corner of the square. The zouaves avenge him by seizing the first houses of the suburb, and, being too few in number to drive the enemy any further, lie in wait there while expecting reinforcements.

Meanwhile, the 33d of the line is forcing the enemy back. In one of the offensive returns of the Austrians, its flag, in danger for an instant, but heroically defended, has its staff broken.

A violent storm which has long been threatening breaks above the scene of combat and deluges it with a torrent of rain. The roar of the thunder mingles with the roar of battle. The wind howls furiously.

Marshal Baraguey d'Hilliers is in the centre of the action, on the church square. His flag-bearer, Quartermaster Franchetti, is wounded at his side.

The 2d division, which had rejoined the troops of the 3d at the Lambro bridge, and had at first been arrested by the depth of the water and the steepness of the banks, has contrived to continue its march, and contributes greatly to the final success.

As to the 1st division, that of General Forey, it had been unable to take part in the fight. Forming a column of his first brigade, the General had pushed on to Riozzo the 74th of the line, the 84th, and the 17th battalion of chasseurs; but the ditches filled with water, the cuttings of the roads and the storm had delayed them, and they had been unable to go further than the Landriano road. As they had been marching since four in the morning, General Forey called a halt. Shortly after he received orders from Marshal Baraguey d'Hilliers to enter Melegnano, which his division reached at half-past ten in the evening.

Now consider the part played by the 2d army corps, that of Marshal MacMahon. After quitting the highroad it moved upon the extreme right and the rear of the enemy, as had been agreed upon by the two marshals. The 2d division, commanded by General Decaen, arrived at Mediglia towards four in the afternoon, followed at a great distance by the 1st division, that of General de La Motterouge, delayed by having to ford the Lambro and by the bad roads.

The Decaen division had camped at Balbiano when the cannon of the 1st corps made it resume and hasten its march. Six battalions, taken by Marshal MacMahon from the two brigades, were at once reunited under arms, without knapsacks, and moved forward, followed by the artillery. This column, on reaching the Mulazzano road, turned to the right, and advanced in a line formed by the massed battalions, across meadows difficult of access. The two batteries of the division were then placed in position, and in spite of the approaching nightfall, in spite of the raging storm, they managed to send several balls after the Austrian columns retreating along the Lodi road.

To sum up, the victors of Melegnano were Marshal Baraguey d'Hilliers, General de Ladmirault and General Bazaine. Seldom has a battle been more bloody. In his report to the Emperor the Marshal wrote: "The losses of the enemy are considerable; the streets and the grounds contiguous to the city are covered with their dead; twelve hundred wounded Austrians have been carried in our ambulances; we have made between eight hundred and nine hundred prisoners and taken a cannon. Our losses amount to nine hundred and forty-three men killed or wounded; but, as in all the previous engagements, the officers have been stricken in large proportion; General Bazaine and General Goze have been bruised; the colonel of the 1st zouaves has been killed; the colonel and the lieutenant-colonel of the 33d have been wounded; in all there are thirteen officers killed and fifty-six wounded."

Alas! among those who had fallen never to rise again, how many still carried in their caps or their buttonholes the flowers which the Milanese women had thrown to them that morning!

CHAPTER XXIV

BEFORE SOLFERINO

IDEAS of triumph and ideas of death met and contended in the mind of Napoleon III. At nine o'clock in the morning of the 9th of June he went to see Marshal Baraguey d'Hilliers at Melegnano, and could not look without anguish at the relics of the carnage of the previous day. Two hours later, he was back at Milan to be present at the chanting of the *Te Deum* in the cathedral.

It is eleven o'clock. All the church bells in the city are jangling. The drums beat the general; the bugles sound. From Bonaparte villa, where the Emperor lodges, as far as the cathedral — the Duomo as it is called — the imperial guard forms a double line in following the Corso. Old tapestries, hangings of silk and velvet, gold fringes blending with the long folds of the flags, cover the walls and droop from the windows.

The imperial and royal cortege approaches. At the head are the hundred-guards. Napoleon III. and Victor Emmanuel come into view at the extremity of the Corso, followed by their brilliant staffs. A rain of flowers falls upon the sovereigns. Milan has laid its gardens waste and robbed its parterres; a perfumed carpet covers the pavements of the Lombard city. In every window, every balcony, are green branches, plaited wreaths, flower petals massed in baskets held by the young girls of Milan as if for the Corpus Christi processions. At one moment the Emperor's horse and that of the King, becoming the target for all the flowery projectiles, begin to prance, and the sovereigns signify to the fair Milanese that a trifle more moderation in their transports of enthusiasm would be agreeable.

The cortege arrives in front of the white marble cathedral, outlining itself majestically against the blue Italian sky, with the inexhaustible wealth of its sculptured ornamentation, the multitude of its staircases and terraces, the audacious spring of its central pyramid, around which is graduated a prodigious forest of turrets, spires, and innumerable statues.

With his white mitre on, the coadjutor-archbishop, M. Caccia, attended by canons, receives the sovereigns at the threshold of the edifice. With excellent taste, the walls of this magnificent church, next to Saint Peter's at Rome the largest in the world, have not been disfigured with draperies. Its mosaic pavement should not be hidden by carpets, nor the five naves, their pointed arches, their columns and festoons of marble, by hangings.

Old inhabitants of Milan are thinking of the ceremony which took place in this very sanctuary fifty-four years ago. Napoleon was crowned here, May 26, 1805, with as much pomp as he had been at Notre Dame of Paris six months before. After Cardinal Caprara had blessed the iron crown with the sacramental words formerly used in crowning Germanic emperors as Italian kings, the great man, placing it on his own head, as he had placed that of the Emperor of the French, pronounced with extreme energy these sacramental words: *Dio me l'ha data, quai a chi la toccerà*, God has given it to me, woe to him who touches it. That is what these old Milanese are thinking of as they watch the heir of the victor of Austerlitz making his entry into the Duomo.

All day and all the evening the city keeps holiday. The Marquis de Massa, an eye-witness, thus describes it: "The restaurants at dinner time would never have been able to accommodate their customers if private individuals, posted at their doorways, had not invited, on the hint of the epaulette, as many guests as their tables could contain. . . . Some persons — I was one of them — had reserved tables in the open air in the garden of the *Albergo Marino*, where we met again, for the most part between habitués of the Maison d'Or or the Café Anglais, General de Ferton with Artus Talon, his orderly officer; General Douay with Gallifet, lieutenant of spahis, arrived from Africa the day before, spite of winds and tides; De Cools and Octave de Bastard, staff-captains; Borrelli, ensign of chasseurs, etc. 'Hold on, what, is that you?'—'Does that astonish you?'—'I heard you were dead.'—'Not yet, and you?'—'Nor I either, as you see.' — 'Here's to your health, then!'—'To yours!' And the corks of Asti wine bottles flew into the air, mingling their dry report with that of the fire-crackers in the street."

The war! What a medley of joys and sorrows, of intoxicating thoughts and bitter ones! While at Milan officers and soldiers were in high glee, at Melegnano they were making doleful reflections on the possibly useless carnage of the previous day. After a fight so bloody, preceded by so long a march, they had not even been able to rest. "The evening and night of June 8-9," writes General Lebrun, "was a dreadful time for the 2d army corps. Rain never stopped falling all the evening; it did stop at night; but our wretched soldiers, wet to the bone, bivouacking in fields covered with water, unable either to lie down or to light fires, never rested for a moment. I remember that on the narrow causeway where Marshal MacMahon and I found ourselves, the Marshal, like another Turenne, lay down on the carriage of a cannon. The ground of the causeway was covered with mud between three and four inches thick. For my part, after wrapping myself in my rubber cloak, I stretched myself on the mud, with half the length of my legs hanging over the dike, above the little canal which bordered it."

It was impossible not to think that Baraguey d'Hilliers had been in too great a hurry to attack. General

Fleury wrote from Milan, June 10 : " If the Marshal had put off his attack until next day, he would have acted with the combined column of Marshal MacMahon and General Niel, and would have obtained as certain a success without wasting so many men. It is evident that the Austrians, seeing their wings threatened, would have quickly decided to retreat. We were at Melegnano yesterday, and the Marshal's army, though proud of its success, seemed to me, nevertheless, somewhat disheartened. The Emperor has strongly advised against any more of these useless feats of strength. The zouaves, for their share, have thirty-eight officers disabled. Now I must admit, from the strategic point of view, that the object has been attained, although too violently. The Austrians instantly evacuated Lodi."

Throughout the 9th of June, at the very moment when religious chants were resounding at Milan beneath the arches of the Duomo, where they were intoning the *Te Deum*, the road from Melegnano to the Lombard capital presented a sorry spectacle. The more wealthy Milanese families had sent their carriages to seek the wounded of the previous day and bring them to their houses, transformed for the time being into hospitals. These carriages came back slowly; on their silken cushions officers and soldiers were lying whose blood-spotted uniforms were still adorned with flowers.

In the evening, Napoleon III. and Victor Emmanuel, acclaimed with frenzy by a crowd intoxicated with joy and enthusiasm, were present at a full-dress representation at the Scala theatre.

The allied army remained the 9th and 10th of June in the positions which they occupied the 8th: the 1st, 2d and 3d corps at Melegnano and its neighborhood; the imperial guard, the 3d army corps, and the King's army at Milan. The troops needed rest, and the Emperor time to prepare the indispensable material means for overcoming the obstacles which the army would encounter on its route. They would have to cross successively all the affluents of the left bank of the Po, descending from the solid mass of the Alps: the Adda, the Serio, the Oglio, the Mella, the Chiesa, before reaching the banks of the Mincio, and it was certain that the retreating enemy would blow up the bridges and employ every effort to retard the march of the allies.

Napoleon III. left Milan for Melegnano in the morning of June 10. He knew that the Austrians had evacuated Lodi and other important positions. The 9th, the Duchess of Parma, yielding to the force of events, had been obliged to leave the duchy where she held the regency in the name of her young son. The 10th, Plaisance was abandoned, and the Austrians, blowing up the forts and block-houses, tore down with their own hands the works they had accumulated before this place, surrounded with a ring of ramparts, and spiked such cannons as they could not load upon barges or tow by steamers. On the 11th they burned the Adda bridge and evacuated Pizzighettone. The same day, the allied army started to pursue them.

The imperial guard, resuming its rôle as a reserve, did not leave Milan until the next day, to go to Gorgonzola, where the Emperor established his headquarters.

The army corps marched at a distance of about three and a half leagues from each other. The clogging of the roads, the dust, the heat, the streams to cross, rendered the march difficult and painful. It was no mean enterprise to move forward, in the face of the enemy, six army corps:—the 1st, 2d, 3d, 4th corps, the imperial guard, and the four divisions of the Sardinian army,—concentrated in a restricted place and ready to rejoin each other in a solid mass at a given signal.

Between the 12th and the 14th of June, the allies crossed the Adda, the Sardinians at Vaprio, the French at Cassano, and there, as at the Sesia and the Tessin, the pontoon men, under the skilful direction of General Lebœuf, gained new titles to the gratitude of the army.

The 18th, the allied troops took their cantonments around Brescia. The Emperor and the guard occupied the city which, renowned for its patriotism and courage, gave the liberating sovereign an enthusiastic reception. All the streets were draped and a rain of flowers descended.

The 19th and 20th of June were days of rest. The

combatants of Magenta and Melegnano received the rewards they had merited.

At noon on the 19th, the 2d zouaves were under arms. Marshal MacMahon arrived, followed by his staff, and the square was formed. "Soldiers of the 2d zouaves," said he, "the Emperor, desiring to retain the customs of the First Empire, has decreed that the eagles of a regiment which has captured an enemy's flag shall be decorated with the Legion of Honor. Zouaves! you all deserve a recompense, for all of you have displayed valor. Your fathers who behold you are proud of you. The flag of your regiment is the first of the army of Italy to be decorated, I am glad that it should be in the 2d army corps, which I command, that such an honor should be paid, and I am proud that it should be you, soldiers of the 2d zouaves, whose reputation has not been belied either in the Crimea, in Africa, or at Magenta, who have deserved it."

Then advancing towards the flag, the Marshal saluted it, and added: "Eagle of the 2d regiment of zouaves, be proud of thy soldiers; in the name of the Emperor, and by the power devolved on me, I give thee the cross of the Legion of Honor." Then he fastened to the eagle the red ribbon from which depended the cross, and shouts of: "Long live the Emperor! Long live the Marshal!" resounded.

The army was rejoined the same day, at Brescia, by a cavalry division of the guard, commanded by General Morris, which, having come by the Corniche road, had been delayed later than the other troops. It was welcome.

The army resumed its march on the 21st. On this side of the Chiesa, two kilometers from Montechiaro, stretches a vast, barren plain which seemed likely to be a battlefield where the Austrian could easily deploy their superb cavalry. This provision was not realized. Continuing their retreat they recrossed the Chiesa, which the allies were also able to cross without resistance.

The decisive moment was approaching. They were nearing the boundaries of Lombardy, to find themselves facing the famous quadrilateral which, formed by the four strongholds of Peschiera, Mantua, Legnano, and Verona, is bordered on one side by an important river, the Mincio, and on the other by the States of the Germanic Confederation. For the Austrians it was a formidable base of operations.

Arriving at Verona as early as the 30th of May, and assisted by Baron Hess, his general chief-of-staff, Francis Joseph had taken command of his reorganized army. His intention in making his troops evacuate Plaisance, Pizzighettone, Pavia, Cremona, Ancona, Bologna, Ferrara, was to concentrate all his forces on the Mincio. He had reunited them into two armies, both under his own orders, but commanded, the one by Count Wimpffen and the other by Count Schlick. Count Giulay had been relieved of his command. The Emperor Francis Joseph established his headquarters at Villafranca. The ensemble of his troops comprised an actual effective force of one hundred and sixty thousand men, a total nearly equal to that of the Franco-Sardinian army. The Austrian sovereign had thought at first of taking the offensive beyond the Mincio and the Chiesa; but he had given up the idea, being unwilling to risk a battle with the Mincio behind him, even with the great number of bridges at his disposal. The recollection of 1848 decided him to follow the example of Field-Marshal Radetzky, and he had just ordered his troops to fall back behind the Mincio to await the enemy from the centre of the quadrilateral and there resume the offensive as the famous Austrian soldier had done in other days.

Meanwhile the Franco-Sardinian army continued its march, amazed at meeting no enemies on its route, and wondering what the schemes of Francis Joseph might be. This forward march occasioned great fatigues and great difficulties.

Listen to General Fleury: —

"The weather is very hot. The army begins to dwindle greatly. The marches, short for a staff, are very long for the army corps, which necessarily follow nearly always the same route in moving to right and left; hence stoppages almost impossible to avoid, needless fatigues, delays of two or three hours for poor fellows loaded like donkeys, and who have eaten scarcely anything. . . . The food question is almost the very first, which is to say that the great art of feeding an army enables one to bring more men to a given day than his enemy, and consequently to have a success. . . . I think this war will end by the loss of our morals. Every one profits by it: one for his advancement, the other for his glory; but one deplores the deaths, one regrets the soldiers sacrificed for a cause not easily comprehensible by the majority of the army."

The letter written by the General to his wife on the eve of the battle of Solferino is full of melancholy and sadness: "For the last two days we have been at Montechiaro, very badly lodged. I have just spent a frightful night. At one o'clock in the morning I was sleeping profoundly when Conneau, his face disturbed, entered my chamber, followed by a valet de chambre carrying a torch, and said to me in a sepulchral tone: 'General de Cotte is dead!' I had just left him before lying down. . . . I could not believe my ears. Finally the valet told me that he had just taken him some despatches, and that after reading two or three, De Cotte sank down saying, 'I see nothing more,' and that he fell back dead as quickly as the extinction of a candle makes you pass from light to darkness. When I apprised the Emperor of this news on his awakening, he seemed thunderstruck. Truly it is a heartbreaking end for a soldier to die like that, when the cannon might at least have given him a glorious death!"

During the day, Napoleon went to Lonato in a carriage to see Victor Emmanuel. He visited Desenzano on Lake Garda. General Fleury says: "There is no finer sight than these mountains and this blue and quiet water which seems saying to you: 'Why all this destruction? Why so many dead? Come rather to enjoy peacefully my lovely sights and my coolness!'"

To this philosophic reflection the General adds: "My idea is that the Emperor is already fatigued by so many material difficulties, and is reconsidering at a longer range the notion of commanding a great army. I think the sight of the wounded and the dead has been painful to him when reflecting that so many heroes have allowed themselves to be killed for a people which does not love us, and for a cause whose future is so doubtful and impenetrable. I think, in fine, that the war he had dreamed of in all its glory has become so hazardous for him that he knows very well that the telegraph which carried you the news of the victory of Magenta narrowly missed taking that of a disastrous defeat. The Emperor has not reflected on all this without recognizing that his stake is too great for the result he is pursuing, and without becoming quite ready morally to limit his winnings in the game he is playing on the green cloth of Lombardy."

It was learned the same day, June 23, that the Austrians had actually retreated beyond the Mincio, abandoning the heights between Lonato and Volta. Whereupon Napoleon III. resolved to take his army there on the 24th. Still, no one believed that the great battle would be fought on that day, and it was supposed that the Austrian Emperor would wait in the centre of the quadrilateral for the Franco-Sardinian army. It was not known that for the third or fourth time Francis Joseph had changed his plan and concluded to go to meet his enemies or else to maintain a purely defensive attitude. Strategic motives and political considerations had brought about the modification which suddenly took place in the sovereign's resolutions.

Garibaldi and General Cialdini, with more than twenty thousand men, were threatening to debouch into the valley of the upper Adige, and by exciting troubles in the Tyrol might make the Austrians anxious about their right wing.

A flotilla of French gunboats intended to assist in the siege of Peschiera was in course of construction at Desenzano and might soon be launched on Lake Garda.

The 5th French army corps, that of Prince Napoleon, reinforced by a Tuscan division, was advancing upon the Austrian left wing.

Finally, the French fleet of the Adriatic was making ready to land a corps of troops in the lagoons of Venice.

The Emperor Francis Joseph feared that the quadrilateral, strong though it was, might find it difficult to withstand a fourfold attack, from Garibaldi and General Cialdini on the north, the Franco-Sardinian grand army on the west, Prince Napoleon on the south, and the French fleet on the east.

On the other hand, he had received at his headquarters a Prussian note, dated June 14, which had driven him to the conclusion that unless he gained an immediate military success Prussia and the entire Germanic Confederation would not decide in his favor. These various reasons determined him to take the offensive. He reflected, moreover, that in case of defeat, he would always have time enough to recross the Mincio and intrench himself behind the strong barrier of the Adige, in the camp of Verona. He selected troops on June 24 to occupy the positions of Lonato and Castiglione, where he believed they would find none but feeble French detachments.

The evening of June 23, the headquarters of the first Austrian army were established at Lonato, the second at Volta, and the imperial one at Valeggio.

Napoleon III. had given orders for his own troops and those of the King to move between two and three o'clock in the morning. Without knowing it, the two armies were marching to meet each other. This meeting brought about the battle of Solferino.

CHAPTER XXV

THE BATTLE OF SOLFERINO

THE allied army leaves its bivouacs between two and three o'clock in the morning, and advances in four columns to reach the positions it is to occupy during the day. Its scouts will presently come into collision with the enemy's outposts along the entire front of the line of march.

The Emperor has spent the night at Montechiaro. He had intended to leave there at seven in the morning. But he will go sooner. Towards half-past five, just as the members of his military household have assembled in the little church to pay the last honors to his aide-de-camp, General de Cotte, two staff officers, one of them sent by Marshal Baraguey d'Hilliers and the other by Marshal MacMahon, come up at full gallop. They announce to Napoleon III. that the enemy is deploying strong columns on the heights of Solferino and Cavriana, that the 1st corps (Baraguey d'Hilliers) and the 2d (MacMahon) are confronted in the plain by considerable masses who dispute the ground with them, that the 4th corps (General Niel) and the 3d (Marshal Canrobert) are still a long way off, but that their cannon are heard in the direction of Medoli and of Castello Goffredo.

The Emperor at once sends orders to the infantry of the guard to accelerate its movement on Castiglione, to the cavalry of the guard to go at a trot to the field of battle and deploy in the plain between the 2d and the 4th corps. Then he enters a postchaise with Generals de Martimprey, de Montebello, and Fleury. His military household and his escort follow him at a gallop. Arriving at half-past seven at Castiglione, which is built on an eminence, he goes up to the top of the church steeple whence he can take in the horizon at a glance. "It is a general battle," he exclaims. Then he goes, at the utmost speed of his horse, to give his orders in person to Marshal Baraguey d'Hilliers and the Duke of Magenta.

It is the 1st corps, commanded by Marshal Baraguey d'Hilliers, which, with its three divisions of infantry (1st, General Forey; 2d, General de Ladmirault; 3d, General Bazaine), is ordered to attack the village of Solferino.

Solferino is a market-town of Lombardy, situated near the right bank of the Mincio, hard by Peschiera to the north and Mantua on the south, and four kilometers to the southeast of Castiglione. From the latter city a considerable chain of hills carries several hamlets on its flanks, then undergoes a slight depression, and presently rises in two mamelons. One is called the mamelon of Cypresses, and the other makes room on its summit for a cemetery, a church, and an old château. Between the two, on an eminence, rises the celebrated tower called the *Spia d'Italia*, the Hope of Italy.

The Forey and Ladmirault divisions advance in parallel lines on Solferino: the first on the right, attacking Mount Fénile, the second on the left, taking away from the enemy the first hills of his position.

The occupation of Mount Fénile by the 84th of the line permits a battery to establish itself there and protect the movement of General Dieu's brigade which descends the rear slope of Mount Fénile and goes towards Solferino, chasing from crest to crest the troops of the enemy, whose numbers incessantly increase. This brigade takes position in face of superior forces, and directs the fire of its artillery upon the mamelon of Cypresses and the height crowned by the *Spia d'Italia*. While the cannonading is in progress, General Dieu receives a wound which will be mortal, and resigns the command of his brigade to Colonel de Cambriels, of the 84th.

On the left, General Ladmirault has succeeded in placing his four pieces of cannon in battery, and their firing facilitates the combined attack of Generals Félix Douay and de Négrier.

General Ladmirault leads the assault himself. Touched in the shoulder by a bullet, he withdraws for a moment to have his wound attended to: then he resumes command and sends forward his four battalions of reserve. Struck by another shot, he is obliged to yield his command to General de Négrier.

The Emperor arrives at the summit of Mount Fénile. Thence embracing the whole extent of the battlefield, he sees that on the right, in the plain, the 3d and 4th corps cannot overcome the obstacles to their march, and learns that, on the left, a portion of the Piedmontese army is retreating before an Austrian army corps which occupies in force the position of San Martiuo, not far from Lake Garda.

It is half-past ten. The result of the battle is altogether uncertain. The 1st corps, under Marshal Baraguey d'Hilliers, is fighting furiously in the plain. His three divisions of infantry (1st, General de Luzy; 2d, General Vinoy; 3d, General de Failly) are stubbornly contesting possession with the enemy of a farm called Casa-Nuova, on the right-hand side of the Gaito highroad, two kilometres from Guidizzolo. A fierce struggle, which is going to last all day, has begun around this farm, at the hamlet of Baite and the village of Rebecco.

Between the 4th corps (General Niel) and the 2d (Marshal MacMahon) there is a wide solution of continuity. Fortunately the interval has been filled by three divisions of cavalry: the Partouneaux division (3d corps), the Desvaux division (1st corps), and the division of the imperial guard, commanded by General Morris. But will not these three divisions be powerless to arrest the masses of Austrian troops which are incessantly renewed? General Niel ardently desires to be supported by Marshal Canrobert's corps, the 3d. But this corps is the farthest back of all, because it is the only one which was obliged to cross the Chiesa in the morning. On the other hand, Marshal Canrobert has been notified by the Emperor that a corps of from twenty to twenty-five thousand Austrians, issuing from Mantua, is moving toward Acqua-Negro. Therefore he has been requested to keep watch in that direction while supporting the right of the 4th corps in another.

As to Marshal MacMahon, who has seized Casa-Marino, he guards provisionally his position on the Mantua road, between the 1st and 4th corps.

The Emperor, on the summit of Mount Fénile, decides to direct his greatest efforts towards the centre of the positions whose key is the heights dominating Solferino.

He orders the D'Alton brigade (2d of the Forey division of the 1st corps), which has not yet been engaged, to go forward, and supports it by four pieces of artillery. General Forey places himself at the head of this brigade, which rushes upon the right of the tower (the Hope of Italy). As it cannot unaided overcome superior forces, the Emperor sends the division of voltigeurs of the guard to its assistance.

This division, commanded by General Camou, and comprising, besides the four regiments of voltigeurs, a battalion of foot chasseurs, is composed of the Manèque and the Picard brigades. The first, supporting the D'Alton brigade, goes to meet the Austrian columns which are coming down from Casa del Monte. The Picard brigade turns towards the heights on the left.

The battalion of chasseurs of the guard skirts the village of Solferino, and some of its companies get to fighting in the streets and seize a flag and eight pieces of cannon.

General Forey, supported by the voltigeurs of the guard, resumes the offensive with vigor. At the same time, two batteries of artillery of the guard, under General Lebœuf, come up at a gallop; they take a position which allows them to cover the village of Solferino with a rain of projectiles. General Forey drives the enemy from the hilltops and takes possession of them, while the D'Alton brigade is seizing the tower heights and the tower itself, that famous *Spia d'Italia* which dominates all the Lombard plains, and whence the eye embraces the horizon from the banks of the Mincio to those of the Po. It is two o'clock in the afternoon when the tricolor floats from the summit of this tower.

The cemetery is carried by assault at the same moment. Marshal Baraguey d'Hilliers has ordered a breach in the walls, and for that purpose has sent an exposed battery of artillery to a most dangerous position some three hundred yards from the wall. After a well-aimed and continuous fire a sufficient gap is made, and General Bazaine takes the cemetery with a rush. The village and the château likewise succumb to the victors.

Now is the time when the 2d corps (MacMahon) is about to take an important part in the contest. Solferino and the surrounding heights are in the hands of the 1st corps. It is essential that the 2d corps should seize the heights and the village of Cavriana. If the attack succeeds, the Austrian army will have to beat a retreat in order to recross the Mincio. The two divisions of infantry, those of General de La Motterouge and General Decaen, rush off impetuously in the direction of Solferino and Cavriana. Simultaneously the Marshal orders the chief of the cavalry of the guard, General Morris, whose twenty-four squadrons have been placed under the Marshal's command by the Emperor, to occupy the interval about to separate the Desvaux division from the 2d corps, whose right flank it will shield by forming in echelons.

The regiment of Algerian tirailleurs, which holds the left of the La Motterouge division, takes the village of San Casciano and scales the very steep cliffs at whose summit lies Cavriana.

Let us listen to Marshal MacMahon's chief of staff, General Lebrun: "We saw our Algerian tirailleurs bound like panthers from summit to summit, halting behind every projection of ground to take breath and discharge a gun, then once more springing farther up. The sight presented to our eyes by this manœuvre, not until then employed in our army, is one never to be forgotten. We admired it for half an hour."

In its ascending movement the regiment of tirailleurs is followed by the 70th of the line. The colonels of both regiments, Laure in command of the first and Douay of the second, are killed.

Now the mounted artillery of the guard comes on the scene, placing itself at the entrance of the valley whose further end is covered by the village of Cavriana. Four pieces are simultaneously despatched to the ridge of Mount Fontana. The teams find difficulty in dragging the cannons, and the gunners support the wheels and push them forward. Moreover, several pieces have to be carried up to a very lofty plateau from which they would be able to give powerful assistance to the other battery. But the slopes are too steep for horses. Whereupon the grenadiers of the guard come to the rescue, and, harnessing themselves to four rifled cannon, succeed in hoisting them to the crest of the hill.

General Morris is impatiently awaiting a chance to set the cavalry of the guard at work. It comes at about half-past three. A column of Austrian cavalry makes its appearance, and he sends General Cassaignoles and the regiment of mounted chasseurs to charge them in flank. The Austrians are driven back.

The Emperor has ordered the Manèque brigade, of the voltigeurs of the guard, supported by General Mellinet's grenadiers, to move from Solferino against Cavriana and support the 2d corps. The enemy can not long resist this double attack, sustained by the fire of the artillery of the guard, and towards five o'clock in the evening, the Manèque brigade and the Algerian tirailleurs enter the village of Cavriana at the same time.

This success coincides with that of the 4th corps. For more than twelve hours its troops have been marching and fighting, without having eaten, on ground completely without water, and in one of those stifling heats which foretell a terrible storm. Worn out by fatigue, they would end by giving in but for the timely assistance of General Trochu, commandant of the 2d division of the 3d corps, who, placing himself at the head of the Bataille brigade, arrives with fresh troops, and, as General Niel afterwards writes, leads them to the enemy in squares, the right wing in front, with as much order and coolness as if on a drill ground. After depriving the Austrians of a company of infantry and two pieces of cannon, he arrives midway between Casa-Nuova and Guidizzolo.

All of a sudden the sky clouds over. A furious wind raises whirlwinds of dust. A formidable storm breaks. The roar of thunder replaces that of cannon. A deluge of rain paralyses all movement and completely suspends fighting. The day has become blacker than night. At ten paces one can distinguish neither men, horses, nor vehicles. "The spectacle," says General Lebrun, "was one of those which are not witnessed twice in a lifetime, and it lasted for more than half an hour. In presence of an atmospheric phenomenon which had made night on the banks of the Mincio, could the Emperor order his army to go in pursuit of the Austrians? I do not think so."

Francis Joseph, whose headquarters had been at Cavriana all day, has just ordered a general retreat of all his troops behind the Mincio. For an instant, Napoleon III. is inclined to pursue them, but Marshal MacMahon calls his attention to the fact that the infantry has not eaten since morning, that most of the knapsacks had been put down on the ground at the time of the different attacks, and that the foot-soldiers would be incapable of supporting the cavalry should it set off in pursuit of the enemy.

When the storm ceased, the Austrian centre had in great part abandoned the field, and was retiring in deep columns towards the points where it had crossed the Mincio the day before. A battery of the French imperial guard, led by Lieutenant-Colonel de Berckheim, on the crest of the last hill taken, opened fire on the flying columns with its long-range guns. In his *Souvenirs et Impressions*, the Marquis de Massa has written: " In the midst of a group of officers who were seeking to open a passage for their generals, Francis Joseph himself, who had been among the last to leave the bravely contested battlefield, was believed to be recognized. At this moment, Napoleon III., coming up at a gallop close to the battery to estimate its terrible effects, seeing the terrible personal risk incurred by his unfortunate adversary, and certain that no offensive return was to be dreaded, ordered the gunners to stop firing. This act of generosity cannot be called in question; I had it from Prince Murat, in whose presence it occurred."

Since that time, France and Austria have never fought against each other. They learned mutual esteem and honor at Solferino and Magenta. Their interests are not antagonistic. Let us hope that the two powers will always comprehend it.

As to the Piedmontese and the Austrians, they were fated to measure swords again. The storm had put an end to the strife between the troops of the two emperors. Those of Victor Emmanuel renewed the combat.

One may say that two distinct battles were delivered simultaneously, the French one at Solferino, and the Piedmontese at San Martino. The five infantry divisions of the royal army, commanded by Generals Durando, Fanti, Mollard, Cialdini, and Cucchiari, were held in check by superior forces, and their situation, not far from Lake Garda, had been critical. The fighting lasted fifteen consecutive hours. In spite of all their valor, the Piedmontese troops had been unable to lend any assistance to the 1st corps of the French army. Nor had they themselves received any except that of a cannonade coming from the French positions, which took momentary effect on the rear of the Austrian columns as they were trying to outflank the right wing of the royal army.

When the storm ended, four Piedmontese batteries opened fire again and prepared the attack of the infantry, which assaulted the positions of San Martino and ended by seizing them. The enemy attempted another offensive return; but a charge of the light-horsemen of Montferrat repulsed them for the last time, and at night the plateau of San Martino remained definitively in the power of Victor Emmanuel's army. General Benedek, who had occupied it throughout the day, had, for that matter, just received orders from the Emperor Francis Joseph to participate in the general retreat. Hence the Austrians claim that the Piedmontese conquered only what they had themselves abandoned. The heroism of the royal troops is none the less incontestable for that. They deserved this eulogy of their brave sovereign: "Soldiers, in previous battles I have frequently had occasion to mention the names of many among you in the order of the day. To-day, I shall mention the entire army."

Napoleon III. had just gained one of the greatest victories of modern times. He had directed all the operations, and, paying bravely with his person, had exposed himself, in the midst of the action, on the different heights visible from Solferino. In the gallery of Versailles, a large canvas by Yvon represents him on Mount Fénile, surrounded by his staff, at the moment when he is sending the voltigeurs of the imperial guard against the tower which dominates the village from which the battle takes its name. Victor all along the line, he gave orders for his troops to bivouac on the conquered positions and take at last a well-earned repose. Then, going to

o

Cavriana, he established his headquarters in the very house where the Austrian Emperor had had his throughout the day. To the horrors and tumult of war succeeded profound tranquillity and the silence of death.

CHAPTER XXVI

AFTER SOLFERINO

THERE are military men who are as accustomed to the sight of human bloodshed as butchers to that of animals, and who view the horrors of war dry-eyed and without a sentiment of compassion for its victims. Napoleon III. bore not the slightest resemblance to such men as these. A philosopher and humanitarian, he did not behold a battle without profound sadness. Baron de Bazancourt has terminated his fine account of the battle of Solferino with this sentence: "When all had become quiet around him, into what a happy slumber must the victor have fallen while thinking that, the next day, France on its awakening would salute with joyous acclamations this new and glorious triumph!" We do not believe that the slumber of Napoleon was "happy." The victory had been purchased by too costly sacrifices. The compassionate sovereign thought he still heard the cries of: 'Long live the Emperor!" coming from the wounded and the dying.

At daybreak on the 25th of June a lamentable spectacle displayed itself before the eyes of the victorious army. Two days before, from the summit of these now dismal and bloody hills, the Austrians had beheld smiling fields, a plain filled with superb harvests, fine trees, vineyards loaded with grapes. Now, all was crushed, trampled, sacked. Nothing was in sight but trees torn up by the roots, rows of mulberries levelled to the ground, farms, outhouses, enclosures riddled with balls; the soil kneaded by the feet of horses and the wheels of gun-carriages. How many farmers and peasants regretted their ruined harvests, their destroyed houses and cabins? Heaps of dead bodies encumbered certain places on the battlefield where the fighting had been especially heavy: the plateau of San Martino, which the Piedmontese and Austrians had furiously disputed; Rebecco and Casa-Nuova, where the 1st French army corps had fought with such violence; the mamelon of the Cypresses, which, to quote M. de La Gorce, seemed to come forward draped in mourning for all the tombs which it would shelter. The cemetery of Solferino was especially provocative of melancholy reflections. Why do not men, in their fratricidal struggles, respect at least the asylum of the eternal slumber? Why do the cries of war disturb the repose of graves?

"To lead our horses to water," says the Marquis de Massa, "we had to cross, between Solferino and Cavriana, one of those furrows of earth where the attack and defence had been most deadly. There lay, extended pell-mell, the enemies of yesterday, united now in the pale fraternity of death: our foot-soldiers and voltigeurs, their long capotes and white gaiters emerging from the red trousers: the Tyrolese and Croatians, with their sky-blue breeches outlining the contours of their sinewy legs, their leather boots laced just above the ankle, some on their backs, others face to the ground, according to the stroke which had mowed them down; most of them bareheaded; the victorious imperial eagle and the double-headed vanquished eagle seemed to be extending their wings sadly on the dinted stars of their helmets or shakos which had rolled to a little distance. Our horses, led by their bridles, distended their nostrils and breathed hard, and seemed unwilling to step over all these corpses, as if conscious of committing a sacrilege."

The churches, public buildings, houses, and silkworm nurseries had been converted into hospitals. But everything was lacking; medicines, stores, even doctors. The *Red Cross* was not then in existence. Philanthropists, acting on their own initiative, came to the battlefield. There they conceived the humanitarian project afterwards realized by the "Society for the help of the wounded."

From an Austrian army comprising not less than one hundred and fifty thousand combatants, and occupying formidable positions, the French army had taken three flags, thirty cannon, and made six thousand prisoners. But at the cost of what a slaughter! Sixteen hundred killed, eighty-five hundred wounded, fifteen hundred men missing, — such was the schedule of its losses. Generals Dieu, Auger, Ladmirault, Forey, Douay, were among the wounded; the first two afterwards died in consequence. Seven colonels and nine lieutenant-colonels had been killed: Colonels Laure, of the Algerian tirailleurs; Waubert de Genlis, of the 8th of the line; Lacroix, of the 30th; Capri, of the 53d; Douay, of the 70th; Broutta, of the 43d; Jourjon, of the engineers; Lieutenant-Colonels Campagnon, of the 2d of the line; Bigot, of the 85th; Herment, of the Algerian tirailleurs; Ducoir, of the 3d grenadiers of the guard; Neuchêze, of the 8th of the line; Vallet, of the 91st; Hémard, of the 61st; Laurans des Ondes, of the 5th hussars; d'Albrantes, chief of staff of the Failly division.

The Piedmontese army had seven hundred dead, thirty-five hundred wounded, twelve hundred missing.

On learning successively of the loss of so many officers apparently destined to a brilliant future, and who had shown such loyalty to him and to France, Napoleon III. was sincerely afflicted. From Cavriana he addressed to his army the following proclamation, which seems to breathe sadness rather than pride:—

"SOLDIERS! The enemy expected to surprise and fling us back beyond the Chiesa; it is they who have recrossed the Mincio instead. You have worthily sustained the honor of France, and the battle of

Solferino equals and even surpasses the memories of Lonato and Castiglione.

"During twelve hours you have repelled the desperate efforts of one hundred and fifty thousand men. Neither the numerous cannon of the enemy, nor the formidable positions they occupied over an extent of three leagues, nor the distressing heat, have diminished your ardor. The grateful fatherland thanks you through my lips for such perseverance and courage; but it weeps with me over those who are dead on the field of honor. We have taken three flags, thirty cannon, and six thousand prisoners. The Sardinian army has fought with like bravery against superior forces; it is well worthy to march beside you. Soldiers, so much spilled blood will not be unavailing for the glory of France and the welfare of peoples.

"NAPOLEON."

All who saw the Emperor the day after the battle of Solferino, agree in saying that his usually impassive face betrayed sadness and moral lassitude. He may already have foreseen the catastrophes to be originated by the war of Italy, and had a presentiment that the Italians would not always behave as brethren to the French. He had probably arrived at the point of wondering whether this war, contrived and prepared for by himself, was in reality as indispensable as he had imagined. One of his most devoted adherents, General Fleury, expressed this anxiety and doubt at Cavriana, June 25: "War is fine at a distance," he wrote on that day. "It is profitable to the commanders-in-chief, it glorifies the country, when there is need of it, but it costs many tears, it makes tears of blood to flow. No war but that of national independence has a right to impose such painful sacrifices. War for influence is not enough to impassion for long even the ambitious men of the army; they fear being unable in their turn to enjoy the promotions made possible by the death of their brethren in arms." And the General added with easily comprehensible melancholy: "Battles excite me, they leave me calm and free to act while they are sporting with corpses; but afterwards, my nerves relax. I reflect on the anguish they leave behind when the fighting is over, and I tell myself that these butcheries are not in keeping with our times."

The fatigue corps grew weary of digging graves. The 25th of June was spent by the allied army in burying the dead and collecting the wounded. On that day, the Emperor appointed General Niel a marshal of France. The commander of the 4th corps, every regiment of which had taken so active a part in the fighting, well deserved this reward. Magenta had made two marshals: MacMahon and Regnaud de Saint-Jean d'Angély; Solferino made a third. Hence a marshal of France found himself at the head of each of the four army corps and of the imperial guard.

During the same day, the French army approached

the Mincio and established itself in the following positions: the 1st corps in the environs of Pozzolongo; the 2d at Cavriana; the 3d at Solferino, leaving one division of infantry at Guidizzolo, with the Desvaux and Partouneaux divisions of cavalry; the 4th at Volta. The Emperor had remained with the guard at Cavriana, and Victor Emmanuel at San Martino. By evening of that day, almost the whole of the Austrian army had recrossed the Mincio, and Francis Joseph had taken up his imperial headquarters at Verona.

CHAPTER XXVII

THE EMPRESS REGENT

NOTHING occurred to disturb the Empress in her functions as regent while Napoleon III. was in Italy. The different parties ceased wrangling and had no intention of playing the foreigner's game.

The Chamber separated at the end of May. On the 26th, the sovereign received at the Tuileries the members of the Senate, the Corps Législatif, and the Council of State. The president of the Senate said to her: "The Senate thanks Your Majesty for the affectionate audience which gives it an opportunity to see this beloved Child, the hope of France. In the absence of the Emperor, each of us experiences a more active devotion towards the cherished persons whom he has confided to the patriotism of the French." The Empress replied: "*Messieurs les Senateurs*, you have desired, before separating, to give a new proof of loyalty to the Emperor by asking to see the Prince Imperial. I am not in the least surprised by this evidence of the solicitude with which I am surrounded; but I am none the less profoundly affected by it; this proceeding, like the counsels of my beloved uncle, gives me precious encouragement and strength."

Count de Morny, president of the Corps Législatif, spoke next: "We are all going back to our departments," said he; "there we shall cultivate the patriotism demanded by existing circumstances; but it will not require much exertion to do that where the hearts of the people always vibrate at the mention of glory and honor. The absence of the Emperor may have caused some anxiety to those who do not know France, but this generous and sensitive nation understands all the delicate sentiments, and when it sees the Emperor departing in order to share the danger of his soldiers and defend the honor of the flag, it displays still more respect, if that were possible, for your authority, and affection and devotion for your person. Rely, then, Madame, on the concurrence of all, and on the sentiments to which you are entitled as regent and as mother."

The Empress replied: "Gentlemen, I am touched by the desire you have expressed to see the Prince Imperial before returning to your departments. I rely upon your enlightened patriotism to cultivate the faith we all ought to have in the energy of the army, and, when the day shall arrive, in the moderation of the Emperor. For me, however heavy my task may be, I shall find in my wholly French heart the necessary courage to accomplish it. I depend, therefore, gentlemen, on your loyal concurrence and the support of the nation which, in the absence of the chief it has chosen, will never be lacking to a woman and a child."

Alas! on September 4, 1870, the Empress will perhaps remember the words she uttered May 26, 1859!

The war which had taken place on the other side of the Alps wrought no change in the appearance of Paris. As usual, the fashionable season did not continue beyond Easter, but the theatres were filled, and every day one saw, at the famous "tour of the lake," a crowd of elegant cavaliers and brilliant equipages. War is as splendid at a distance as it is horrible close at hand. In 1859, it gave Parisians more diversion than anxiety. It recalled celebrated places and the names of victories. Its scene was that poetic and illustrious Italy which has played so great a part in the annals of French glory. People bought maps on which they stuck pins surmounted by tiny French, Piedmontese, and Austrian flags which indicated the positions of the three armies. There were optimists then in all classes of society. The thought of a disaster never occurred to anybody. Even the enemies of Napoleon III. believed in his luck, in his fortunate star. The French nation, infatuated with itself since its successes in the Crimea, considered itself invincible.

The Empress fulfilled her duties as regent very conscientiously. Her ministers were in raptures over her zeal, her intelligence, her aptitude to comprehend difficult questions. She had installed herself in the château of Saint-Cloud, and was living there in seclusion, engrossed in studying the most arduous of political subjects. The Countess Stéphanie de La Pagerie summarizes thus the life led by the sovereign at this time: "She presides over three ministerial councils every week, two of which are at the Tuileries; she supports valiantly the emotions of the situation. She even adapts herself so well to this grave and serious work that she sometimes says that when the regency is over she is afraid she shall be very dull, so captivated is she with these interesting and important occupations. In the evening she assembles a few persons, the Count and Countess Walewski, the Marquis de Cadore, and several ladies of the palace. They chat while making lint and drinking tea. Minds are in Italy, at the scene of war, and there is a lack of news."

The people of Paris do not hear of the victory of Magenta until the evening of June 5. The same day, at a quarter past four in the afternoon, the Emperor had sent the Empress the following telegram: "This is the summary, so far as known, of the battle of Magenta: seven thousand prisoners at least; twenty thousand Austrians disabled; three cannon and two flags taken. To-day the army is resting and reorganizing. Our losses amount to about three thousand men killed and one cannon taken by the enemy."

Salvos of artillery from the Invalides announced the victory to the Parisians at eight o'clock in the evening. Between nine and ten, the Empress and the Princess Clotilde passed through the boulevards and the rue de Rivoli in an open carriage. They were everywhere greeted by shouts of: "Long live the Emperor! Long live the Empress! Long live the Princess Clotilde!" Public buildings and many private houses were illuminated.

A *Te Deum* was chanted at Notre Dame, June 7, in presence of the Regent, King Jerome, the Princess Clotilde, and the Princess Mathilde. The streets and squares through which the cortege of the sovereign passed were draped with French and Sardinian flags. The line was formed by the national guard and the troops of the line. Received under the dais by the clergy of Notre Dame, the Empress was conducted processionally to the estrade prepared for her in the choir. At her entry as at her exit from the church she was greeted by the liveliest applause.

Before leaving Milan, Napoleon III. raised one of his orderlies, Commandant Schmitz, to the rank of lieutenant-colonel, and sent him to the Empress with the two Austrian flags taken at Magenta. This officer reached Saint-Cloud June 13. The sovereign gave him the accolade, and after receiving the glorious gift with profound emotion, she asked the messenger many questions about the great events he had just witnessed.

June 24, Napoleon III. addressed a telegram to the Empress worded as follows: "Cavriana, June 24, 9.15 P.M. Great battle and great victory. All the Austrian army has given in. The line of battle was five leagues in length. We have carried all the positions, taken many cannon, flags, and prisoners. The battle lasted from four in the morning until eight in the evening."

The Empress was in bed at the château of Saint-Cloud when the despatch arrived during the night. She rose at once, dressed as quickly as possible, went down into the garden and announced the victory herself to the sentries and soldiers of the guard.

I remember the morning of June 25 at Paris. I had just arrived at the boulevard des Capucines when I saw the shops and houses being draped with flags. That was how I learned the news of the victory. The superb weather was in harmony with the patriotic joy with which all hearts were throbbing. In the evening the streets and public places were filled with countless crowds.

July 1, the Minister of Worship and Public Instruction addressed the following circular to the rectors of academies: "I think myself bound to express the desire that all the bulletins of the army of Italy published in the *Moniteur* shall be read before the pupils of lyceums and colleges, and posted up in the interior of these establishments. Youth responds quickly to noble sentiments; its heart is touched by great things and devoted to the dynasties which know how to comprehend them; it will rejoice in the new glories of the imperial standard; it will learn also, in listening to the daily history of this heroic campaign of Italy, how well labor and study form intelligent and strong generations."

July 2, at the Tuileries, Commandant d'Andlau, one of the Emperor's orderlies, presented to the Empress the Austrian flags taken at the battle of Solferino.

Enthusiasm was general. The Crimean War, fought on a distant scene, and for little known and ill-defined diplomatic interests, had not so greatly excited public imagination. There is no resemblance between the monotony of a long siege and a series of swift battles like those of the war of Italy.

The telegraph brought none but good news. All letters from officers or soldiers breathed enthusiasm, gaiety, confidence. All the bulletins were tales of victories. Lugubrious, lamentable, horrible when its sufferings are not compensated for by victories, war assumes an aspect of continual gladness when it is merely a succession of triumphs. Even mothers hardly dare to weep.

July 3 had been fixed on for the chanting of the *Te Deum* at Notre Dame in celebration of the victory of Solferino and in thanksgiving to the God of armies. The Empress Regent, who had gone without her son to the *Te Deum* chanted for Magenta, concluded to take him to that of July 3. When the child was told this good news he was delighted, and asked many questions about the fine ceremony in course of preparation. Favored by fine weather, it was magnificent. The procession left the Tuileries at eleven o'clock in the morning, the Empress having with her, in an open carriage, the Prince Imperial, the Princess Clotilde, and the Princess Mathilde. She was met at the threshold of the cathedral by the Cardinal Archbishop of Paris, grand almoner to the Emperor, and by the metropolitan chapter, and, leading her son by the hand, was conducted processionally under a canopy to the estrade prepared for her in the middle of the choir. The ancient basilica was magnificently decorated. The escutcheons of France and Sardinia were visible on pillars draped with red velvet and gold fringe; from the vaulted roof hung flags, oriflammes, and banners. I was present at this solemnity. I seem still to hear the chants of the Church, the cries of: "Long live the Emperor! Long live the Empress! Long live the Prince Imperial!" Standing in the choir, a few steps behind the Empress, I was looking at the little Prince, who, paying great attention to all the movements of his mother, sat, stood up, and kneeled down whenever she did. Nothing could be more gracious than this child of three years in his white piqué dress and his belt of blue watered silk. "This was the first time," said the *Moniteur*, "that the Emperor's son united officially with the nation. God has permitted him to do so under the auspices of victory." On leaving the cathedral, General de Lawoëstine, commander-in-chief of the national guard of the Seine, offered the Empress a superb bouquet, and the cavalry of the same troops presented her with a wreath of golden laurels with clasps of real pearls. The ovation on the return of the procession was still more cordial than that which greeted it as it went. The applauded sovereign saluted the crowd with emotion and the little Prince threw kisses to it.

CHAPTER XXVIII

PRINCE NAPOLEON

ON the day when the *Te Deum* for the victory of Solferino was being chanted at Notre Dame, the Emperor, who was continuing his forward march and had just crossed the Mincio, was rejoined by Prince Napoleon. The Prince brought with him the 5th corps, comprising the d'Autemarre and Ulrich infantry divisions, the brigade of light cavalry commanded by General de Lapérouse, and the Tuscan division under General Ulloa. The total effective was about thirty thousand men and two thousand horses.

Prince Napoleon, commander of the 5th corps, had landed at Genoa, May 12, with the Emperor. One of his divisions, the d'Autemarre, was detached from the corps and placed under the orders of Marshal Baraguey d'Hilliers, commander of the 1st corps, and two of its regiments, the 93d of the line and the 3d zouaves, took part respectively in the battle of Montebello and that of Palestro. All that remained with the Prince was the Ulrich division and the Lapérouse brigade of cavalry, with which the Emperor directed him to embark for Leghorn and occupy Tuscany.

A revolution had broken out in Florence as far back as April 27. The train for it having been laid even more remotely by the Sardinian minister in that city, M. de Buoncampagni, it was effected without violence or bloodshed. During the night the Tuscan troops had assumed the Italian cockade, and at seven in the evening the Grand Duke Leopold had quitted his capital in the midst of a crowd that seemed more indifferent than hostile to him. Each of the foreign ministries sent one of its secretaries to escort him and his family as far as the frontier, and the municipality offered him a guard of honor. Before leaving, the Grand Duchess said to Count de Rayneval, secretary of the French legation: "I hope that the Emperor of the French will protect us; I have the letters he wrote me in 1848, and they testify his friendly sentiments for our family." Not a threat, not an insult was uttered against the Grand Duke during his journey. At the frontier, when M. de Rayneval came up to take leave of the Grand Duchess, she repeated that she relied on the Emperor's protection, and the hereditary Prince, who had been the guest of Their Imperial Majesties at Compiègne, in 1856, expressed his desire to be remembered to them.

The very day of the Grand Duke's departure from his States, M. Buoncampagni had assumed power, with the title of commissioner of King Victor Emmanuel, and the tri-colored Italian flag had been run up.

Prince Napoleon landed at Leghorn, May 23. His antagonism with the Marquis de Ferrière-le-Vayer, minister of France in Tuscany, became evident as soon as he reached the city. The French diplomat showed himself as averse to the annexation of the grand duchy to Sardinia as the Prince was in favor of it. The former wrote to Count Walewski, May 24: "Prince Napoleon arrived at Leghorn yesterday with part of his army corps, and has been received with the utmost enthusiasm. I had been invited by His Imperial Highness to call upon him, and M. Buoncampagni having received a similar invitation, we went together. The Prince told both of us that the annexation of this country to Sardinia had been decided on at headquarters, and that we must prepare people's minds for it; that it was necessary to have done with a would-be ambition to reign at Florence, and that the best way to accomplish this was to destroy the autonomy of Tuscany by handing it over to Piedmont. I ventured to defend the cause of Tuscan autonomy against Prince Napoleon. I said that the opinion of all the aristocratic nobilities, scientists, literary men, and politicians of the country, was arrayed more than ever on its side, and would be increasingly so if it were seriously threatened."

The Marquis de Ferrière-le-Vayer added in the same despatch: "If the annexation must be consummated — and I ask myself by what right — I do not see what claim a minister of the Emperor could have to remain here; and, if this minister must remain for the purpose of accustoming minds to this measure, it is evident that I would be quite incapable of executing, with propriety or success, instructions contrary to opinions which everybody here knows me to hold. Hence I would beg Your Excellency, if this thing must be, to authorize my return to France as soon as possible."

Count Walewski had been the Emperor's minister at Florence, and, like the Marquis de Ferrière-le-Vayer, he was a convinced partisan of Tuscan autonomy. May 25, he sent the latter this telegram in cipher: "I made haste to acquaint the Emperor that Prince Napoleon declared that His Majesty had decided on the annexation of Tuscany to Piedmont. The Emperor replied this morning that if his cousin had employed such language, it was contrary to his instructions. Tell Prince Napoleon so. It is all the more essential that no misunderstanding should exist on this head since the despatches I have sent you within the last few days are contradictory of what the Prince has said."

We reproduce some extracts from two despatches addressed to Count Walewski by the Marquis de Ferrière le-Vayer: —

"*Florence, June* 9, 1859. — Prince Napoleon's presence has done much harm. It has been made use of by the Sardinian party. . . . Baron Ricasoli and the advocate Salvagnoli have each told me within a few days that the temporal sovereignty of the Pope must be radically abolished. It really is a little too strong to see these persons, puffed up by their chance functions, settling in this way one of the greatest questions that can present itself before the victorious sword and lofty intelligence of the Emperor. . . . I repeat it, Count, if the question of Tuscany is to be kept intact, it is not a prince with an army corps, but five or six hundred Frenchmen who should be sent here, expressly charged to maintain substantial order, and the royal commissioner and his ministers should be enjoined to await the definitive arrangements which will be adopted after the war, without pretending to prejudge them."

The second despatch, dated June 14, was an actual plea against Italian unity. Among other things, it said: "The unity of Italy would entail the fall of the temporal sovereignty of the Popes, linked so closely with the traditions of our country since the origin of its monarchy, that, without mentioning the consequences to the Catholic world, this fall would at once open an abyss in front of France; and, moreover, it would create a first-class power on the Mediterranean which, once constituted, would be more inclined to become England's ally than ours should war break out between us, were it only to resume possession of Corsica, as is demanded by MM. Guerrazzi and Salvagnoli in their novels and brochures."

The despatch concluded thus: "It would be better for us to give up the prospect of gaining Savoy, and thus by our disinterestedness acquire the right to impose moderation on Sardinia, than to procure for it an increase of territory which might introduce such serious disturbances in our political and religious sphere. Henry IV. and Richelieu, whose authority has so often been evoked within the last few months, dreamed of dismembering the great powers neighboring to France and not of reuniting their scattered fragments in order to constitute another State on our frontier."

Meanwhile, unitary ideas were making rapid progress, not merely in Tuscany, but in Parma, Modena, and the Romagna.

The Duchess of Parma, sister of the Count de Chambord, had vainly tried to save her son's throne by observing strict neutrality between Austria and Sardinia. The Austrians having evacuated Plaisance, June 10, she felt that she was ruined. June 16, M. Pallieri was appointed governor of the duchy of Parma by the Piedmontese government. The 27th, the Duchess left for Switzerland after announcing in a proclamation that, placed under the necessity of taking part in a war said to be one of nationality or else violating her pledges to Austria, she withdrew to avoid the alternative of acting contrary to the wishes of Italy, or of failing in her engagements.

Francis, Duke of Modena, had not been more fortunate. The provinces of Massa and Carrara had declared against him as early as April 27. He withdrew into his fortress of Brescello, and caused Modena and Reggio to be occupied by the Austrians.

They having evacuated the two cities, June 12, he took refuge in Austria, and on the 19th M. Farini installed himself at Modena as Piedmontese commissioner.

The Romagnas had a similar fate. The Austrians left there June 11-12. Bologna at once elected a junta one of whose members was Marquis Joachim Popoli, grandson of King Murat, cousin of Napoleon III., and husband of a princess of the blood-royal of Prussia, the daughter of Prince Hohenzollern, then president of the Ministerial Council of Berlin. The first act of this junta was to proclaim the dictatorship of Victor Emmanuel, who made haste to send M. d'Azeglio into the Romagna as commissioner extraordinary. June 15, Cardinal Antonelli protested against what he called "a felony which horrifies everybody."

Prince Napoleon's policy triumphed, and the Emperor, though desiring the federation of Italy, took no steps to oppose that unity for which the signal was boldly given by the attitude of the Piedmontese government in Tuscany, Parma, Modena, and the Romagna.

All central Italy having been evacuated by the Austrians, Prince Napoleon was ordered to reassemble all the troops of the 5th corps and rejoin with them the army commanded by the Emperor. He arrived at Goito on the 30th. The junction being made, the concentration of the 5th army corps with the imperial guard was effected.

CHAPTER XXIX

THE DIPLOMATIC SITUATION

PRINCE NAPOLEON, who had been so urgent for war, suddenly became the impassioned advocate of peace. General Fleury wrote to his wife June 30: "What a changeable mind ours is! Prince Napoleon is the exaggerated type of it. He says quite frankly that the Emperor is as much bound to return to Paris as the Austrian Emperor to Vienna, and that the time to negotiate has come."

Another letter of July 1: "I have talked much and at length with Prince Napoleon. He seemed to me not merely reasonable, anxious to see the Emperor profit by his victory in order to assure the basis of peace, but singularly alarmed by the gravity and extent which the war must inevitably assume if a timely end is not put to it. . . . From all of which it results that the Prince is not a bad adviser *for the moment.*"

It was no longer possible to delude one's self. All Germany was about to declare against France, and Russia would not take up arms against Germany. The Prussian army was in movement to concentrate itself upon the Rhine, lending a hand meanwhile to several other corps of the federal army, and the corps of observation, reunited at Nancy under Marshal Pélissier, was not large enough to withstand an attack from Prussia and the other States of the Germanic Confederation.

Napoleon III. has been often reproached for halting in the midst of the struggle, and it has been asserted that if he had kept on, he might have counted on the assured support of Russia. We are about to reproduce a despatch which proves this to be a capital error. As early as June 25, the Duke of Montebello, ambassador of France at Saint Petersburg, wrote to Count Walewski: "The news of the mobilization of six corps of the Prussian army has produced the most unpleasant impression on the Russian cabinet. Prince Gortchakoff has not concealed his uneasiness from me. Prussia intends to send an army to the Rhine and another to the Main. The Prince concludes that in order to avert the terrible extremity of a war with Germany, we should make haste to come to negotiations. He is extremely desirous that these may be based on just foundations, such as may assure a lasting peace, and in conformity with the legitimate wishes of Italy, the interest of Europe, and the situation of the belligerent parties. He is intimately persuaded that the war will become general if it is prolonged; he foresees that in our ulterior operations it will be difficult for us not to borrow German territory. In this situation full of incalculable dangers, the cabinet of Saint Petersburg places its confidence in the moderation of which the Emperor has given so many proofs, and which should be easy after victory. Prince Gortchakoff has said to me that if France agrees to negotiate, its views will be upheld by Russia; if it refuses, all that Russia can do is to reconcile itself sadly to resignation and abstention."

The Emperor Alexander acted with frankness and loyalty. He sent Count Schouvaloff to Napoleon III. with a letter in which he described the situation with the utmost precision. General Fleury wrote from Valeggio, July 1: "We have a newcomer to the general staff, the young Count Schouvaloff, aide-de-camp of the Russian Emperor, who is going to follow the operations of the campaign. He is a very nice and intelligent young colonel, and one can get something out of him. He told me that in passing through Berlin he had seen the Grand Duchess Hélène, and learned from her that the Prince of Prussia was positively jealous of the laurels and influence of the Emperor Napoleon; that he spent his time in studying his map, sticking pins in it, and in getting ready to play the part of a great warrior in his turn. . . . As to the effective and immediate assistance against Austria which the public for an instant believed would be given by Russia, all hope of it must be abandoned. . . . Beware of a general war; then beware the desertion of England, and beware above all the revolution and the desertion of France!"

Count Walewski had been always opposed to the

war, and did all in his power to induce the Emperor to cut it short by sending him the most alarming reports. All the representatives of France at Berlin, Frankfort, and in the secondary States of Germany were unanimous in considering the situation as very menacing. The passions of 1813 were reviving. All the efforts made by Napoleon III. to reassure the Germans had been useless. The Prince of Prussia persisted in saying that the Emperor was deceiving everybody, and that it was the duty of Prussia, and of all Germans, to get ready to face the danger. All the States of the Confederation declared against France, and it would have been impossible to find one among them with the slightest sympathy for the Italian cause.

In the general crisis which seemed impending, could the Italians count at least upon the English? Not in the least. The Tory ministry led by Lord Derby had been overthrown by a parliamentary vote June 10, and replaced by a Whig ministry in which Lord Palmerston was Prime Minister, and Lord John Russell chief of the foreign office. On seeing these two former champions of their cause arrive at power, the Italians cherished great illusions and hoped that English fleets might perhaps assist to deliver Venice. At the moment when the vote of the Commons, which overthrew the Tory ministry, was announced, Marquis Emmanuel d'Azeglio, who was in the lobby, was seen to toss his hat up and utter cries of joy. "Never," said Lord Malmesbury, "could one have imagined an ambassador, even an Italian one, abandoning himself to such extravagant actions." A few days later, the Marquis, still full of confidence, laid before Lord Palmerston the plan of a kingdom of Italy which should include Lombardy, Venetia, the Romagna, and the duchies. The Prime Minister contented himself with replying: "The question is to know whether France would like to establish a second Prussia on her flank."

Menaced by Germany, Napoleon III. and Victor Emmanuel had not for a single moment the idea of relying on the armed assistance of England. Could they at least count upon her moral support? Not the least in the world. The war once over, Italian demonstrations in London were noisy enough. But during and before it, not a single voice was raised in England to favor the abolition of the treaties of 1815, the maintenance of which was demanded by the Queen, Prince Albert, and the Whigs as well as by the Tories. It never occurred to any one to dream of seeing the English flag in the Adriatic as an ally in the deliverance of Venice.

Napoleon III., too much inclined to believe in the friendly intentions of England, fancied that she would assist him, if not to continue the war, at least in making peace. He hoped that his old friend, Lord Palmerston, would lend his good offices to extricate him from a situation which daily grew more critical. He had his ambassador, Count de Persigny, try the ground. The latter hinted, as a personal suggestion, at an arrangement which should assign Lombardy to Piedmont, and create for one of the archdukes a separate kingdom comprising Venetia and the duchy of Modena. "Those," replied Lord Palmerston, "are propositions which would displease both sides. The Austrians would not cede Venetia which they still occupy. As to the Italians, they are hoping for the liberty of their whole country, and they will not believe they have got it so long as an archduke reigns over Venice and Modena." All hope of English mediation was quickly dispelled.

Lord Palmerston, once a great admirer of Napoleon III., had arrived at sharing the suspicions of Germany in his regard, and at speaking disdainfully of his policy. "His head," said he, "is like a warren, ideas swarm in it like rabbits." He responded in no kindly tone to the applications of Count Persigny. "If the Emperor thinks the war has lasted long enough," said he, "or finds the task too difficult, let him make explicit personal offers to the Emperor of Austria, and not ask us to take his suggestions under our responsibility." This advice was to be followed more expeditiously than the English statesman could have believed. Seeing that he had nothing to hope from London, Napoleon III. resolved to address himself directly to the Emperor of Austria, and to make peace suddenly at the very moment when everybody looked forward to a continuation of the war. He liked unexpected things. Dramatic strokes pleased him.

CHAPTER XXX

THE LAST DAYS OF THE WAR

NAPOLEON III. put in practice the old adage: If you want peace, prepare for war. At the very time when he desired a peaceful solution, he took care to conceal his innermost thoughts, and to show increasing activity in his bellicose preparations. Far from diminishing his effective forces, he enlarged them. His army on the Mincio received daily reinforcements. Besides the corps of Prince Napoleon, which had lately joined it, a division from France was expected. July 1, the Minister of War had sent an order in this sense to Marshal de Castellane, who designated the division of General d'Hugues to leave the army of Lyons and rejoin the army of Italy at Brescia, its mission being to cover the outlets of the Alps, while acting as reserves for Garibaldi and General Cialdini.

The allied army was convinced that it was about to attack in front the formidable quadrilateral which, formed by the four cities of Peschiera, Mantua, Verona, and Legnano, constituted one of the strongest strategic situations in the world. They had already begun the siege of Peschiera, situated on the

Mincio, at the point where that stream issues from Lake Garda, twenty-four kilometers from Verona. On the left bank the investment was complete, and on the right bank the work of countervallation had been started.

The Emperor spent his days in visiting the most advanced positions occupied by his troops, and in superintending the engineering and artillery works on the Mincio. He was seen everywhere, making personal investigation of the least details. Throughout the campaign he displayed perfect evenness of temper, the utmost kindliness towards the chiefs of the army, and an incessant solicitude for the condition of officers and soldiers. Enduring fatigue very well, he set a good example to all. His gentleness and courtesy inspired affection. Still, the sanitary conditions continued to disturb him. At the beginning of July there were twenty-five thousand sick men in the hospitals or infirmaries. A rather large number of Austrian prisoners had been transferred to Genoa. Napoleon III. had given orders that they should be well treated and advances of money made to officers who needed it. The pain caused him by the calamities of war and his desire to lessen them was shown on every occasion. A messenger from the Emperor of Austria having come to reclaim the body of Prince Windischgratz, gloriously slain at Solferino, he received him with extreme kindness, and asked him to thank the Emperor Francis Joseph for his good treatment of the French prisoners.

However, no one as yet believed that the humane sentiments of Napoleon III. would make him lay down his arms before he had executed his programme: Italy free from the Alps to the Adriatic. The moment seemed approaching when, according to all previsions, Austria would be attacked at once by land and sea, and the navy men believed that they, too, would have a great part to play. In the Adriatic, a blockading fleet, composed of six ships of the line, two screw-frigates, two corvettes, and several transports, had been placed under the orders of Vice-Admiral Romain-Desfossés, and, since June 1, Rear-Admiral Jurien de La Gravière had been blockading Venice with four vessels. Moreover, the Emperor had decided that the blockading fleet should be assisted by a besieging one composed of three floating batteries and twenty-one gunboats, under command of Rear-Admiral Bouët-Willaumez.

As a base of operations for the fleet, Napoleon III. had designated the island of Lossini, whose port, bestriding the two shores of the Adriatic, is an excellent shelter for vessels. Situated some twenty leagues from Venice, at the extremity of the archipelago of Quarnero, the island of Lossini is very nearly the central point between Venice, Trieste, Pola, Fiume, and Zora, which are the principal maritime establishments on the Adriatic. July 3, the French squadron, commanded by Vice-Admiral Romain-Desfossés, occupied the island of Lossini. The Austrians had not offered the slightest resistance.

Full of ardor and self-reliance, the fleet believed itself about to force the canals of Venice, enter the lagoons, and seize the forts dominating the city. Of the three principal entries which give access to the city of the doges from the sea, the Lido, Malamocco, and Chioggia, the latter had already been fixed upon as the point of attack. General de Wimpffen, made general of division after the battle of Magenta, had been selected as commander of a corps of all arms intended to effect a landing on the shores of the Adriatic. Arriving at Rimini by way of Leghorn and Florence, he had at once placed himself in relations with the fleet, which merely awaited a signal to open the attack. The Venetian partisans of Victor Emmanuel were trembling with joy and expectation.

All seemed in readiness for a general and decisive action. The park of artillery, intended to operate against the quadrilateral, was completed. Since July 3, the first pieces had been at Pozzolongo. At the same time, the railway brought to Desenzano the unshipped gunboats which were to assist in the siege of Peschiera.

To sum up, the Emperor had arranged the following combinations for attacking Venice : 1. On the left wing, to menace the Austrian right and disturb the line of the upper Adige by the operations of Garibaldi and General Cialdini in the mountains; 2, on the right wing, to take Venice by the fleet and throw into it a strong detachment which, under cover of the fort of Malghera and the French vessels, might undertake incursions on the Austrian line of retreat; 3, at the centre, with Peschiera as a base of operations and the intervention of three hundred siege guns, to begin the siege of Verona.

On July 6, all the commanders-in-chief of army corps, as well as those of the artillery and engineers, had received a precise and detailed order of movement from the Emperor. Everything was minutely provided for. Never had the sovereign fulfilled more zealously and conscientiously his rôle as commander-in-chief.

Dated from Valeggio, the order of movement began as follows: "The siege of Peschiera is an operation to which I attach great importance; but it is clear that we cannot perform it with safety until after we have repelled an attack of the Austrians. According to the information I have received, it seems very probable that we shall be attacked to-morrow, in front and in flank, by the army from Verona and by another from the upper Adige. The Austrians occupied Pastrengo this morning. It is expedient, therefore, that to-morrow morning at daybreak the troops should take their position." Next the Emperor indicated the place assigned to each army corps. The order of movement terminated as follows: "No baggage to be taken. The canteens to be filled with brandy and water; a light battalion to be left in charge of the camps. The men to take their knapsacks, containing nothing but biscuits and cartridges. All to leave their coats in camp and wear only their jackets. As soon as the enemy is in sight, artillery firing to begin. When the ground will admit of it, the infantry lines to be drawn up alternately in deployed battalions and double columned battalions. Useless skirmishes to be avoided, and, while the deployed battalions are making a file fire, the others will sound the charge and attack the enemy with the bayonet."

A great battle seemed imminent and certain.

CHAPTER XXXI

THE ARMISTICE

NAPOLEON III. had made a long reconnoissance on the heights of Somma-Compagna, July 6. Listen to General Fleury who accompanied him: "The heat was horrible; the Emperor seemed anxious and preoccupied. We met several bands of soldiers on fatigue duty marching painfully. The atmosphere was heavy, and everything seemed ominous of great difficulties for the long sieges awaiting us. . . . Hardly had we re-entered Valeggio and alighted from our horses when the major-general, Marshal Vaillant, summoned me. 'There is a delicate mission to perform,' he said to me, 'and a man of initiative is needed to perform it. The Emperor sends you to Verona; be ready to start in ten minutes, order the carriage, and go to the Emperor who is waiting for you.'"

The General at once ordered a postchaise, a mounted postilion to conduct it, and a trumpeter of guides who would sound the call to a parley at the outposts. Then, going upstairs to the Emperor, whom he found with Victor Emmanuel, he told them he was ready to set off. Napoleon III. said, "Here

is a letter you are to carry to the Emperor of Austria.
. . . I am appealing to his sentiments of humanity and proposing a cessation of hostilities in order to leave time for diplomacy to negotiate conditions of peace." He added: "I needed an ambassador who would be amiable and intelligent. I have chosen you."

General Fleury had all the needful qualities for accomplishing the mission entrusted to him. Courteous, attractive, full of tact, better adapted to the diplomatic than the military career, he was a courtier in the best sense of the word. He pleased every sovereign with whom he came into relations. Personally he might possibly have had something to gain by the continuation of the war. But, like all who were acquainted with the diplomatic situation, he understood the danger, and knew very well that if Napoleon III. should engage in a struggle with Austria backed by all Germany, in case of defeat he would be likely to lose his crown. Hence the General ardently desired his mission to be successful. We learn its details from the letters he sent to his wife.

He left Valeggio, July 6, at seven o'clock in the evening, accompanied by his aide-de-camp, M. de Verdière, in an imperial post carriage. On the seat behind were a courier and a trumpeter of guides carrying a flag of truce. As soon as he had left the French outguards behind him, he was escorted by Austrian foot-soldiers, and then by uhlans. In a few minutes the carriage rolled across the drawbridge of Verona and entered the city, whose gaslighted streets contained promenaders and officers, all much surprised by the sight of a carriage bearing the arms of the Emperor of the French. On arriving at the palace occupied by Francis Joseph, the General was courteously received by Field-Marshal Hesse and Count Grünne, first aide-de-camp and grand equerry of the sovereign. The Emperor had already gone to bed, but he sent word that he would get up and receive him in an instant. In fact, at the end of a quarter of an hour Francis Joseph appeared.

The letter of Napoleon III., written in lofty and chivalrous terms, was calculated to please the young monarch. After reading it, he said: "My dear General, this is a very serious matter that you have brought me. I cannot give you a reply at once. I must reflect; be good enough to wait until eight o'clock to-morrow morning, I must collect my thoughts." First replying that he was at His Majesty's orders, the General went on to urge the considerations militating in favor of the armistice, concluding as follows: "Whatever may be the decision of Your Majesty, permit me to say that it is urgent that the answer should be prompt, since, as you perhaps are not aware, the French fleet is at present occupying the island of Lossini. At the first signal the attacks on the littoral of Venetia will commence. An expeditionary corps of four thousand men, under General Wimpffen, has rejoined Vice-Admiral Romain-Desfossés."

"In fact," replied the Emperor, "I have just learned of the occupation of Lossini by French troops. But I have received nothing official from the courts, and I need to reflect. To-morrow morning, General, I will give you my answer."

In reality, Francis Joseph incurred fewer risks from a continuation of the war than Napoleon III., for even if he were completely vanquished, the sovereign of an old monarchy like Austria was not in danger of losing his throne, while the Emperor of the French, the chief of a young dynasty, needed to be always successful in order to maintain his position. If Francis Joseph inclined to peace, that was doubtless on account of his repugnance to the policy of the cabinet of Berlin. He felt on one hand that the assistance of Prussia would be indispensable if he were to succeed, and on the other he disliked to owe anything to this rival power whose greed he dreaded. All that might augment the influence and favor the ambition of the Hohenzollerns awakened the instinctive suspicion of the head of the house of Hapsburg.

Let us add that, like Napoleon III., the Austrian monarch had been deeply affected by the lamentable aspect of battlefields, and that his essentially humane and generous character made him ardently desire the cessation of such calamities.

It is curious to observe that the war which had just caused such torrents of blood to flow had created no personal animosity between the two sovereigns, and even in the thickest of the struggle, neither had said a bitter word against the other!

General Fleury anxiously awaited the reply of the Emperor Francis. Treated with much attention by Marshal Hesse and the officers of the military household, he passed the night in the chamber of Count Grünne, courteously ceded to him by the latter. At five o'clock in the morning, Prince Richard Metternich, son of the illustrious chancellor, came to him there. The Prince was then thirty years old. In great favor with Francis Joseph, he acted as intermediary between the sovereign and the Minister of Foreign Affairs. He had formed part of the Austrian embassy to Paris, and, during that time, had maintained very cordial relations with General Fleury. "If peace is the result of the armistice," said the General to him, "as I hope it may be, the only thing I desire is to see you ambassador in France." This wish was to be realized.

Towards eight o'clock in the morning, Francis Joseph sent for the envoy of Napoleon III., and read him his very noble and dignified reply. He accepted the armistice and begged the Emperor of the French to name the place where conditions of peace might be discussed. Then, after sealing the letter, he expressed his wish that the French fleet might be notified at once of the cessation of hostilities just agreed upon. Having already received from Napoleon III. the necessary authorization, General Fleury complied with the Emperor's desire, and wrote on the sovereign's own table to Vice-Admiral Romain-Desfossés that he was obliged to countermand his orders. This letter, forwarded immediately to the governor-general of Venetia, at Venice, was sent the same day to Rear-Admiral Jurien de La Gravieère, then cruising on the Venetian coast, and transmitted to Vice-Admiral Romain-Desfossés, who was much amazed the next morning by receiving it at the very moment when he was expecting to quit the isle of Lossini and attack Venice with the whole fleet.

General Fleury is again the narrator: "Another word about the Emperor of Austria, whose attitude and bearing completely won me. Knowing how devoted I am to the Emperor, he entered into the most intimate details, asking about his health and habits, all with an air of deference which greatly pleased me. We had afterwards a rather long talk about the battle, and I took my leave. Some minutes later, one of the aides-de-camp came and told me that, knowing that my aide-de-camp was with me, His Majesty desired to see him, and Verdière had the honor of being presented." Much flattered by this attention, and retaining a most respectful and grateful souvenir of Francis Joseph, General Fleury set out for Valeggio, no longer as a protected envoy to an enemy, but as a messenger of his sovereign, his carriage with its windows open and blinds raised, and the uhlans acting as an escort of honor. At the village of Santa-Lucia he drank with an Austrian general to the approaching peace and the glory of both nations. At eleven o'clock in the morning he passed the French outposts.

All the troops had been under arms since daybreak. At four o'clock in the morning Napoleon III. had passed through the different lines with his staff on his way to the left of the 2d corps, commanded by Marshal Canrobert and occupying the space between Valeggio and the slopes of Venturelli. Then, surveying in person the execution of the orders he had given the day before, he had followed at the head of the line of battle all the crests occupied by the different army corps.

Neither on June 4, the day of the battle of Magenta, nor on the 24th, that of Solferino, had the troops on rising in the morning suspected that a general battle would be fought before night. On July 8, on the contrary, every member of the army believed that a great battle would take place. No one suspected the pacific mission of General Fleury, and at half-past eleven, the moment when he returned to Valeggio, the troops could not understand why they had not yet encountered the enemy.

General Fleury thus describes his arrival at the Emperor's headquarters at Valeggio: "I was expected with great impatience. . . . So when I said the words, Good news, and when I made the motion of taking from my pocket the letter which I carried, before speaking, I saw what pleasure the certainty of a response already gave the Emperor.

It was all very well for him to resume his usual tranquillity after this first emotion which he had been unable to control, but I had surprised on his features, in a flash as it were, the impression of a great relief and a real satisfaction. . . . I handed him the letter of the Emperor of Austria, which he read with eagerness, and gave him all the details of my mission. Kind and affectionate, as he always is, he rewarded me with the most flattering compliments."

Towards one o'clock, to its great astonishment, the army received orders to leave its fighting positions and go back to its cantonments. The taking of arms that morning had been its last warlike service in this campaign.

The village of Villafranca, midway between Valeggio and Verona, was named as the meeting place for the delegates commissioned to settle the conditions of the armistice. For Austria these were Field-Marshal Baron Hesse, chief of staff of the Austrian army, and General Count de Mensdorf-Pouilly; for France, Marshal Vaillant, major-general of the French army, and General de Martimprey, assistant major-general; for Sardinia, Lieutenant-General Count della Rocca, first aide-de-camp of Victor Emmanuel and major-general of the Sardinian army.

The delegates met at Villafranca, July 8, and settled the conditions of the armistice. Article 1 of the convention stipulated the suspension of arms. Article 2 provided that this suspension should last until August 15, without notice, and that in consequence the hostilities, should occasion arise, would recommence without previous warning at noon on August 16. The works of attack and defence of Peschiera would remain during the suspension of arms in their present condition. The arrangement indicated lines of demarkation to be strictly observed by the armies. Hostilities would cease at once by sea and land, and merchant vessels, without distinction of flags, might circulate freely in the Adriatic.

The convention, signed July 8 by the delegates of the three powers, was ratified the same day by the three sovereigns.

The next day, Napoleon III. announced the armistice to the troops by the following order of the day, dated from his imperial headquarters of Valeggio:

"SOLDIERS,— A suspension of arms was concluded, July 8, between the belligerent parties until the fifteenth of next August. This truce will permit you to rest from your glorious labors and, if needful, to imbibe new strength to renew the work you have so brilliantly inaugurated by your courage and devotion. I return to Paris, leaving the provisional command of my army to Marshal Vaillant, major-general; but, when the hour of combat sounds, you will again see me among you to share your dangers."

At Paris, people read in the *Moniteur:* "There must be no misunderstanding of the meaning of the suspension of arms agreed upon by the Emperor of the French and the Emperor of Austria. It is simply a truce between the belligerent armies, a truce which in clearing the ground for negotiations does not as yet permit the end of the war to be anticipated."

For the French the armistice was a surprise, and for the Italians, a disappointment. Venice, which had believed the hour of her deliverance was about to strike, was inconsolable, and Count Cavour trembled with rage. Victor Emmanuel, more politic, concealed his discontent. Napoleon III., to console him, told him at Valeggio that it was only a question of a truce, and that Austria would doubtless refuse the propositions that would be made to her. The King assembled his generals at his headquarters in Monzambano, and repeated the words of Napoleon III. However, Victor Emmanuel was under no illusion; he was convinced that a peaceful solution would result from the interview which his powerful ally was about to have with the Emperor Francis Joseph.

CHAPTER XXXII

THE INTERVIEW OF VILLAFRANCA

PRINCE ALEXANDER of Hesse having come to the grand headquarters of the French army to confer with Napoleon III., it was learned that the two monarchs would meet during the morning of July 11.

On the 10th, General Fleury wrote to his wife: "I think the young Emperor of Austria has consented to the interview only because he accepts the bases of the negotiations. That means peace, and the return of the army from here before very long. This is enormous news; it is the dramatic stroke of moderation. . . . The Emperor seems enraptured, and so does everybody else. We shall not disturb ourselves any more for politics. The main thing is accomplished, and we have no further concern with it. I will describe to-morrow's interview for you as best I can. We are all going, the entire military household, with two squadrons, one of hundred-guards and one of guides. You may fancy whether we are getting ready to look fine." The General, who had been colonel of the regiment of guides, added: " My poor guides who have not had a chance to make a charge! I am doubly sorry for it, first because I cannot have Mirandole made a general, and then on account of the regret I feel in not seeing my children able to brag a little."

During the night of July 10–11, Francis Joseph sent one of his aides-de-camp, young Prince Hohenlohe, to Valeggio to ask Napoleon III. to settle the question of the uniform in which Their Majesties and the two staffs should present themselves at the interview, and also the number and composition of the escorts. It was agreed that the sovereigns and their military households should be in field uniform and the escorts in full dress. The Emperors met at Villafranca at ten o'clock in the morning of July 11.

July 11, 7.15 A. M. — Napoleon III. leaves Valeggio on horseback, with Marshal Vaillant on his left. Like all his staff, he wears the kepi. His military household is behind him. Thirty paces in the rear follow the hundred-guards.

9 A. M. — Napoleon III. reaches Villafranca. Francis Joseph, a trifle late, not having arrived as yet, the Emperor of the French goes on towards Verona, intending, as an act of courtesy, to leave the place of rendezvous behind him and go to meet the Emperor of Austria. After covering in this way about the space of a kilometer, he perceives Francis Joseph, riding, like himself, at full gallop. The sovereigns stop, salute in military fashion, and then shake hands. With his usual tact, Napoleon III.

rides at the left of the Emperor of Austria, and they move towards Villafranca, accompanied by the military households and escorts. Arriving in the principal street, they alight and go up to the first story of a house belonging to M. Gaudini-Morelli. A small salon has been made ready for them. The escorts get into line of battle in the street to left and right of the doorway. In front of this door all the aides-de-camp smoke and chat.

The two monarchs are in presence of each other. Never, perhaps, has there been so important a meeting of sovereigns since that of Tilsit between the Emperors Napoleon I. and Alexander. On what Francis Joseph and Napoleon III. are going to say, on the mutual impression which they produce, depends peace or renewed slaughters, possibly a general conflagration extending over the greater part of Europe. The emperors open the conversation with perfect courtesy and calmness, like two accomplished gentlemen. One of them will be twenty-nine on the 18th of the following August; the other had been fifty-one the 20th of April. They had come to power in the same month of the same year, one having ascended the throne December 2, 1848, the other elected president of the Republic on the 10th. Both have had an experience of men and things which is already long, and at certain moments painful; both have made disagreeable reflections on the caprices of fortune and the responsibilities of supreme rank. Napoleon III. does not in the least assume the tone and manners of a victor. His language gives no suggestion of an ultimatum or a menace. He is touched by the youth, the misfortunes, and the dignity of his interlocutor, who must, at this moment, find the weight of a sceptre very heavy. On his side Francis Joseph is affected by the softness of Napoleon's voice, and by the affability and kindness depicted on his countenance. The Emperor of the French does not dictate conditions; contenting himself with expressing wishes, he proposes the cession of Lombardy to Sardinia, the creation of a kingdom of Venetia under an Austrian prince, the establishment of an Italian Confederation under the presidency of the Pope, the concession of reforms in the Pontifical States, and, lastly, a Congress to settle the details of questions. Whereupon the Austrian monarch says: "I wish for peace, and I am about to give Your Majesty a proof of confidence by indicating the extent of the concessions I can make. . . . I have lost Lombardy, but I will not give it to Sardinia. The utmost I can do is to cede it to France, which will do what she pleases with it. As to Venice, I still occupy it, and I cannot abandon what has not yet been conquered. Still, I feel that great changes there are necessary; I will accomplish them, and Venice will be not merely satisfied but happy under my sceptre."

Napoleon III. has not conquered Venetia; he has not even invaded it. Hence he cannot insist. He limits himself to assuming that Venetia will form part of the Italian Confederation under the dominion of the Emperor of Austria. To this confederation, of which the Holy Father would have the presidency, Francis Joseph makes no absolute objection, but the details of its organization remain in the air. He also agrees to join France in asking the Pope for reforms, expressing, however, some doubts as to their urgency and also concerning the means of putting them into execution. The point he has most at heart is the restoration to their states of the Grand-Duke of Tuscany and the Duke of Modena, both of whom have associated themselves with his fortune, and who are both Archdukes of Austria. This for His Imperial and Royal Apostolic Majesty is a question of honor. Napoleon III. seems to comprehend it, and promises to do all in his power to reinstate the two princes in their dominions, while granting a general amnesty and a Constitution. But what form shall the intervention of the two emperors take? Ought it to be purely platonic, or, in case of need, a resort to force? To insist on this point might endanger the result of the interview. Hence nothing is defined. The sovereigns declare themselves satisfied to have traced the great lines of their agreement. For the moment they demand nothing further. There is a table with pens, ink, and paper in front of them. They do not use it, but confine themselves to speech. They mutually confide in their good faith and their memory. The interview has lasted a little less than an hour.

After coming out of the house where their interview has taken place, Napoleon III. and Francis Joseph present to each other by name the members of their military households. The French monarch is extremely amiable to Field-Marshal Baron Hesse, who, born in 1788, is the veteran of the Austrian army.

"Sir Marshal," he says, "I am proud of having been able to make war in face of a glorious soldier of Wagram." The valiant warrior has retained the bearing of a young man. The fifty years which have elapsed between Wagram and Solferino seem barely to have touched him.

Like Napoleon III. Francis Joseph has brought as escort only two squadrons, one of Court gendarmes and the other of uhlans. The Emperor of the French passes them in review and declares they are magnificent. The Emperor of Austria, after inspecting the squadron of hundred-guards and that of guides, eulogizes them as highly.

General Fleury writes in his *Souvenirs:* "I greatly fear that such fine troops will never be seen in France again. All the army uniforms have been reduced to a democratic level. Infantry, cavalry, wagon-trains, all look alike. It is scarcely observed that, under pretext of simplifying the provision of clothing, our War Ministers — who are changed every year — are in this way destroying the esprit de corps, that self-love of a regiment which, at a given moment, engenders extraordinary feats."

Wishing to return the politeness shown by Napoleon III. in going beyond Villafranca to meet him, Francis Joseph rides about a kilometer on the road from Villafranca to Valeggio with the French sovereign. The emperors take friendly leave of each other. Thus, at the very moment when so many victims have just been flung into the graves common to the combatants of the three armies, at the moment when a great number of sick and wounded are suffering and dying in the hospitals where they have been huddled, the two sovereigns who caused the war, are amicably shaking hands.

CHAPTER XXXIII

THE PRELIMINARIES OF PEACE

ON his return to Valeggio, Napoleon III. found Victor Emmanuel, to whom he related all that had just taken place. The abrupt solution, which did not more than half realize his expectations, was a great disappointment to the King. But this monarch, very shrewd and subtle under his rude exterior, was too politic to endeavor to shun the inevitable. He offered neither objection nor recrimination to his powerful ally, and contented himself with saying: "Whatever may be the decision of Your Majesty, I shall be eternally grateful for what you have done for the cause of Italian independence, and you may rely in all circumstances on my entire fidelity."

Nothing had been written at Villafranca. At Valeggio, Napoleon III. took a paper on which he put the conditions which, if his memory were faithful, had been agreed upon between him and the Emperor of Austria. He charged Prince Napoleon to carry this to Francis Joseph at Verona, and return with the signature of the sovereign. This was not a mere formality, and Napoleon III. dreaded lest difficulties might arise when there was no longer question of a conversation, but of a written agreement.

At Paris, the cousin of the Emperor was often accused of too democratic manners. Abroad, he was always very correct, and whenever he found himself in relations with sovereigns or princes, there was nothing to criticise in his bearing or his language. Moreover, he was very intelligent, very apt, extremely conversant with diplomatic affairs and the usages of courts. In designating him for this delicate and important mission, the Emperor did something that pleased Victor Emmanuel, who, knowing the ideas and sentiments of his son-in-law concerning Italy, was well aware that the Prince would do all he could for her.

There was no time to be lost. As Marshal Moltke has written in his history of the Italian campaign of 1859, "Prussia was completely armed. The mobilization of two-thirds of her military forces was completed. The rest was on a war footing. The troops were already on the march towards the first places of assembly. It was no longer a secret that the transport of soldiers by railway towards the Rhine was to begin on July 15, and that within a very short time an army of two hundred and fifty thousand men would be gathered there, which the contingents of other German States were ready to join."

French and Bonaparte on his father's side, but

German through his mother, the daughter of the first King of Würtemberg, Prince Napoleon knew Germany perfectly. He had been brought up there, and knew all that might be dreaded from it. The extent and gravity of the danger did not escape him; he desired to make every effort to dispel it without losing a minute.

Napoleon III. had re-entered Valeggio at one o'clock in the afternoon. At half-past two, a post-chaise with four horses took Prince Napoleon to Verona, which he reached two hours later, and presented himself at the imperial headquarters. Francis Joseph affably extended his hand and led him into his study. The Prince gave the details to Baron de Bazancourt, who has introduced them into his remarkable history of the campaign of Italy.

The Austrian Emperor expressed himself as follows: "I set the example of frankness this morning by telling the Emperor Napoleon explicitly what were the limits of the concessions I could make consistently with my honor and the interests of my crown. But, be well assured that if you have a public opinion to conciliate, I have one also, and it is all the more exacting because it is I who am making all the sacrifices."

The paper drawn up by Napoleon III. contained seven paragraphs. Francis Joseph and Prince Napoleon examined them one by one.

1. *The two sovereigns will favor the formation of an Italian Confederation.*

This paragraph roused no objection. The Confederation was established in principle. Its organization was to be regulated by a Congress.

2. *This Confederation will be under the honorary presidency of the Pope.*

Francis Joseph desired the word *honorary* to be expunged. The Prince persuaded him to allow it to stand.

3. *The Emperor of Austria cedes his rights over Lombardy to the Emperor of the French, who, in accordance with the wishes of the inhabitants, will resign them to the King of Sardinia.*

This paragraph gave rise to grave disputes. Francis Joseph would not accept the words: *in accordance with the wishes of the inhabitants.* "For my part," said he, "I know no rights but those written in the treaties. According to those, Lombardy is mine. The fortune of war being against me, I agree to cede that province to the Emperor Napoleon, but I do not recognize the 'wishes of the inhabitants,' which, to my mind, means the right of revolution. If you choose to employ that expression in addressing the King of Sardinia, it is no affair of mine, but you can understand that the Emperor of Austria is unable to accept such language."

Prince Napoleon did not insist, and the words were suppressed.

A still more serious question came up. The Emperor of Austria declared in peremptory terms that the two fortified cities of Peschiera and Mantua were not included in the cession of Lombardy. He said: "I cannot oblige my army to evacuate fortified towns which it occupies and retains possession of; honor forbids me. I could understand the Emperor's demanding to keep Peschiera if the allied army had seized it; but my troops are there still. Make it plain to him that, even if such were my personal wish, it would be impossible for me to cede any of my fortresses."

4. *Venetia forms part of the Italian Confederation, remaining, however, under the crown of the Emperor of Austria.*

This paragraph was adopted without discussion.

5. *The two sovereigns will make every effort, recourse to arms excepted, to maintain the Grand-Duke of Tuscany and the Duke of Modena in their dominions, they giving a Constitution and a general amnesty.*

This was the delicate point, and unless something were clearly specified, no mutual understanding could be arrived at.

The words, *recourse to arms excepted*, were not admitted by Francis Joseph. He saw in them an indirect appeal to insurrection and an encouragement to the people to persevere in the path of revolution. On the other hand, he knew that nothing would induce Napoleon III. to resort to force for the sake of reinstating the two princes. How then could it be accomplished? The difficulty was insurmountable.

The Emperor of Austria did not go so far as to require that the two relatives in whom he was so greatly interested, and who, in their quality as archdukes, were considered as actually his lieutenants, should be reinstated by either Austrian or French bayonets. But he said that the Duke of Modena hoped to be able to re-establish himself in his duchy by means of the battalions which had remained loyal to him, and that the Grand-Duke of Tuscany was not far from arriving at an understanding with his subjects. For the moment the emperors must confine themselves to recognizing the principle of the restoration of the princes.

6. *The two sovereigns will ask the Holy Father to introduce the necessary reforms in his States, and to separate the Legations administratively from the rest of the States of the Church.*

Francis Joseph admitted the reforms, and even substituted the word *indispensable* for *necessary*, but he requested the suppression of the second part of the sentence, on the ground that only a Congress could decide whether the Legation must be separated administratively from the rest of the Pontifical dominions.

7. *Full and complete amnesty is accorded on both sides to persons compromised by recent events in the territories of the belligerent parties.*

This final paragraph was in accordance with the general sentiments of both emperors, and was accepted without the slightest hesitation.

No mention, it will be observed, was made of the duchy of Parma in either paragraph. As the duchess-regent, the sister of the Count of Chambord, had never been willing to submit herself to Austrian policy, Francis Joseph did not feel bound to defend the rights of her son. Hence Prince Napoleon sought to induce him to recognize the annexation of the duchy to Sardinia, but the Emperor of Austria would have nothing to do with it. All he said was: "There must be no question of the duchy of Parma in these preliminaries. The duchess-regent is not a princess of my family. But I cannot cede States which do not belong to me."

Meanwhile, the interview had already lasted more than two hours without an agreement having been reached on several of the essential points. Prince Napoleon remarked that his sovereign had ordered him to be back at Valeggio by ten o'clock at latest. "Very well," said the Emperor, rising, "you shall have my answer presently." And he showed his interlocutor to the apartment that had been made ready for him. A dinner was served to His Imperial Highness, at which two officers of the military household of the Emperor bore him company.

The sovereign came to the Prince at half-past seven in the evening. "Here is my written reply," said he; "you may carry it to the Emperor Napoleon." The text of it was as follows: —

1. The two sovereigns will favor the creation of an Italian Confederation;

2. This Confederation will be under the honorary presidency of the Holy Father;

3. The Emperor of Austria cedes his rights over Lombardy to the Emperor of the French, with the exception of the fortresses of Mantua and Peschiera, so that the frontier of the Austrian possessions shall start from the extremity of the fortress of Peschiera and extend in a straight line along the Mincio as far as Grazie; from there to Scarzarola and Suzana on the Po, whence the existing frontiers will continue to form the boundaries of Austria. The Emperor of the French will remit the ceded territory to the King of Sardinia;

4. Venetia will form part of the Italian Confederation, remaining, however, under the Austrian crown;

5. The Grand-Duke of Tuscany and the Duke of Modena will return to their States, giving a general amnesty;

6. The two emperors will ask the Holy Father to introduce the indispensable reforms in his States;

7. Full and complete amnesty is accorded on both sides to persons compromised on account of recent events in the territories of the belligerent parties.

Prince Napoleon perceived that this was Francis Joseph's last word, and that he would accept no modification of his text. Hence he asked him to sign it. The sovereign replied: "I cannot pledge myself if the Emperor Napoleon does not do the same. It is impossible for me to sign such conditions without being certain that they will be accepted by him." Prince Napoleon replied: "Sire, I give Your Majesty my word of honor as an honest man, that you will receive this very paper to-morrow morning with the signature of the Emperor Napoleon."

Francis Joseph then concluded to sign. Afterwards he said: "I am making a great sacrifice in ceding one of my finest provinces like this. But, if we can come to an understanding about Italian affairs with the Emperor Napoleon, there will be no further cause of dissension between us."

The clock struck eight. The sovereign and the Prince remained together for some moments longer, but without exchanging a further word on politics. Then Francis Joseph went to the head of the stairs with the cousin of Napoleon III. and held out his hand, saying: "Till we meet, Prince; I hope it will be no longer as enemies."

Prince Napoleon was back at Valeggio at ten o'clock. As soon as the Emperor had read the paper signed by Francis Joseph, his face lighted up with joy, and he embraced his cousin warmly. The next day he signed the paper and sent it to the Emperor of Austria with an autograph letter. The preliminaries of peace were definitively concluded.

CHAPTER XXXIV

THE RESIGNATION OF CAVOUR

THE man who had most ardently desired the continuation of the war was Count Cavour. His revolutionary policy was roundly blamed by the minister of France at Turin, Prince de La Tour d'Auvergne. This essentially conservative diplomatist, extremely hostile to the project of Italian unity, wrote to Count Walewski, July 8, 1859, concerning the Piedmontese minister, who was already making open preparations for annexations: " The devouring activity of his mind, his ambition, the adventurous character of his genius, nearly always get the better of his reason. Hence, whatever appearances may be, it would be a singular delusion to fancy that M. Cavour is sincerely abandoning the more or less loyal and regular methods to which he has too often resorted, and which, one must admit, have sometimes been successful. For my part, I am under no manner of illusion. I have made frequent experience of my powerlessness, and I know of but one really serious means of opposing the impatiences and whims of M. de Cavour, and that is the firm and categorical will of the Emperor. With that exception, I see no remedy."

COUNT CAVOUR

No sooner had the Prime Minister learned by a letter from General de La Marmora that the armistice just concluded was a long truce which might lead to peace, than, concealing neither his vexation nor his anger, he set off for the camp, hoping to induce the King and the Emperor to abandon all pacific intentions. At daybreak, July 10, he arrived from Turin at Desenzano, and during the day at Mozambano, headquarters of the Sardinian army. Victor Emmanuel was at the Melchiarri villa, where he received the minister, but was not in the least affected by his rage. Cavour vainly entreated his master to refuse incomplete enfranchisement, to summon all Italy to his aid, and to go on with the war even without the support of Napoleon III. Victor Emmanuel took good care not to accept such bad advice. The same day the foolhardy minister saw Prince Napoleon, who gave him no hope, but he was not admitted to an audience with the Emperor. The next day, July 11, he tried to see Prince Napoleon again; but the Prince had gone to Verona to arrive at an understanding with Francis Joseph on the preliminaries of peace. Cavour knew the text of these in the evening, and the morning of July 12, after handing in his resignation, he departed in great exasperation. The violence of the minister had ended by making the sovereign weary. He said to him, "Peace is being made without me; I am not the strongest; do not bother me."

Victor Emmanuel frequently needed Cavour, but

did not really like him. Very jealous of his authority and proud of his race, the head of the house of Savoy could not accustom himself to the presuming manners and dominating tone of his ambitious minister, and was unwilling to seem a new Louis XIII. obliged to wear the yoke of a Richelieu. Victor Emmanuel was a sovereign who allowed no one to lead him. When he thought it necessary, he was able to make his subjects take his own view, and to prove to all men the strength of his will. Moreover, the King was in the right, for nothing could have been more fatal to Piedmont than a broil with Napoleon III.

Cavour was doubtless a clever statesman; nevertheless, as a disciple of Machiavelli he was inferior to Victor Emmanuel, who, the day after the preliminaries of Villafranca, comprehended the situation far better than his minister. He remembered that "Patience and delay do more than force or fury." Instead of facing great difficulties, he eluded them, he put them off. Forced to bow to accomplished facts, he was careful, even while giving his adhesion to the preliminaries of Villafranca, to stipulate to his advantage his future freedom of action, *liberta d'operare*, as he called it. " I approve as far as I am concerned," was his reply to the Emperor. This meant that he reserved to the Tuscans, Modenese, Parmesans, and Romagnols the faculty of disposing of their destiny. If, instead of confining himself to this mental reservation, he had broken violently with Napoleon III. as Count Cavour advised, he would have placed his kingdom between the hammer and anvil of France and Austria.

The King made a formal entry into Milan by the eastern gate and the Corso, July 13, towards five o'clock in the afternoon. The division of French infantry, under General d'Hugues, had just arrived from Lyons. Its troops formed the line on the Duomo square. Entering the palace, Victor Emmanuel received the French generals d' Hugues, de Bailliencourt, de Béville, and Suau. In an interesting volume entitled: *Military Leaves*, General de Bailliencourt has given some curious details concerning this reception. He says: "The King, still covered with noble dust, in a very untidy uniform, affected the attitudes of a captain of hussars of the First Empire. . . . Raising his eyes to the ceiling, holding his head absurdly high, he said to us: 'Well! gentlemen, I am not content, and you ought not to be so either, for all you have done is to come here, and the peace deprives you of all hope of witnessing such victories as we have gained! Your army has rendered us great service; . . . yours and mine have fought like two sisters; . . . I am only a soldier; I do not like lawyers, I do not care much about my kingdom, all I like is battles. I had built castles in the air; I expected to make war for two years, and I have only been allowed to do so for two months; I hoped to go round the world with the French soldiers. I would have been willing to have several ribs broken on condition of being able to go on fighting. . . . At the battle of Solferino, it was I who had them fire the last guns of the day, with thirty-eight pieces in battery."

Reverting finally to the idea he had first expressed, the valiant monarch said: "I do not like lawyers. Do you, General?" addressing himself to General d'Hugues. The latter replied, "Your Majesty is right, lawyers belong to a degenerate age." Victor Emmanuel returned: "And yet I am going to have a new affair with them. All the same, I shall be able to put them in their place. . . . That Cavour, I made him, and now he comes here with his resignation! I gave him a very bad reception. Better still, he is going to make speeches in a café to increase his popularity! What would you have me do with such a lawyer as that? . . . All the same, he had better be careful, I shall keep my eyes open. . . . He won't lose anything by waiting. I will contrive something for him."

To this story, which one would scarcely believe to be authentic but for the perfect respectability of its narrator, General de Bailliencourt adds: "We went out, unable to believe either our eyes or our ears. . . I made a note of it at once, and so did my companions, wishing to keep exact the memory of this very original interview, and to preserve its every feature with scrupulous care." On returning to Turin, Cavour said that he was not merely no longer president of the Council, but that he would sooner become a conspirator than lend a hand to such a bargain as had just been concluded. However, his compatriots put no faith in his definitive retirement. "Cavour is going away," said they, "but he has a return ticket in his pocket."

CHAPTER XXXV

THE EMPEROR'S RETURN

NAPOLEON III. made ready to go back to France. July 12, he resigned the chief command of the army of Italy to Marshal Vaillant and issued the following proclamation to the troops from the imperial headquarters of Valeggio: —

"Soldiers!

"The bases of peace are agreed upon with the Emperor of Austria; the chief object of the war has been attained. For the first time Italy is about to become a nation.

"A Confederation of all the States of Italy, under the honorary presidency of the Holy Father, will reunite in group the members of a single family. Venetia remains, it is true, under the Austrian sceptre; nevertheless it will be an Italian province and form part of the Confederation.

"The reunion of Lombardy to Piedmont creates for us on this side of the Alps a powerful ally which will be our debtor for its independence; governments remaining outside of the movement, or reinstated in their possessions, will comprehend the necessity of salutary reforms.

"A general amnesty will remove the traces of civil discords. Mistress henceforward of her own destiny, Italy will have no one but herself to blame if she does not make uniform progress in order and liberty.

"You will soon return to France; the grateful country will receive with transports the soldiers who have carried so high the glory of our arms at Montebello, Palestro, Turbigo, Magenta, Marignan, and Solferino; who in two months have liberated Piedmont and Lombardy, and who have halted only because the war was about to assume proportions no longer in relation with the interests which France had in this formidable struggle.

"Be proud, then, of your success, proud of the results obtained, proud above all of being the beloved children of that France which will always be the great nation so long as she has a heart that can understand great causes and men like you to defend them."

The Emperor left his headquarters at Valeggio the same day. The guard was ordered to go into its first encampments at Desenzano, and the different army corps began leaving the banks of the Mincio, where their concentration was no longer useful, in order to be distributed in the great centres of Lombardy.

Napoleon III. made a halt at Desenzano. The tranquil beauty of the place seemed grateful to him after the painful emotions awakened by the horrid sights of war. On the shore of Lake Garda were the now useless gunboats prepared at great expense for the siege of Peschiera. These he presented to Victor Emmanuel.

July 14, the Emperor made an entry at Milan which was not less brilliant than that of June 8. The railway station was adorned as for a fête. At a little after five o'clock, Prince Carignan arrived there to meet the two sovereigns. The French and Piedmontese troops made the line with the national militia. On their way to the Royal Palace Their Majesties, riding in an open carriage, were vehemently applauded by a crowd whose enthusiasm amounted to frenzy. "The Emperor seemed calm," writes General de Bailliencourt, an eye-witness, "and it pleased me to see once more on his countenance that poetic expression which is peculiarly his own."

On reaching the Royal Palace, Napoleon III. immediately received the generals who came to escort him. As they were expressing their admiration for his triumphs, he answered with profound sadness: "But what losses! What bloodshed!"

A dinner of one hundred covers was served at half-past six in the magnificent gallery of the palace. "Seated almost opposite the Emperor," adds General de Bailliencourt, "I did not lose a movement of the principal actors in the great drama just enacted. Napoleon III. had Victor Emmanuel on his right and Prince Napoleon on his left. He seemed visibly preoccupied. The King, always unreserved and petulant, loudly regretted the two years of campaigning he had been counting on. War is a game for him, on much the same footing as the chase. . . . The Emperor, addressing himself to all, inquired with great interest for news of Marshal de Castellane (commander-in-chief of the army of Lyons), quoting for us several passages from the admirable letter he had received from him, requesting to be allowed to march under no matter what command."

The generals quitted the palace at half-past eight. The city was splendid. The illuminated houses, the thousands of parti-colored lanterns waving in the breeze, produced a magical effect. "A curious, enormous crowd," says General de Bailliencourt again, "encumbers the square through which we pass. People throng about us; children cling to the tails of our coats; women hang on our arms and kiss our hands, while men want to carry us in triumph."

Milan has retained an affectionate and grateful memory of Napoleon III. and of France. The same has not always been true of other great Italian cities.

On returning to the Gonfalonieri palace where he lodged, General de Bailliencourt learned that a despatch from Turin, which came that evening, announced that the turbulent disposition of the population was displaying hostility to the Emperor, who was expected there. Angry demonstrations had occurred. Portraits of His Majesty in the shops had been torn down by a crowd who substituted those of Mazzini and Orsini in their stead. Apprised of these details, Napoleon III. had just ordered General de Bailliencourt's brigade to start for Turin at once.

The same day, July 14, Prince de La Tour d'Auvergne, minister of France in that city, wrote to Count Walewski: "The news that peace has been signed has caused a profound sensation at Turin. The clauses relating to Venetia have created especial dissatisfaction. Austria's possession of this province and the fortresses of Mantua, Peschiera, Verona, and Legnano is considered as a continual menace for the security and independence of Piedmont. Nor do people entertain more favorably the idea of an Italian Confederation which obliges Piedmont to live in close alliance with Austria. . . . A rumor is being circulated that England will refuse to recognize a state of things in the arrangement of which she has not intervened. Count Cavour's resignation has been the cap sheaf. The disturbance is greater to-day than it was yesterday. Orsini's portrait has been substituted for that of the Emperor in every picture-shop in the city. The attitude of the press is equally hostile. It should be the part of the Government under such circumstances to tranquillize public opinion by enlightening it, but it has abstained from intervention. It is greatly to be desired that Count Arese, who has agreed to accept Cavour's place, may succeed in recalling to order the evidently distracted public mind."

At three o'clock in the afternoon of July 15, Prince de La Tour d'Auvergne sent this telegraphic despatch to Count Walewski: "The Emperor is to arrive at Turin about five o'clock. The people are in a better humor. A notification of the syndic inviting the inhabitants to illuminate their houses in honor of the coming of Their Majesties is read quietly. The portraits of Orsini have been withdrawn. M. Irvoy (chief of police charged to secure the Emperor's safety) begs you to communicate this despatch to the Minister of the Interior."

Meanwhile Napoleon III. and Victor Emmanuel were on the way to Turin by rail. The train passed Magenta. The Emperor, much affected, glanced at the city station and the Naviglio Grande. He recalled the prodigies of valor performed by his guard at this spot, and the cruel perplexities, the anguish he had himself endured at the moment when victory seemed so doubtful, even so improbable. It is a striking spectacle to find a battlefield calm and empty which one has seen in the midst of all the agitations and horrors of carnage. Impassible and serene, nature has forgotten it all. The song of birds has replaced the noise of cannon, shells, and bullets. Grass has covered over the trenches where the victims of war are sleeping their last slumber. What a contrast between two aspects of a single place!

Towards four o'clock in the afternoon of July 15, the troops formed the line in the principal streets of Turin. A number of Piedmontese generals, under command of old General de Sonnaz, were awaiting the two sovereigns. Cavour, in an elegant carriage drawn by fine English horses, had also gone to the station. One of his horses was seized with vertigo and fell, nearly upsetting the carriage. Cavour had to go a little way on foot, and more than one superstitious Italian saw a bad omen in this slight accident.

The clocks were striking five when the imperial and royal train arrived. Napoleon III. shook hands with the ex-Prime Minister, but without speaking. A rumor had been spread that there would be national guards along the route taken by the sovereigns, who would lower their arms and utter offensive cries. Nothing of the kind occurred, but it was undeniable that the crowd cheered the King much more than the Emperor. The procession halted in the second court of the palace, and Napoleon III. occupied the fine apartments on the ground floor formerly inhabited by King Charles Albert. There was a grand dinner at which Cavour was not present. But the Emperor had him summoned during the evening and conversed very kindly with him.

"I am unwilling," he said to him, "that we should part on ill terms. It is not strictly true that I may have refused to receive you. Only, what could I have said to you? . . . It would have taken three hundred thousand men to go on with the campaign, and I did not have them." Cavour having laid stress on the forlorn situation of the abandoned provinces, Napoleon III. replied, "I will have their cause pleaded in the Congress." Then the two former associates of Plombières separated, never again to meet.

The Emperor left the Piedmontese capital at six o'clock the next morning. Possibly he had selected this early hour because he had no confidence in the good dispositions of the inhabitants so far as he was concerned. Not a flag was in any window. The streets were almost empty. Acclamations were very few. Victor Emmanuel, his staff, Prince de Carignan, and the members of the French legation accompanied the Emperor to Suse, where the macadamized road ended. There, after cordially embracing Victor Emmanuel and Prince Carignan, and shaking hands with those surrounding them, Napoleon III. entered a travelling carriage which ascended Mont Cenis and redescended towards Saint-Jean de Maurienne, where he boarded a train. His passage through Chambéry gave occasion for manifestations which seemed like a first omen of the annexation of Savoy to France. M. Grand Thorane, French consul at Chambéry, wrote to Prince de La Tour d'Auvergne: "The Emperor has been received here with enthusiasm by all that is good in the population, which is certainly the immense majority, and it is certain that there would have been a much larger crowd had the intendant-general taken care to apprise the people of the time of his arrival. If it had been known in the neighboring communes, there would have been a still greater throng on the roads by which he came. The syndic would not permit the firemen to go to the station, because the corps is composed of orderly men whose sentiments towards the Emperor are well known, and he was not anxious for him to hear their unanimous acclamations. The archbishop and the first president of the court of appeals, who went to the station, had not been notified."

Napoleon III. noticed that Savoy was well-inclined towards him and his empire. Perhaps, after having done a great deal for Italy, he was now thinking of doing something for France.

CHAPTER XXXVI

SAINT-CLOUD

AFTER passing through Savoy, which he was to annex to France the following year, the Emperor went on to Saint-Cloud without further delay. In spite of the incognito he preserved on his rapid journey, the people assembled at the railway stations and acclaimed the victorious sovereign as he passed. July 17, at ten in the morning, he arrived by the enclosed railway at the palace of Saint-Cloud, where he was received on alighting from the train by the Empress and the Prince Imperial, whom he embraced with much affection. When the Emperor asked the little Prince if he recognized his father, the child seemed rather humiliated by such a doubt. There were tears of joy in the eyes of all present.

Napoleon III. possessed the family feelings in a very high degree. Under a cold exterior and a mask of absolute impassibility, he concealed an almost womanly sensitiveness and a very affectionate nature. A melancholy impression blended with his happiness. He was thinking of so many others, less fortunate than he, who would never return, and whose mothers, wives, and children were even now weeping for them. The château of Saint-Cloud, with the sweet coolness of its venerable shades, its cascades, and its fountains, did not make him forget the prostrating heat of the Italian battlefields, the clouds of dust, the agonies of the fight, the horrors of the carnage. At noon he heard Mass in the chapel in thanksgiving to God. He afterwards received the imperial family, the members of the privy council, the ministers, the persons of his household and that of the Empress.

Countess Stéphanie de Tascher de La Pagerie was present at this reception. "The Emperor," she says, "was calm, content, unaffected as usual. He looked well, his tanned complexion showed that he had been exposed to the ardors of the sun of Italy. He went from one to another, kindly, affectionate, and while moving about told us certain details. But he insisted on one point, namely, that on finding himself here again, it seemed that all this campaign, so rich in incidents, in episodes of all descriptions, had been a dream. . . . What a dream!"

All the news the Emperor received, all the reflections he made upon the situation of Europe, inclined him to congratulate himself on having tempted fortune no further. He knew that if he had not made haste to sign the preliminaries of peace, the entrance of Prussia and all the other States of the Germanic Confederation upon the scene would have been merely a question of days, of hours. The French generals surrounding him criticised the Prussian landwehr, some of them going so far as to compare it with the national guard. Napoleon III., who had been brought up in Germany, knew how erroneous such an appreciation was. He was aware that the landwehr was a real army, and he recognized that the present effective forces of the French troops were not large enough to permit them to triumph simultaneously on the Adige and the Rhine. When he closely considered the matter, he was amazed that the Emperor of Austria, who occupied formidable positions in the quadrilateral, should have given up the struggle. Despatches from Saint Petersburg proved that in spite of his sympathies for France, the Czar would not have gone to the length of drawing the sword in her defence. The pleasure with which the Russian government learned that preliminaries of peace had been concluded, confirmed Napoleon III. in the conviction that he had done well in halting midway.

The Duke of Montebello, ambassador of France at Saint Petersburg, wrote to Count Walewski, July 14: "The telegraphic despatches of Your Excellency, dated the 12th of this month, brought news that peace had been signed between the Emperor Napoleon and the Emperor of Austria, and I hastened to announce it at Peterhof, where the Emperor Alexander and Prince Gortchakoff are at present. The satisfaction displayed by the Prince was sincere and complete. Above all, he expressed most warmly his

T

admiration for the profound sagacity of His Imperial Majesty's policy. As soon as it was known at Saint Petersburg that an armistice had been concluded, to expire the 15th of August, the Russian Cabinet began to hope that hostilities would not be renewed, and that a definitive arrangement would be the consequence of the suspension of arms. But it had not expected that the two sovereigns would bring about so quickly the realization of its hopes. The surprise has merely augmented its satisfaction. The Emperor Alexander, to whom Prince Gortchakoff transmitted the news immediately, sent me word that he desired to see me at once, and His Majesty displayed with equal vivacity the sentiments by which his minister had just shown himself to be animated. . . . The bases agreed upon are considered by the Russian government well adapted to serve as the foundation of a lasting peace. The Emperor Alexander and Prince Gortchakoff recognize that in confining to these limits the sacrifices which the success of his arms might have imposed upon the Court of Vienna, the Emperor has shown himself as profound a politician in negotiation as he has proved himself a great captain on fields of battle."

On the other hand, Napoleon III. foreboded the difficulties originated by the war, and their future developments incessantly disquieted him. He was under no illusion as to the obscurities of the preliminaries of peace and the obstacles to be encountered before it could be rendered final. Questions pertaining to the central Italian States, especially to those of the Holy Father, were far from being settled, and the Emperor was well aware that one of the most arduous problems would be to establish any sort of harmony between the clerical and the revolutionary parties, the one as ardent and as ultra as the other. Anxieties for the future mingled therefore in the sovereign's mind with the gladness of present success.

July 19, at half-past eight in the evening, at Saint-Cloud, the great bodies of State entered the salon of Mars to congratulate the victorious monarch. M. Troplong, Count Morny, and M. Baroche, the first of whom was president of the Senate, the second of the Corps Législatif, the third of the Council of State, vied with each other in protestations and praise.

According to M. Troplong, "When Scipio had vanquished Hannibal at Zama, he might have destroyed Carthage; he would not do it, although he had pledged himself to subvert the Carthaginian power. Prudent politician as well as skilful general, he knew that to ruin an enemy too completely is often equivalent to ruining one's self." Napoleon III. was rather surprised at finding himself thus compared to Scipio.

"Sire," said M. de Morny, "what prodigies in three months! . . . But the finest of all the victories is the one you have gained over yourself. In the intoxication of triumph you have shown yourself to be as generous an enemy as you are a faithful and disinterested ally. Surrounded by victorious and ardent soldiers, you thought of nothing but how to spare their precious blood. You have given true liberty to Italy by freeing it from despotism and restraining it from revolutionary proceedings. In fine, with that marvellous moderation which characterizes you, you have gone as far as the honor of France required, no farther than her interests demanded."

"God be thanked," said M. Baroche, "for bringing you back safe and sound to this France of which you are the saviour and the hope, to this august wife whose firm courage and lofty intelligence we have tested during your absence, and to this noble child who is already learning to thank Heaven for the triumphs of his father."

The Emperor replied: —

"Gentlemen, in finding myself once more amongst you who have surrounded the Empress and my son with so much devotion during my absence, I feel the necessity of thanking you in the first place, and then of explaining to you the motive of my conduct.

"When after a two months' fortunate campaign, the French and Sardinian armies found themselves under the walls of Verona, the struggle was about inevitably to change its character, both with respect to military matters and to politics.

"I had no choice but to attack in front an enemy entrenched behind great fortresses, and protected against all flank movements by the neutrality of surrounding territories; and in commencing the long and fruitless war of sieges I was confronted by Europe in arms, and ready either to dispute our success or to aggravate our reverses.

"Yet the difficulties of the enterprise would not have shaken my resolution or the enthusiasm of my army, if the means had not been disproportionate with the results to be expected.

"It was necessary to determine on breaking through the obstacles opposed by the neutral territories, and then to accept war on the Rhine as well as on the Adige. It was necessary, above all, to avail one's self frankly of the support of the revolution. It was necessary to shed more precious blood when too much had been spilled already. In a word, in order to succeed, it was necessary to risk what it is not permissible for a sovereign to put at stake for anything but the independence of his country.

"If I stayed my hand, it was not, therefore, through lassitude or exhaustion, nor through desertion of the noble cause I had desired to serve, but because there was something in my heart which spoke more loudly still — the interest of France."

Thus the Emperor sought to justify rather than to glorify himself. His speech was a sort of public confession, a skilful plea to prove that he was right in laying down arms.

On the other hand, he was fully aware that Venice had been cruelly disappointed at the moment when she thought the hour of her deliverance had come. He knew Italian passions too well and in youth had shared them too profoundly not to be extremely afflicted at his failure to realize more than half of his liberating programme.

"Can you believe," continued the crowned orator, "that it has cost me nothing to bridle the ardor of soldiers excited by victory and merely asking permission to go on? Can you believe it has cost me nothing to eliminate openly from my programme, in the face of Europe, the territory extending from the Mincio to the Adriatic? Can you believe it has cost me nothing to behold the wreck of noble illusions and patriotic hopes in honest hearts?

"I made war against the will of Europe in order to aid Italian independence; as soon as the destinies of my own country were endangered, I made peace."

The Emperor ended his speech as follows, as if seeking to console and reassure himself: —

"Can it now be said that our efforts and sacrifices have been totally wasted? No. As I said in taking leave of our soldiers, we have a right to be proud of this brief campaign. In four combats and two battles, a numerous army, second to none in organization and bravery, has been vanquished. The King of Piedmont, formerly styled the guardian of the Alps, has seen his frontiers extended from the Tessin to the Mincio. The idea of an Italian nationality is admitted by those who antagonize it. All the sovereigns of the peninsula finally comprehend the imperious necessity of salutary reforms.

"Thus, after having given a new proof of the

military strength of France, the peace I have just concluded will be fruitful in fortunate results; the future will reveal them more fully day by day, for the welfare of Italy, the influence of France, and the repose of Europe."

The diplomatic corps having signified its desire for an audience, it was received by the Emperor at Saint-Cloud, July 21. "Sire," said the Nuncio, "the diplomatic corps experienced the necessity of asking Your Majesty to receive its cordial and sincere felicitations on your happy return and the prompt conclusion of peace."

Napoleon III. replied, but, in spite of his habitual courtesy, without wholly concealing a certain feeling of bitterness. "Europe in general," he said, "was so unjust to me at the beginning of the war, that as soon as the honor and interests of France had been secured, I was glad to be able to conclude peace, and to prove that I had entertained no intention of convulsing Europe and stirring up a general war. I hope that now all causes of dissension will vanish, and the peace be of long duration. I thank the diplomatic corps for its congratulations."

The impressions of the public had been complex, and at first the tidings of peace caused only moderate satisfaction. Countess Stéphanie de Tascher de La Pagerie remarked this. "Such a notion," she says, "had been formed of this war, which had flattered our national pride in many ways, that people almost regretted so speedy a denouement. In general, these strokes of see-saw policy which bewilder public opinion and bring about solutions different from what had been expected, are not much liked."

At the first moment, there had been perhaps more surprise than satisfaction. But a little reflection sufficed to put things in their proper light. It seems to us that M. Eugene Fourcade, the chronicler of the fortnight in the *Revue des Deux Mondes* of July 15, was a faithful interpreter of the prevailing sentiment. "The war," said he, "has just given the world a proof of French power which assuredly was not needed, since foreigners are perhaps even more keenly alive to our strength than we ourselves, but which has been singularly agreeable to our national pride. Thus far, all we have tasted of war appears to be the sweetness of its honeymoon, the marvellous and swift successes obtained by our soldiers, with wonderful enthusiasm and contagious good humor, over enemies worthy of esteem. But the shortness of a war is its greatest charm, and thanks to the peace which has had for France almost the delight of a surprise, it is, at this moment, the one she seems to relish with most pleasure. However, we must beware of accepting war and peace in this way with epicurean carelessness. In addition to the precious lives sacrificed, war entails charges and responsibilities which stretch far into the future."

Diplomatists and politicians already foresaw approaching difficulties and complications. But the general public abandoned itself to a perfectly natural joy. Business men were so quickly reassured that within a few days public funds went up five francs. The Catholics, lately so alarmed, resumed confidence. At that time there existed in the Republican party, and even in that of the Orleanists as well, very pronounced Italian sympathies. It was the Duke of Aumale who had obtained from Victor Emmanuel an authorization for the Duke of Chartres to serve under the Piedmontese flag at the side of the French army. Many men who were afterwards hostile to Italian unity beheld the deliverance of Milan with pleasure. M. de La Gorce was right in saying, " France, afterwards so pitiless towards Napoleon III., was at this time more indulgent to him than he was to himself." France loves its leaders only so long as they are fortunate. At the conclusion of the Italian War, the Emperor had had nothing but successes since his accession to the throne. He was popular.

Sunday, August 7, the victor of Magenta and Solferino left Saint-Cloud to spend some days at the camp of Châlons, where he was received by General Schramm, commanding officer of the camp. The following morning, at seven o'clock, he witnessed the manœuvres. In the afternoon he visited the agricultural establishments constructed by the engineers. Surprising the soldiers in their ordinary tasks or while resting, he was everywhere received with spontaneous ovations which deeply affected him. Napoleon III. loved the army and acknowledged himself its debtor for his prestige and his throne. Never did he feel himself better understood and served than by his troops. When he returned to headquarters from the left wing of the camp that evening at half-past six, soldiers were seen running across the fields at the double-quick to reach the road and form in ranks in order to acclaim their Emperor once more. On August 11 he instituted the medal of Italy, intended for officers and soldiers who had made the Italian campaign. Surrounded by a laurel wreath, this medal bore on one side an effigy of the sovereign, with the words: Napoleon III., Emperor; and on the other the titles of the six victories: Montebello, Palestro, Turbigo, Magenta, Marignan, Solferino.

CHAPTER XXXVII

THE RETURN OF THE TROOPS

NAPOLEON III. had determined to postpone his triumph until his troops should return from Italy. He knew how much he owed them. His own glory was not so near his heart as that of his army.

July 23, all the troops who had made the campaign, with the exception of five divisions of infantry and two brigades of cavalry which were to remain until peace was finally concluded, were ordered home from Italy. On their arrival they went into camp at Saint-Maurice, where they were constantly visited by Parisians anxious to see them under their tents, until Sunday, August 14, the day fixed on for their ceremonious entrance into the capital. It was to be the happiest day of the Second Empire.

The troops were to time their departure from Camp Saint-Maur so that the head of the column, passing through the faubourg Saint-Antoine, would reach Bastille Place at nine in the morning. Thence the procession would begin to move in the following order: —

The Emperor with his military household, and his suite;

The four Austrian flags, the first carried by a light-infantry man of the imperial guard and escorted by two soldiers from each regiment of the guard, and the three others by soldiers of the 1st, 3d, and 4th corps;

The forty Austrian cannons;

Marshal Regnaud de Saint-Jean d'Angély, at the head of the infantry of the guard, foot chasseurs, voltigeurs, zouaves, grenadiers, and the foot and mounted artillery;

Marshal Baraguey d'Hilliers and the 1st corps;

Marshal MacMahon, Duke of Magenta, and the 2d;

Marshal Canrobert and the 3d;

Marshal Niel and the 4th.

The cavalry of the guard were to close the procession.

The Emperor advances at the head of his army. A truce to party spirit! There are none but Frenchmen now, joyful, enthusiastic, frenzied in the applause they give to other Frenchmen who are conquerors. Even those who yesterday were blaming the war of Italy, think of nothing to-day but the delight of victory. The crowd is transported, electrified. A cloud of flowers falls from windows and balconies; the streets are strewn with wreaths. The triumphal procession advances under a rain of roses, over a carpet of foliage. Bouquets are stuck on the points of bayonets; the horses are loaded with garlands.

There are persons who force their way through the standing lines, glide up to the soldiers and offer them cigars, tobacco, glasses of beer and wine.

In order to afford the wounded who are marching a little rest, the Emperor orders a halt of a few minutes near rue Peletier, after which the cortege goes on again. They pass beneath the windows of the Jockey Club, then occupying a house on the boulevard des Italiens, at the corner of rue Gramont. The Marquis de Massa says: "The military element was already numerous in it, some forty of its members having made this short but decisive campaign. Every time one of these passed under the club balcony at the head of his command, he was welcomed with hearty cheers. Among its dead, the club reckoned Colonel Paulze d'Ivoy, of the 1st zouaves, killed gloriously at Marignan; among the severely wounded, Staff-Captain de Champlouis, Count Alfred de Gramont, commander of an infantry battalion, and François de La Rochefoucauld, Duke de Liancourt, appointed two years afterwards lieutenant-colonel of the Empress's dragoons. The majority of the members of the Jockey Club were legitimists rather than imperialists, but they were too patriotic not to rejoice over the success of our armies."

In front of the ministry of Justice, opposite the Vendôme column, had been erected a tribune supported by an architectural projection in the Tuscan style, which was intended for the Empress. At a quarter of ten, four gala carriages, preceded by outriders in the imperial livery, enter the square. They contain the sovereign, the young Prince, and their suite. Radiant with beauty, the Empress wears a white robe and a black mantle with blue embroideries, caught up by a spray of diamonds. The little Prince is in the uniform of the grenadiers of the guard, with a blue and red police helmet. Greeted with universal applause, the mother and child leave the carriage and take their places in the tribune.

All eyes turn towards rue de la Paix, where the Emperor and his army are to debouch. Presently the hundred-guards, with drums and trumpets, make their appearance between columns surmounted with golden victories. They precede by a few paces the sovereign, who comes forward on a magnificent chestnut horse. He wears the uniform of a general of division with the white-plumed chapeau and broad ribbon of the Legion of Honor. All the spectators are on their feet. An immense cry of: "Long live the Emperor!" resounds. They are saluting the commander-in-chief as well as the sovereign.

Napoleon III. halts, still on horseback, under the balcony where the Empress is. The troops are going to march past him. As soon as the Prince Imperial sees them, he rises, draws his little sword out of its scabbard, and brandishing it, salutes them. The infantile gesture is received with a long round of applause.

Here come the four Austrian standards, borne by

the soldiers who took them. The crowd respects these noble trophies, defended and seized so bravely. It remembers what was said by Napoleon I., after the battle of Austerlitz: "Honor to unfortunate courage!" And here, the forty Austrian cannons with their teams. Next, after a platoon of sunburnt guides, and preceded by three chaplains, come those of the wounded who have been able to march from Bastille Place. They stretch their legs, trying to keep step. Their mutilated hands can scarcely hold the wreaths and bouquets which the crowd flings at their heads. One pale young officer has both arms in a sling. These wounded, how pleased the people are to see them marching like this in spite of their sufferings! How they admire, how they love them! How they would like to ease their pains! When they are passing a long murmur of compassion and tenderness can be heard! For their part, they seem amazed by the ovation they receive. Heroes think nothing more simple and natural than heroism.

Here comes the commander-in-chief of the imperial guard, Regnaud de Saint-Jean d'Angély, who owes his marshal's baton to the battle of Magenta; here are the two divisions of the infantry of the guard: Mellinet, whose grenadiers and zouaves, to the number of four thousand, resisted for more than three hours forty thousand Austrians on the banks of the Naviglio Grande; Camou, whose voltigeurs and foot chasseurs carried the tower of Solferino and the surrounding heights. How beautiful they are, these choice troops, and how proud the Emperor must be of his guard! Each of the regiments composing it returns its flag to him as it goes by, the bands playing meanwhile at the foot of the column.

Now comes Baraguey d'Hilliers, marshal since the taking of Bomarsund, who is marching at the head of the 1st corps. Then the 2d corps, with its commander-in-chief, MacMahon, whom victory has made marshal of France, and Duke of Magenta; among his troops, look at the Algerian tirailleurs, the Turcos, marching behind the chaplains, three Catholic priests, respected by them in spite of the difference of religion; here they come in sky-blue uniforms braided with yellow, their types including all the races of northern Africa, from the negro to the Arab; on their guidons you may see the crescent of Islam and the open hand, that preservative against the evil eye still scuptured on the keystone of the arch of the first door of the Alhambra.

Here comes Marshal Canrobert, marshal since the Crimean War, with the 3d corps. And here the 4th corps, commanded by Niel, who gained his marshal's baton at Solferino, where his regiments, without exception, fought in a heroic manner throughout the day.

The march by is about to close. The Prince Imperial, who had incessantly clapped his hands, is taken down from the tribune by his equerry, M. Bachon, and carried to Napoleon III., who embraces his son and sets him for a few minutes in front of him on the saddle, to repeated cries of: "Long live the Emperor! Long live the Empress! Long live the Prince Imperial!"

In the evening, the Emperor gives a dinner at the Louvre in honor of the army of Italy, and afterwards makes a speech. His very strong and sonorous voice resounds through the vaulted Hall of States, and not a syllable of his harangue is lost. "Gentlemen," he says, " the joy I feel in meeting again the majority of the leaders of the army of Italy would be complete if it were not mingled with regret because the elements of so well-organized and redoubtable a force are to separate so soon. As sovereign and as commander-in-chief, I once more thank you for your confidence. It was flattering for me, who had never commanded an army, to find such obedience on the part of those who had had such large experience of war. If success has crowned our efforts, it pleases me to attribute the greater part of it to the skilful and devoted generals who rendered command easy for me, because, animated by the sacred fire, they always set the example of duty and of contempt for death."

To these simple and modest words, Napoleon III. added: "Part of our soldiers are about returning to their homes; you yourselves will resume the occupations of peace. But let us not forget what we have done together. May the recollection of obstacles surmounted, of perils averted, of imperfections pointed out, recur often to your memory; for, to every military man, memory is science itself.

U

"In commemoration of the Italian campaign, I am going to distribute a medal to all who have taken part in it, and I wish you to be to-day the first to wear it. May it remind you of me sometimes, and in reading the glorious names inscribed upon it, may each say, 'If France has done so much for a friendly people, what will she not do for her independence?'"

The following day, August 15, was the Emperor's fête, and it was celebrated with unparalleled splendor. In addition to the usual religious ceremonies in the churches, there were free spectacles at all the theatres, fireworks, and illuminations on a grand scale. Nor were the rejoicings confined to Paris. The Italians still required the assistance of the victor of Solferino, and Milan and Turin united in the celebration of his fête. The advocates of Italian unity were bent on making use of him, with his will or against it, in the realization of their programme, and they were not slow to recognize that in France lay their only safeguard against an offensive return from Austria. Lombards and Piedmontese were as zealous on August 15 as if they had been the subjects of Napoleon III. One might have fancied himself back in the days when his uncle was at once Emperor of the French and King of Italy.

On reaching the summit of his fortune, Napoleon III. sought to efface all remaining traces of the civil wars. He remembered the unlucky citizens who were victims of the insurrections of 1848, 1849, and the *coup d'État* of 1851. Eighteen hundred of these were still undergoing such penalties as police surveillance, exile or confinement, in the prisons of Algeria and Guiana. The Emperor resolved to restore to liberty and their country even those who were unwilling to ask pardon, and who had irrevocably determined to abate neither their passions nor their grudges. August 16 he signed a decree worded as follows: "Full and complete amnesty is granted to all individuals who have been condemned for political crimes and misdemeanors, or who have been the object of measures of public security." To judge only by the surface, one might have fancied that all parties in France were reconciled. Unhappily, while the exiled Republicans were coming back from Belgium, Switzerland, and England, the doors of the fatherland still remained closed against the princes and princesses of both branches of the Bourbon family. There were proscripts still.

CHAPTER XXXVIII

TUSCANY

THE war was gloriously ended, but the era of political difficulties was only just begun, and the situation of Italy was still in utter confusion and obscurity. Were the arrangements of Villafranca to be put into execution, or were they a dead letter? Would there be an Italian Confederation? Were the sovereigns of central Italy to be restored to their thrones? Would the Pope preserve the integrity of his States? Were the partisans of Italian unity to be forced to renounce their plans, or would they be found continuing successfully their propaganda? Would a congress assemble, or would European diplomacy be left to say the last word? Such were the questions which presented themselves and which were to cause Napoleon III. the most serious preoccupations.

The Emperor has been accused of duplicity with regard to Italian affairs. Still, he may have been sincere in expressing his desire to keep the promises he had made to Francis Joseph. But it was understood that the people were not to be forced, and that their right to dispose of their destiny should be respected. The dogma of national sovereignty was the basis of the doctrines of Napoleon III., and he was resolutely determined to defend it against all comers. This reservation made, he was bound to put no hindrance in the way of the restoration of the dispossessed princes. Italian unity did not enter into his views, and he particularly desired the maintenance of Tuscan autonomy.

Victor Emmanuel, pretending at first to wish for the scrupulous performance of the stipulations of Villafranca, recalled the four Piedmontese commissioners, Buoncampagni, Pallieri, Farini, and d'Azeglio, from Florence, Parma, Modena, and Bologna. At Florence, the partisans of Piedmont were at first very much alarmed. A grand-ducal restoration seemed impending. There was some disturbance at the Palazzo Vecchio and under the porticos. General de La Marmora having sent from the Piedmontese camp a hint to Baron Ricasoli that silence and resignation were in order, the latter exclaimed, addressing the bearer of the message: "Tell La Marmora that I tore his letter to pieces." But the partisans of Victor Emmanuel soon regained courage. It having been rumored that Napoleon III. had said: "The treaty sanctions the restoration of the princes, but not by force," all friends of Piedmont felt reassured. As to the adherents of the dynasty of Lorraine, they had induced the Grand Duke Leopold to abdicate, July 21, in favor of his son, Prince Ferdinand, who had been the guest of Napoleon III. at Compiègne, and they hoped he would ascend the Tuscan throne.

This combination was cordially supported by the Ministry of Foreign Affairs at Paris. The husband of a Florentine, and formerly minister of France at Florence, Count Walewski was keenly interested in the dynasty of Lorraine and in Tuscan autonomy. July 23, he sent the following telegraphic despatch to the Marquis de Ferrière-le-Vayer, minister of France at Florence: " The Grand Duke has just abdicated in his son's favor. We all hope that the latter will give a constitution, and perhaps that he will even take the Italian flag. The Emperor thinks the Tuscans, in their own interest, should make haste to assume the initiative in recalling the hereditary Grand Duke themselves. Annexation to Piedmont is an impossibility; I have reason to believe that the Sardinian government will not delay in making this understood in Florence. Do your utmost to promote explicitly the intentions of the Emperor."

The Marquis de Ferrière-le-Vayer desired the maintenance of the Lorraine dynasty as keenly as Count Walewski, but he was under no illusion. He replied by telegraph, July 24: " I have tried the ground. Impossible to obtain from Tuscany the recall of the young Grand Duke. The revolutionary spring is too tense, and the national sentiment too much offended. A restoration would be impossible without the presence of French troops, but what a complication! The hereditary Grand Duke would have had some chance if Prince Napoleon had not stopped in Florence, if Tuscany had not been abandoned two months ago under intimidation from the clubs and the pressure of an annexationist government, and if the princes had not been in the enemy's camp; they have no more use for the son than for the father; they would admit anything rather than the dynasty."

Tuscan autonomy, if not the dynasty of Lorraine, had numerous partisans still, but they were intimidated by a Florentine, Baron Ricasoli, who was more Piedmontese than the Piedmontese themselves. Bearing an illustrious name, and possessing a considerable fortune, this democratic noble, a fanatical advocate of Italian unity, was ready to sacrifice all to the triumph of his ideas, and to solicit the aid of the boldest and most advanced revolutionists for their realization. With his rigid countenance, his sharp features, his austere and ardent eloquence, he had the physiognomy and the temperament of a dissenter. He was one of those men whom nothing frightens or discourages, and who, in spite of every obstacle, pursue their object with indomitable energy and tenacity. After the departure of M. Buoncompagni, he proclaimed himself president of the Council of ministers on his own authority, and got into working order a government whose only programme was the annexation of Tuscany to Piedmont. The Marquis de Ferrière-le-Vayer well knew that such a man would yield to nothing but force.

The young Grand Duke had hastened to make a

proclamation to the Tuscans in which he declared that he would adopt the Italian colors, grant a constitution, and recognize the rights of the nation. Baron Ricasoli replied by calling the people to arms against the vanquished man of Solferino, as he styled the young Prince.

The Marquis de Ferrière-le-Vayer wrote to Count Walewski, July 26: "To give you an idea of public opinion, I will say that the Marquis Ginori has read me two letters, one from Prince Strozzo, and the other from Count Ugolino della Gherardesca, both of whom, notwithstanding they have always professed the most monarchical sentiments, now declare that no one should try to bring back the dynasty of Lorraine." This dynasty, therefore, could no longer count on the great families which had so long supported it. The French minister added: "If the means employed are condemnable, the result has none the less been what was desired, the tension of the revolutionary spring and the increase of the annexation party, to which the conduct of the archdukes, their presence in the Austrian army, and the uncontradicted report of their participation in the battle of Solferino, have added all those who naturally dislike to witness the return to Florence of princes who have been fighting in the camp of the enemies of Italy. If there had only been a French battalion at Florence, which was what I expressed a wish for, nothing of this kind would have occurred. Of course the unionists, and the impression produced by the regrettable attitude of the archdukes, would still have to be reckoned with; but there would not have been this general rout of the timid and the uncertain, produced by the peculiar moral state of a society, probably the most impressionable and peaceful in the world, abandoned without defence to a party which has the revolution for its auxiliary."

The revolution! Every day it was making a wholly unimpeded progress. In another despatch, dated August 10, the Marquis de Ferrière-le-Vayer thus expressed himself: "The partisans of the dynasty serve it very little since its fall, after serving it very badly before. They speak of nothing but their alarms, when they might talk about their plans, and come to see me only to ask for passports which I pitilessly refuse. When they tell me they are threatened with imprisonment and being killed, I tell them that a party which keeps quiet under menaces of that sort scarcely deserves attention, and that if some of them should allow themselves to be put to death for their princes it would make their cause more interesting, but they prefer to fold their arms and rely on Austria or France, groaning meanwhile in the privacy of their villas or in the letters they write me, and getting more frightened by words and articles than people anywhere else would be by the bayonets of soldiers or the executioner's axe. Singular country, where thrones are upset with ribbons and music, and where a reign of terror is no longer inaugurated by the guillotine but by a newspaper article and three words: *Morte ai codini!* charcoaled on a wall! Singular country, but very soft and very tame to resist the contact of Sardinia without foreign aid! And yet I think that from the French, the Italian, and the Catholic point of view, reasons of state demand, — especially if we do not have Savoy, — that we should not allow Piedmont to seize Tuscany and arrive at the Pontifical and Neapolitan frontiers, emboldened to dare anything by the success of its policy."

Count Walewski fancied that persuasion, friendly advice, and semi-official missions might exert some influence. Count Walewski was under a delusion. At intervals of several days he sent two emissaries to Florence, Count de Reiset and Prince Joseph Poniatowski, whose mission it was, as the minister said, to assist in bringing public opinion back to views more in conformity with those of the government of the Emperor.

As men of the world, the two messengers were received most courteously in Florence, but, as their mission was merely semi-official, no one affected to attach the slightest diplomatic importance to it. With a politeness slightly sarcastic, they were invited to travel through the country, question the inhabitants, test public opinion, and thus enable themselves to estimate the sympathies which the princes of the house of Lorraine had left behind them.

I knew Prince Joseph Poniatowski. He was

one of the most amiable and attractive men that I have ever met. An accomplished gentleman, by turns soldier, diplomat, singer, and composer of music, he had everywhere and always achieved success. He was the nephew of the celebrated Prince Poniatowski, the hero of the imperial epic, the Polish Bayard who was made marshal of France on the Leipsic battlefield, and was drowned three days afterwards in the river Elster. Like his uncle, Prince Joseph Poniatowski had served under the banners of France. After distinguishing himself in several Algerian campaigns, he entered Tuscan diplomacy and had been the Grand Duke Leopold's minister at Paris. Then naturalized a Frenchman, he had been made a senator by Napoleon III. at the close of 1854. When, in August, 1859, he arrived at Florence, where he had none but friends, the society man was greeted with great cordiality, but no account was made of the diplomat. And yet to strengthen this mission and increase its chances of success, Count Walewski had written, August 10, to the Marquis de Ferrière-le-Vayer: "The Emperor authorizes you to deliver a copy of a despatch advising the recall of the hereditary Grand Duke, who will give, on his part, all desirable guarantees."

The next day, August 11, the Tuscan Assembly, convoked by the government of Baron Ricasoli, met at Florence. Out of a population of one million eight hundred thousand souls, Tuscany had sixty-seven thousand electors, forty-five thousand of whom had voted. Their choice fell upon the most notable men in the country, without distinction of origin, providing only that they should have signified their intention to reject the Lorraine dynasty. On August 16, its downfall was pronounced by all the members present. Four days later, by a vote which lacked only three of being unanimous, the Assembly decreed the annexation of Tuscany to Piedmont.

But all was not yet done. It remained to be known whether Victor Emmanuel would accept this vote, and especially whether Napoleon III. and the great powers would permit its realization.

Prince de La Tour d'Auvergne, minister of France at Turin, wrote to Count Walewski, August 30: "The unanimous vote of the Tuscan Assembly in favor of annexation to Piedmont, an example which will inevitably be followed by the duchies of Parma and Modena, and the Legations, singularly complicates the situation and greatly embarrasses the government of King Victor Emmanuel. His Majesty's first impulse was flatly to refuse compliance with the vote of the Tuscan Assembly, but this way of considering the question was speedily modified by earnest solicitations, to which ambition and self-love naturally added further weight."

The Tuscan delegates arrived at Turin, September 3. The municipal body and a large number of senators and deputies went to the station to receive them. The four legions of the national guard formed the line through which they passed. All the streets were draped with the national colors. The delegates went to the royal palace and formally presented Victor Emmanuel with the minutes of the deliberations of the Assembly. In his reply, the King vaunted the necessity of a strong realm which would assure national independence, and openly expressed his desire to group all the populations of Tuscany under his sceptre. But, having many things to consider, he prudently added: "The realization of my wishes cannot be effected except by means of the negotiations which are to take place concerning the affairs of Italy. Strong in the rights conferred on me by your resolution, I shall support your cause with the powers, and above all with the magnanimous Emperor of the French, who has done so much for the Italian nation. I hope Europe will not refuse to accomplish that reparatory work for Tuscany, which, under less favorable circumstances, she accomplished not long ago for Greece, Belgium, and the Principalities."

Two days later, September 5, Prince de La Tour d'Auvergne wrote to Count Walewski: "The form and signification of the King's reply, modified as much as possible in the sense of our observations by the Minister of Foreign Affairs, General Dabormida, have in general obtained the approval of moderate people and those of such of my diplomatic colleagues as I have been able to exchange opinions with; but the liberal press can hardly conceal its disappointment, and I am assured that even the Tuscan delegation, in spite of the many marks of sympathy it has received, is far from being satisfied."

In a word, all was still in suspense. Everybody was wondering what would be decided on by the Congress, the assembling of which was then considered near and inevitable. Napoleon III. had not spoken his last word. All eyes turned towards him. It was perfectly well recognized that he was in reality master of the situation.

CHAPTER XXXIX

PARMA

THERE was one throne in Italy, that of the Duke of Parma, which Napoleon III. and the Empress Eugénie would have greatly liked to see respected. Born July 9, 1848, the Duke was not quite eleven years old when the war of Italy broke out. His mother, Louise of France, granddaughter of Charles X., daughter of the Duke and Duchess of Berry, widow of Duke Charles III., had governed as regent since March 27, 1854, on which day that Prince had been assassinated.

In our volume entitled: *Last Years of the Duchess of Berry*, we have spoken at length of this amiable and attractive Princess who had remained so French in mind and heart. She was born September 21, 1819, a year before her brother, the Count of Chambord. Old residents of Paris remembered seeing her as a child, when she was called *Mademoiselle* and attracted all eyes by her prettiness. Napoleon III., who likewise felt himself threatened by assassins, had been impressed by the fate of Charles III., and took real interest in a princess who had had a grandfather dethroned, a brother deprived of his heritage, a father and a husband assassinated. The Empress Eugénie, possibly foreboding that she might have to exercise the regency under painful circumstances, felt the sympathy of a woman and a sovereign for the Duchess. She admired her virtues, her intelligence, and her courage. The ministers of France in Tuscany were likewise accredited to Parma, and none of them had anything but praise for the regent, whose government, as was said by Lord Clarendon, " was a mild, moderate power, characterized by indulgence and good sense." The Empress Eugénie interested herself in the Princess, at first through generosity of feeling, and then because she comprehended what the gratitude of the French legitimists would be if the Emperor should lend his support to the sister of the Count of Chambord.

Moreover, the policy of the Duchess of Parma was in conformity with the views of Napoleon III. What she desired in Italy was the establishment of a Confederation independent of all foreign influence. Since she had been regent she had sought every occasion of being agreeable to France and its sovereign. She had been complained of more than once at Vienna for being too liberal, too French, and too Italian.

June 9, 1859, when the Duchess quitted Parma, never to see it again, her departure was full of dignity, as all her regency had been. After bidding her people and her soldiers a noble and affecting farewell, she quietly left her palace in a carriage, as if she were going on an ordinary excursion, and departed, saluted and respected by all.

A few days later, — June 23, — a secretary of the French legation, Count de Mosbourg, who had just been through central Italy to get an idea of the situation, wrote to Count Walewski: "Arriving June 17, at Milan, I left there on the 20th for Plaisance and Parma. The population had a sincere liking for the Duchess. I was easily convinced of this by the manner in which they speak of her in this country which has not driven her away, but which she has quitted, terminating her government by acts whose wisdom and moderation are praised by everybody. The Duchess of Parma went away leaving a million and a half in the State treasury, and without taking with her a single one of the objects, even the most personal, which filled the elegant palace in which she lived. She departed, leaving numerous and keen regrets, and surrounded as she went by marks of affection and esteem. Chance has permitted me to collect some interesting details of her journey. She stopped at Verona, where the Emperor of Austria called upon and spent several minutes alone with her. Immediately after this visit she wished to go on, and as no train was near, she declared to her suite that she would not spend the night in Verona, and took a special train to continue her route. This detail I have from a Spanish diplomat who was my colleague at Vienna, and who accompanied the Duchess as far as Switzerland."

In the same report, Count de Mosbourg remarked that, unlike the Duchess of Parma, the Duke of Modena had taken all he could possibly carry; leaving nothing behind but the four walls of his palace, and bringing fifty political prisoners in his suite to Mantua.

The attitude of the Duke of Modena and that of the Duchess of Parma were completely different. The Duke established himself on Austrian territory; the Duchess took refuge in Switzerland. The Duke sought to draw more close the already binding ties which united his duchy to Austria; the Duchess would have liked that of her son to be entirely independent. This was why the Emperor Francis Joseph, who took such pains to plead the cause of his relatives, the Grand-Duke of Tuscany and the Duke of Modena, did not concern himself with Parma, and passed over in silence the young sovereign of that duchy.

The Duchess Regent might have hoped to find Victor Emmanuel favorably disposed towards her. Brought up with the King, Duke Charles III., her husband, had spent his youth at Turin and served in the Piedmontese army. She herself was closely connected with the King's wife, Queen Adelaide, Archduchess of Austria, who died in January, 1855. But the Duchess of Parma was soon to recognize that politics has no pity on the widow and the orphan.

Meanwhile, the unhappy mother relied on France,

and perhaps more still on Russia. The Duke of Montebello, ambassador of Napoleon III. at Saint Petersburg, had written to Count Walewski, July 29: "The fate of the duchy of Parma, not mentioned in the preliminaries of Villafranca, greatly preoccupies the cabinet of Saint Petersburg. The Duchess of Parma has written to the Emperor of Russia recommending to him the cause of her son. Prince Gortchakoff has no doubt that the sovereignty of the young Prince will be maintained. He has told me that he knows the Emperor to be most favorably disposed towards him. He thinks, also, that Europe could not recognize the right of the belligerent powers to dispose of an Italian sovereignty."

Meanwhile the Piedmontese government had decided to consider the sympathies which Napoleon III. and Alexander II. might express in favor of the young Duke of Parma as null and void. As early as June 16 it had appointed M. Pallieri governor of the duchy in the name of King Victor Emmanuel, and M. Pallieri did at Parma what Baron Ricasoli and M. Farini were doing in Florence and Modena. As the preliminaries of Villafranca made no mention of the Parmesan duchy, it seemed to be believed at Turin that this silence signified annexation. Count Cavour telegraphed to M. Pallieri July 13: "Parma must remain annexed to Sardinia. Have the oath to the king taken, and act with the greatest energy." But Cavour having resigned, the Piedmontese government, not yet daring to throw off the mask, was obliged to take down the escutcheon of Savoy from the public buildings of Parma and recall M. Pallieri to Turin. Before departing, under pretext of maintaining order, the latter left a substitute in the duchy, M. Manfredi, whose only care was to prepare it for annexation to Sardinia. The sole remaining hope of the Duchess of Parma lay in the Congress.

CHAPTER XL

MODENA

IF Napoleon III. had sympathies for the young Duke of Parma, and especially for his mother, he had none at all for Francis V., Duke of Modena.

Of all European dynasties the most reactionary, most intransigent, most opposed to the Napoleonic ideas, liberalism, and parliamentary institutions was the dynasty of Modena. It held the Italian and the French tricolor in equal abhorrence. When Francis IV., father of Francis V., ascended the ducal throne in July, 1814, his first care was to abolish the Code Napoleon in his duchy. The Parisian revolution of 1830 had inspired him with boundless wrath and indignation. While the Courts of Turin, Florence, and Naples felt obliged to use circumspection in their dealings with Louis Philippe, the Duke of Modena gloried in defying him, and was the sole European sovereign who refused to recognize the King of the French, whom he persisted in considering a mere usurper. He had offered the Duchess of Berry an asylum in his ducal château of Massa, where, surrounded by a little court of the most ardent and fanatical legitimists, she openly prepared the Vendéan rising of 1832.

Francis V., who ascended the throne in January, 1846, had followed the paternal footsteps in every point. His sister was married to the Count of Chambord; but the Duke was infinitely more absolutist than his brother-in-law, the head of the elder branch of the Bourbons. While all the Courts of Europe were lavish of advances to Napoleon III., he maintained the most frigid and reserved attitude toward the Emperor of the French. He went so far as to refuse to those of his subjects who had served under Napoleon I. the authorization to wear the Saint Helena medal.

Francis V. felt in honor bound to act under all circumstances as a good archduke, a lieutenant devoted to the head of his family, the Emperor of Austria, a general of the imperial and royal family. As soon as the war of Italy broke out, he made haste to have Modena and Reggio occupied by the Austrians, shutting himself up meanwhile, with a small army on which he thought he might rely, in his fortress of Brescella, whither he had carried, and whence he afterwards transported to Venetia, sixty thousand livres of treasure, the crown jewels, the medals from the museums, and the precious manuscripts from the libraries. When the news of the battle of Magenta came he no longer considered himself safe in his fortress, and took refuge on Austrian territory, M. Farini arriving meanwhile at Modena in the capacity of Piedmontese commissioner.

M. Farini was a pupil of Cavour; but, coming of

an obscure stock, necessitous even to poverty, an ardent and fanatical sectary, he was further advanced in demagogy than his master. There were few revolutionists in Europe as fiery and impetuous as this conspirator, to whom politics was both a passion and a means of livelihood. The news of the preliminaries of Villafranca threw him literally into a fury. "Do not leave me without instructions," he wrote by telegraph to Count Cavour. "Know that if, in consequence of some agreement unknown to me, the Duke makes any attempt, I will treat him as an enemy of the King and the country." When this telegram reached him Cavour had already resigned. He replied in a single sentence: "The minister is dead; the friend applauds your decision." Shortly afterwards M. Farini received his order of recall from the government of Turin. He paid no attention to it, and after taking off his uniform as a Piedmontese commissioner, he went up to the balcony of the Este palace and proclaimed himself dictator before the assembled crowd.

The Austrians, however, could not easily anticipate that Napoleon would support in good earnest the cause of a prince whose antecedents and principles were those of the Duke of Modena. To ask that prince to enter into an Italian confederation founded on liberal and parliamentary principles was to ask an impossibility. Posing as a victim of Solferino, he had decided never to come to terms with the conquerors.

On the other hand, if Napoleon III. had retained no disagreeable memories of Tuscany, where his father and his eldest brother, exiled from France, had received generous hospitality, and where the grand-ducal family had treated them with kindness, it was also true that the duchy of Modena awakened none but unpleasant impressions in his mind. He had not forgotten the apprehensions, the anguish he had endured in passing through the territory with his mother, by means of forged passports, when he was escaping after his lamentable participation in the insurrection of the Romagnas in 1831. Francis IV. had just delivered several Italian patriots to the executioners, and Louis Napoleon, their accomplice, had every reason to fear that if he were recognized and arrested he would share their fate.

French sympathies seeming so alienated from Francis V., those of the Emperor of Austria should have been inclined to lay greater stress on the rights of a relative who in time of trial had shown him such confidence, devotion, and fidelity. It is even surprising that Francis Joseph was not more persistent in supporting a sovereign in whom he found rather a subject than an ally.

If the Emperor had been as hardy a conservative as M. Farini was a revolutionist, he would have assisted the Duke of Modena to equip several trusty foreign regiments by whose means he might have regained his duchy. M. Farini acted rashly in braving this Prince, for Francis V. kept close to the frontier, anxiously awaiting an opportunity to reenter his dominions, and relying on the assistance of Austria; but Austria lent him no assistance.

Possibly the Emperor Francis Joseph believed that the French troops left in Lombardy would oppose all attempts at restoration. Still, it was not certain that Napoleon III., once more very peacefully inclined, would incur the risk of renewing war in order to maintain the dictatorship of M. Farini. The latter, finding that he could tranquilly continue his work, convoked an assembly at Modena, which decreed the downfall of the Duke and annexation to Sardinia by a unanimous vote on the 16th of August.

Napoleon III. did not in the least desire the restoration of Francis V., but he recommended the preservation of Modenese autonomy. There was even question for a moment of annexing the dominions of the Duke of Parma to Sardinia, and giving the duchy of Modena to the young sovereign by way of compensation. Such an arrangement had very little chance of success. Austria might think, in fact, that nothing could be more contrary to its legitimist principles than such a substitution. In accepting it for her son would not the Duchess Regent have made herself jointly responsible for the Piedmontese usurpations and placed revolutionary right above divine right. Although the Duchess of Parma was the sister of the Count of Chambord, she could not forget that this Prince was the brother-in-law of the Duke of Modena. Moreover, she remembered all the services rendered to her mother, the Duchess of Berry, by the father of the Duke, Francis IV. The combination could not succeed; it was soon abandoned, and M. Farini, more audacious than before, encountered no further obstacles on his path.

XLI

THE ROMAGNAS

THE name of Romagnas is given to those territories in the States of the Church comprising the six Legations: Velletri, Urbino-and-Pesaro, Forli, Bologna, Ravenna, Ferrara. At the time when war broke out, Rome was occupied by a French corps, and the Austrians were garrisoned in the Romagnas. The States of the Church were a neutral ground where the Austrian, French, and Piedmontese armies were not to enter into contest. Throughout the duration of the war, no manifestation or trouble of any kind occurred in the Eternal City. Order was maintained under the shadow of the flag of France, and Pius IX. had absolutely nothing to fear. The Romagnas would also have remained tranquil had the Austrians continued to occupy them, as was their undoubted right.

Napoleon III. has often been accused of being the author of the annexation of the Romagnas to the kingdom of Victor Emmanuel. He certainly did contribute to it; but we believe the Emperor of Austria possibly contributed still more. In causing his troops to evacuate the six Legations, June 11-12, which he was not in the least obliged to do, he left the ground open to the revolution and put an end himself to Austrian influence, not simply in the States of the Church but throughout central Italy. It was evident, in fact, that if the Pope lost the Romagnas, the Grand Duke of Tuscany, the Duke of Parma, and the Duke of Modena would be dispossessed.

No sooner had the Austrian troops evacuated Bologna than the pontifical escutcheons were torn down, and a junta in which figured the Marquis Joachim Pepoli, grandson of Murat and cousin of Napoleon III., proclaimed the dictatorship of Victor Emmanuel. Imola, Faenza, Ferrara, and Ravenna followed the example of Bologna, and the Pope lost all the Romagnas. He never regained them.

Victor Emmanuel did not dare at first to assume the dictatorship. He contented himself with resorting to an expedient, appointing as commissioner the Marquis d'Azeglio, who in 1845 had published the famous brochure entitled, *I Casi delle Romagne*. The King felt obliged to recall him after the preliminaries of Villafranca. But this recall was only a feint. Instead of concentrating his troops for the evacuation, as his official instructions prescribed, M. d'Azeglio divided them among the former Austrian garrisons, occupied Bologna in force, and then delegated his powers to his chief of staff, Colonel Falicon, who governed in his room and stead. On returning to Turin he said to the King: "Sire, I have disobeyed

Your Majesty. Have me brought before a council of war!" Victor Emmanuel replied, "You have done very well." In spite of the contrary advice of Napoleon III., the Piedmontese troops were maintained at Bologna, and the King's minister of finances, by large and secretly granted subsidies, enabled the Romagnol authorities to provide for public services. This assistance, denied at first, was afterwards openly proclaimed.

However, the Emperor of Austria and the Emperor of the French had declared that the Pope would be the honorary president of the Italian Confederation, and people were wondering what would be the practical result of such a combination. It is permissible to believe that if the chair of Saint Peter had then been occupied by a diplomatist as skilful as Leo XIII., the Holy See, placing itself frankly at the head of the Confederation, might possibly have overcome the political difficulties and saved the whole of its temporal power. But Pius IX., disgusted with liberal ideas by bitter experience, considered the title of honorary president of a Confederation a snare, and made no effort to enter into the views of Napoleon III. Influences opposed to France, and especially to the Emperor, were in the ascendant at Rome, and rendered all agreement impossible, to the great distress of a Catholic so fervent as the Empress Eugénie.

Pius IX. was displeased with Napoleon III. for having demanded of Francis Joseph, at the interview of Villafranca, the administrative separation of the Legations from the States of the Church. He was equally displeased at his giving the epithet of honorary, — which Francis Joseph had also wished to suppress, — to the presidency of the Italian Confederation, and he concluded that this *honorariat* was merely a flattering appearance which cloaked evil designs. Yet it may be affirmed that Napoleon III., averse to Italian unity, desired in principle the maintenance of the pontifical power. But, on the other hand, he was convinced that Pius IX. could not keep possession of the Romagnas without secularizing the government.

Count de Sainte-Aulaire, Louis Philippe's ambassador at Rome, had criticised as follows the situation of these territories in a despatch dated March 6, 1831: "Withdrawn from pontifical authority for nearly twenty years, the Legations found themselves under a government based upon the great principles of modern civilization. The Vienna Congress replaced them under Roman domination. An enlightened policy would have taken account of the situation which had lasted for so considerable a space of time, and circumspectly granted institutions which should resemble as closely as possible those they had just lost. Far from this, they were not even granted the privileges they had been enjoying down to 1797. In 1828, the French government, in the instructions given to M. de Chateaubriand, pointed out the dangers of such a fatal system in energetic terms."

In the question of the Romagnas Napoleon III. was hampered by his youthful antecedents. Although not literally affiliated to the sect of the Carbonari, he had shared in 1831 the passions of the Italian patriots, and taken part in the insurrection of the Romagnas. But he could say that even then, what he had desired was not the suppression of the power of the popes, but the secularization of their government. What he aimed at was a reforming and anti-Austrian papacy which should place itself at the head of ideas of emancipation. Such was likewise the idea of his mother, Queen Hortense, who wrote in 1831: "If the Pope were capable of making suitable concessions, he would be the leader of all Italy to-morrow. He might possibly dictate the laws in Europe, and restore to religion, allied to liberty, the splendor it had of old."

Napoleon III. was still cherishing this dream when in 1859 he tried to place the Italian Confederation under the invocation, so to say, of the Sovereign Pontiff. But the scheme was purely chimerical, and Pius IX. absolutely refused to secularize the whole or any part of his States.

On the other hand, the Emperor had not changed in any way the ideas expressed by him in a letter, written August 18, 1849, to his orderly officer, Colonel Edgard Ney, who formed part of the Roman expedition: "The French Republic has not sent an army to Rome to stifle Italian liberty, but on the contrary to regulate by preserving it from its own excesses, and to give it a stable foundation by restoring to the pontifical throne the Prince who was the first to place himself boldly at the head of all useful reforms. . . . I summarize as follows the re-establishment of the Pope's temporal power: general amity. Secularization of the administration. The Code Napoleon and a liberal government." The conclusion of this famous letter ran as follows: "When our armies made the tour of Europe, they left everywhere, in token of their passage, destruction of the abuses of feudality and the germs of liberty; it shall not be said that in 1849 a French army could have acted in a contrary sense and to bring about different results." Ten years later, the Emperor had absolutely the same programme as the President of the French Republic.

The divergency of views existing between Pius IX. and Napoleon III. could not be other than favorable to the progress of the revolution in the Romagnas. The principal act of Colonel Falicon's government was to put the Code Napoleon in force. After having emitted a national loan of six million lira and created a court of accounts, he retired August 1, and a man who was supposed to enjoy the Emperor's good will, M. Cipriani, was made governor-general. He decreed equality of religious, civil, and political rights. August 6, the electors were summoned to the colleges. The Assembly was opened September 1. Among its one hundred and twenty-four members were two princes, seven marquises, thirty counts, three knights, twenty-seven physicians, seventeen lawyers, twelve professors, and three military men, the rest being merchants or men of independent means.

Hence the aristocracy constituted nearly half of this Assembly. Nevertheless, it cast one hundred and twenty-one votes in favor of deposing the government of the Holy See and annexing the Romagnas to Sardinia.

People wondered anxiously whether Victor Emmanuel would dare to accept this annexation. September 15, deputations from Parma and Modena came to notify him of the annexationist votes cast by the Assemblies of those two duchies. Count San Vitali was at the head of the Parmesan deputation, and the celebrated composer Verdi among its members. Counsellor Muratori led the deputies of Modena. The King's reply to the two addresses produced very little sensation, because it scarcely differed from that given to the Tuscan deputation. Great anxiety was felt, however, as to what he would say to the Romagnols. He received them at Monza, September 24: "I am grateful," said he, "for the wishes formed by the inhabitants of the Romagnas, of which you are the interpreters. As a Catholic Prince I shall always preserve the most profound and unalterable respect for the supreme hierarchy of the Church. As an Italian Prince I must remember that Europe, considering that the existing condition of the Romagnas demands prompt and efficacious measures, has contracted formal obligations with your country. I welcome these desires, and, strong in the rights conferred upon me, I will maintain your cause before the great powers. Confide in their justice, confide in the generous patriotism of the Emperor, who will complete the great work of reparation which he has so powerfully begun, and which will assure to him the gratitude of Italy. Europe will recognize that it is a common interest and duty to prevent disorder by granting satisfaction to the legitimate desires of peoples." Hence Victor Emmanuel admitted that it belonged to Europe to settle the question beyond appeal.

Two days later, Prince de La Tour d'Auvergne wrote to Count Walewski: "The deputation from the Romagnas, guided doubtless by the advice of General Dabormida, has refused the invitation of the municipality of Turin to visit that capital before returning to Bologna. It seems they have also given up the notion of going to France to present the Emperor with the vote of the Bolognese Assembly. They will confine themselves to sending a person to the Emperor who will submit the result of the deliberations of that Assembly to His Majesty in an entirely private manner. General Dabormida has expressed to me his satisfaction in having succeeded in dissuading the Romagnese envoys from a proceeding which would have caused too great a commotion and certainly have given rise, under existing circumstances, to unpleasant interpretations."

Victor Emmanuel and Napoleon III. had already a presentiment of the difficulties of every kind which would be created for them by the Roman question. They were well aware that it would be difficult, if not impossible, to solve the problems presented by this most difficult of subjects from the religious, political, and social points of view. To both of them the controversies and passions it excited must have been a perpetual cause of sadness and preoccupation. Throughout the entire reign of the two monarchs there was not one hour in which the affairs of Rome did not nourish and maintain a troubled condition of interests and consciences which, after thirty-nine years, is existing still.

CHAPTER XLII

SAINT-SAUVEUR

NAPOLEON III. did not allow the flatteries of his courtiers to make him lose his head. The ovations awarded him and his troops had not cast into oblivion either the horrible side that war presents even to the conquerors, or the almost insoluble problems raised by recent events. His humanitarian sentiments had suggested more than one painful reflection. His imagination continued to be haunted by the scenes of carnage he had witnessed, and he began to be doubtful of the gratitude of Italy. His moral lassitude was greater than his physical fatigue. He needed repose and self-concentration and wished to meditate in peace upon the difficult questions which Providence had made it incumbent on him to study. He thought that mountain air would be good, not merely for him but for the Empress, who had also experienced many emotions, and he resolved to spend some weeks in the Pyrenees, first at Saint-Sauveur and afterwards at Biarritz.

Saint-Sauveur is a very tiny village in the department of the Upper Pyrenees. It consists of a single street ascending the slope of the Som de Laze, above the gorge in which boil the waters of the mountain stream of Gavarnie. Here the sovereigns lived as private persons, enjoying the beauties of nature and making daily excursions in the vicinity. Nevertheless Napoleon III. sought in vain to escape from his absorbing preoccupations. While at Saint-Sauveur he received, at an interval of a few days, two visits which disturbed him. One of these was from Count Arese, the other from Prince Metternich, the first being the advocate of the Italian cause, the second of that of Austria, and it was not an easy task to be agreeable to both. The Emperor contrived to discourage neither.

To Napoleon III. Count Arese had been a youthful companion, a friend in exile, and a courtier in misfortune. This great Milanese noble, who asked nothing for himself but all for Italy, had given Louis Bonaparte proofs of loyalty which Napoleon III. by no means forgot. In 1836, the Prince being transported to the United States after the fiasco of Strasburg, Arese had gone to Liverpool in all haste, taken ship, and, unknown to the Prince, had reached America before him, so that on landing the first countenance the Prince beheld was that of a friend.

The Italian cause could have no better advocate than Count Arese. As early as July he had written to the Emperor: "Sire, authorized and encouraged by your kindness, I come to rob you of a few moments and speak to you as unreservedly as in the days of Arenenberg and New York. In the first place, I want to be reassured concerning your health after such fatigue of body and mind, and also about that of the Empress, whose affection has made her a sharer in all the chances of the campaign." Count Arese tried as follows to prove that Italy would not be ungrateful: " Rely on my frankness, with which you are well acquainted. After the first astonishment felt by all on hearing of the unexpected peace which mutilated so many brilliant hopes, people have made an evident return to the reality of the situation and comprehended all you have done, all that you may still do for this unhappy Italy, which since your early youth has counted you among its most sincere and devoted friends. . . . I adjure you, Sire, take our cause into your own hands and it will succeed. You will acquire new glory, and new titles to the admiration and gratitude of Italy and of posterity."

The Empress was greatly attached to Count Arese, but he found it more difficult to convince her than her husband. Not yet knowing that he was coming to Saint-Sauveur, she had written him, August 26: " I am trying *as hard as I can* to become an Italian. . . . Are you not afraid of convincing Europe that the rôle of redeemer is the trade of fools? . . . The Emperor himself has been for an instant *against the sentiment of his own country*, and he has been obliged to revive the sentiment of generosity and glory in order to make this country, fatigued already by the hard trials it has undergone, accept a struggle in which all it had to expect was gratitude, and in which a reverse might have proved a cruel blow."

Count Arese arrived at Saint-Sauveur August 30. The chief object of his mission was the reply which Victor Emmanuel would have to make to the Tuscan delegates. He tried to prove that the annexations of central Italy were inevitable, and he went away the bearer of certain encouragements, if not of promises. But he had scarcely quitted Saint-Sauveur when Prince Metternich arrived as the envoy of the Emperor Francis Joseph, and strongly insisted on the maintenance of the arrangements of Villafranca, adding that any derogation from them would result in an indefinite adjournment of his master's generous intentions relative to Venetia.

Greatly embarrassed, Napoleon III. hesitated between the two roads that he might take. September 5 he wrote to Count Arese: "My dear Arese, since your departure I have seen Prince Metternich. I was very well satisfied with his conversation, and I wish to tell you the result in confidence, so that you can impart it to the King. However, I must repeat, it is necessary that it should remain very confidential for the present.

"I think that if Tuscany recalled the Grand Duke we might reunite Parma and Plaisance to Piedmont, place the Duchess of Parma at Modena, and obtain for the Venetians an Italian administration, an Italian army, and a provincial council. The Austrians, as a result, would be relegated to the other side of the Alps. Such advantages deserve, I think, to be examined; this is why I have written the King to be very prudent in his language to the Tuscan deputation. I saw the deputation from Modena to-day. I spoke to them in that sense. I hope that as a final result the peace of Villafranca will have enfranchised Italy. It is my dearest wish. I am getting up an article for the *Moniteur* which will explain clearly, I hope, the motives of my conduct."

This article, which appeared in the *Moniteur* of September 9, is very curious. It proves that Napoleon III. had been sincere in signing the treaty of Villafranca, and that he continued to aim at the establishment of the Italian Confederation, in which Venetia would form a part. The Emperor thus expressed himself in the article, his personal work: "If the treaty were sincerely executed, Austria would no longer be a power inimical to the Peninsula, opposing all the national aspirations from Parma to Rome, and from Florence to Naples; but would, on the contrary, become a friendly power, having consented of its own free will to cease to be a German power on this side of the Alps, and to develop Italian nationality as far as the shores of the Adriatic."

The note, after blaming the men who, "more preoccupied with small and partial successes than with the future of the common country," were hindering the consequences of the treaty of Villafranca, went on to say: "What could be simpler and more patriotic than to say to Austria: 'You desire the return of the archdukes? Well, have it so! But then you must loyally carry out your promises concerning Venetia. Let her receive a life of her own; let her have an Italian army and administration; in a word, let the Emperor of Austria be simply the Grand Duke of Venetia, just as the King of the Low Countries is only the Grand Duke of Luxembourg.' The French government has declared that the archdukes shall not be restored to their dominions by force of arms, but if a part of the conditions of the peace of Villafranca remains unexecuted, the Emperor of Austria will think himself discharged from all the pledges given in favor of Venetia. Disturbed by hostile demonstrations on the right bank of the Po, he will remain in a state of war on the left bank, and we shall find a policy of distrust and hatred reviving, which will bring about new troubles and misfortunes."

Broaching afterwards the question of the Congress, the author thus expressed himself: "People seem to hope much from a European Congress; we also heartily desire it; but we greatly doubt whether a Congress could obtain better conditions for Italy. A Congress will only demand what is just, and would it be just to ask a great power for important concessions without offering it equitable concessions in exchange? The only means would be war; but Italy must not deceive herself, France is the only power in

Europe which makes war for an idea, and France has fulfilled her task."

The victor of Magenta and Solferino seemed to doubt sometimes the results of his victories. The note we have just reproduced gives an inkling of the perplexities and anxieties which preoccupied him during his stay at Saint-Sauveur. This document, stamped to the utmost with the impress of his style and character, allows one to read a sentiment of sadness and almost of discouragement between its lines.

CHAPTER XLIII

BIARRITZ AND BORDEAUX

THE Emperor and Empress left Saint-Sauveur, September 12, spent the night at Tarbes, and arrived the 13th at Biarritz, where they gladly found the Prince Imperial. September 18th they received the King of the Belgians and the Grand Duke of Oldenburg in their villa, as well as many foreigners of distinction, Russian and Spanish. The 19th they made an excursion on board the *Aigle*, a new imperial yacht constructed with all the modern improvements. They landed towards six o'clock at Cape Breton, where the population came *en masse* to thank the sovereign for the improvements he had ordered and which would ensure the future of the port.

Their stay at Biarritz gave great pleasure to Their Majesties, who had been there already in 1857. But the Emperor continued to be disturbed by Italian affairs. He was dissatisfied with the obstacles opposed by the Piedmontese government to the execution of the treaty of Villafranca, and it vexed him to find that government apparently resolved not merely to annex central Italy but to refuse, as a compensation in this hypothesis, to annex Savoy and Nice to

France. Napoleon III. did not conceal from Count Arese the painful impression produced on him by such a state of things. He sent him from Biarritz the following letter, dated October 3 : "I write you to-day to communicate one of the many reports I am receiving from Italy, all of which denote the lack of firmness in the Piedmontese government. A people is not regenerated with lanterns and flowers ; that demands firmness and justice. How do you explain the fact that the government, so patient when France and its chief are insulted, is so decided in Savoy against the press when it asks for annexation to France? I beg you to remonstrate seriously with the ministry. I shall soon write to the King on the subject of the great affairs which must be brought to a conclusion."

The next day, October 4, a second letter, still more severe : "My dear Arese, I write you again to-day to communicate another note which I have received from Milan. I repeat that it pains me to see the heedlessness of the Sardinian government, because it must necessarily lead to a coolness between us, and I say it to you *without presumption*, but there is not a soul here *except myself* who is devoted to the Italian cause.

"The Sardinian government cannot allege its impotence where the press is concerned, since in Savoy it is quite able to suppress the journals which do not agree with it.

"It is sad to think that while I am constantly

laboring here in favor of Piedmont, they allow me to be insulted in every way on the other side of the Alps."

Napoleon III. was not better pleased with Rome than with Turin. The Pope declared that he would not hear of an Italian Confederation so long as he remained dispossessed of the Romagnas, and relations between the Vatican and the French government were becoming still more strained. On his return from Biarritz, the Emperor stopped at Bordeaux, where the discourses exchanged between him and the Cardinal-archbishop of the city brought into clear light all the difficulties of the question.

Their Majesties arrived at Bordeaux with the Prince Imperial, October 10. In spite of the bad weather, the inhabitants of the city and the surrounding country thronged around them with hearty acclamations. The next day, the Emperor received the authorities. The Cardinal-archbishop, Mgr. Donnet, a prelate very popular in his diocese and in great favor at the Tuileries, delivered an address which attested the fears of the Catholic world even while expressing profound loyalty to the sovereign.

"Sire," said the Cardinal, "eight years ago, when the city of Bordeaux welcomed you with such enthusiasm that the arches of our old basilica shook with the acclamations of the crowd, my priests and I beheld with joy what seemed to us like the baptism of the new Empire. At that time we prayed for him who had arrested the ever rising flood of the revolution, who had renewed the aureole of honor on the forehead of the Church and her clergy of which others had sought to deprive them, and who had inaugurated his great destiny by restoring to the Vicar of Jesus Christ his city, his people, and the integrity of his dominions. To-day we are still praying, Sire, that God may furnish you with the means, as He has given you the will, to remain faithful to this Christian policy which calls blessings on your name, and which is perhaps the secret of the prosperity and the source of the glories of your reign. We pray with a persistent confidence, a hope which deplorable events and brutal sacrileges cannot discourage, and the motive of this hope whose realization now seems so difficult, after God, is you, Sire, who have been, and who still wish to be, the eldest son of the Church, who have uttered these memorable words: 'The temporal sovereignty of the head of the Church is bound up with the splendor of Catholicism, as with the liberty and independence of Italy.'"

In concluding, the Cardinal entreated the Emperor to assure the triumph of Christ in the person of His Vicar, and added that "this triumph would put an end to the anxieties of the Catholic world, who would salute him with transport."

Napoleon III. replied: "I thank Your Eminence for the sentiments you have just expressed. You render justice to my sentiments, yet without misunderstanding the difficulties which hamper them, and you seem to me to comprehend your lofty mission well when you seek to strengthen confidence rather than to spread alarms. I thank you for recalling my words, for it is my firm hope that a new era of glory for the Church will begin on the day when the whole world shares my conviction that the temporal power of the Holy Father is not opposed to the independence of Italy."

After this optimistic beginning, the response of the Emperor left an opening for the greatest fears. "The Holy Father," said he, "has reason to be anxious about the day, which cannot be far distant, when Rome will be evacuated by our troops. For Europe cannot permit the occupation which has lasted for ten years to be prolonged indefinitely, and when our army withdraws, what will it leave behind it, anarchy, terror, or peace? These are questions to whose importance nobody is blind. But, be very sure that at the epoch in which we live, in order to solve them, it is necessary to seek truth with calmness and to entreat Providence to enlighten peoples and kings concerning the wise exercise of their rights as well as the extent of their duties, and not to make an appeal to ardent passions. I have no doubt that the prayers of Your Eminence and of your clergy will continue to draw down the blessings of heaven upon the Empress, my son, and me."

The Emperor received an excellent welcome at Bordeaux, as he had in 1852. But the situation was felt to be less favorable, and the harmony between the throne and the altar had not the same solidity. It was certain that to the Italian question, already so perplexing, was added the Roman question, more grave and arduous still. The reply of the Emperor to the discourse of the Archbishop was, in fine, very disquieting. An era of difficulties was beginning which was to continue to the end of the reign, and which has survived it. Napoleon III. had a presentiment of this.

On returning to Saint-Cloud, October 12, the Emperor found there a sort of congress of Italian notables, as they were then called, who sought to make the sphinx talk. He gave them audience on the 16th. He expressed his wish to see Parma annexed to Piedmont, and the young sovereign of that duchy transferred to Modena and later on affianced to a niece of Duke Francis V. As to Tuscany, he declared that the restoration of the Grand Duke was obligatory, with the grant of a constitution and the adoption of the national flag. October 20 he addressed a letter to Victor Emmanuel which did not appear in the *Moniteur* but was published in the *Times*, and then by the *Constitutionnel*, a semi-official sheet. In this letter he maintained the stipulations of Villafranca, except on one point, the duchy of Modena, which should be given to the Duke of Parma as compensation for the loss of his duchy, annexed to Piedmont. He manifested his hope that, if Italian pretensions were thus limited, the Emperor Francis Joseph would accord a large autonomy to

Venetia. Things stood at this point when Napoleon left Saint-Cloud for the château of Compiègne, where a series of brilliant receptions took place, which lasted until the Imperial family returned to Paris on December 4.

CHAPTER XLIV

THE CLOSE OF 1859

WHILE the Emperor was at Compiègne the definitive treaty of peace had been signed at Zurich, November 10, by Austria, France, and Sardinia. The signers for Austria were Count Kariloji and Baron de Meysenberg; for France, Baron de Bourqueney and Marquis de Banneville; for Sardinia, MM. des Ambrois and Jacteau. The three powers pledged themselves to "favor with all their efforts the creation of a Confederation between the Italian States, which should be placed under the honorary presidency of the Holy Father, and whose object should be to maintain the independence and inviolability of the confederated States, to assure the development of their moral and material interests, and to guarantee the interior and exterior security of Italy by the existence of a federal army. Venetia, which remains under the crown of His Imperial and Royal Apostolic Majesty, will form one of the States of this Confederation and participate in the obligations as well as in the rights resulting from the federal pact, the clauses of which will be determined by an assembly composed of representatives from all the Italian States."

The article relating to the dispossessed princes ran as follows: "The territorial boundaries of the independent States of Italy which were not parties to the late war, not being liable to change except with the concurrence of the powers which presided at their formation, the rights of the Grand Duke of Tuscany and of the Duke of Parma are expressly reserved between the high contracting parties."

The peace signed at Zurich resulted in the appointment of Prince Metternich as ambassador of Francis Joseph at the court of Napoleon III. The new ambassador presented his credentials December 14. The Emperor said: "I firmly hope that the relations happily re-established between the Emperor of Austria and myself cannot but become more friendly by an attentive examination of the interests of the two countries. For my part, since I have seen the Emperor, I attach great value to his personal friendship."

Prince Metternich was thirty years old; the Princess, twenty-three. They were bound to shine at court in virtue of their youth, lofty position, and personal charm. Napoleon III. was seeking a difficult thing: to stand well at the same time with Vienna and Turin.

In reality, the treaty of Zurich left everything at loose ends. One of the signers, Baron de Bourqueney, said on returning to Paris: "I bring back *a peace*, but not peace." Emboldened by the impunity accorded to its actions, the Piedmontese government had placed all the central Italian States and the Legations under the authority of its commissioner, M. Buoncompagni. The partisans of the former legal title had but one hope remaining: the Congress. Napoleon III. had written from Compiègne, November 9, to Victor Emmanuel: "The Congress is going to be convoked; nothing else can settle existing difficulties. . . . Show some energy and prove that the peace signed is a serious matter. By acting in any other way you will lose Italy." It was believed that the Congress would meet at Paris in January. The great powers, the Pope, and all the Italian sovereigns were to be represented in it.

Count Cavour was getting ready to go to Paris as Victor Emmanuel's first plenipotentiary. He wrote to one of his friends, M. de La Rive: "If you come to Paris this winter you will find me at the Hotel Bristol; I have taken the same apartment occupied in 1856 by Count Buol, for you know I have always liked to invade Austrian territory."

In a despatch addressed to Count Walewski, Prince de La Tour d'Auvergne, minister of France at Turin, said: "The appointment of Count Cavour as plenipotentiary, greatly desired by liberal opinion in Italy, has been not less favorably received by moderate men. The Whist Society of Turin, most of whose members belong to the higher aristocracy of Piedmont, and which has until now been extremely averse to his policy, has just elected him its president. . . . In talking with me, he has not concealed his satisfaction at having to represent Italy in a European Congress. He told me that his confidence in the Emperor was entire, that he was persuaded that His Majesty would finish the work he had begun, and defend the cause of Italy to the very end before the Congress. Alluding subsequently to his personal relations with the Emperor at a former period, he assured me that he retained sentiments of most respectful gratitude towards His Majesty, and denied energetically the violent remarks attributed to him after the peace of Villafranca. . . . He said a few days ago, to General de La Marmora, that if at that time he had thought for a moment that things were going as they have done, he would not have thought it necessary to resign."

At the very time when all Europe believed in the near convocation of the Congress, Napoleon had become convinced that this diplomatic assemblage would put him into a very embarrassing position and oblige him to break with either Austria or Piedmont. According to the cabinet of Vienna, the programme must be laid down in advance, and no one could diverge from it under any pretext; its object would be to confirm the former agreements, not to destroy them.

The Prussian government made it plainly evident that the Prince Regent's attachment to legitimist principles would not permit approbation of the recent enterprises. As to Russia, in the name of the solidarity of crowned heads it stood out against annexations contrary to international law.

All the Italian sovereigns, with the exception of Victor Emmanuel, considered by them an usurper, were on the side of Austria. Since May 22, Francis II., a young sovereign attached to the Court of Vienna by every sympathetic tie, had been reigning at Naples. He had married a sister of the wife of Francis Joseph. Threatened by the revolution, he held the Piedmontese policy in horror, and regarded Victor Emmanuel as an adept and an accomplice of Mazzini. Special bonds of amity existed between the Courts of Russia and Naples. The Emperor Nicholas had been the friend of King Ferdinand, father of Francis II., and the Emperor Alexander showed great interest in the young sovereign. Upheld by Russia and by Austria, the King of Naples would inevitably make common cause with the princes of central Italy and with the Pope. As to Pius IX., he demanded first of all that the Legations should be given back to him, and recognized neither in a Congress nor in any human power the right to despoil him of his States.

Hampered by the promises made to Francis Joseph at the interview of Villafranca, and by the quite recent stipulations of the Zurich treaty, Napoleon III. could not have supported the ambitions of Victor Emmanuel in a Congress without being accused of double dealing. As to England, she seemed to support Italian aspirations; but when the day came to proceed from words to acts and lend effective concurrence to Piedmont, she would be certain to find no more pressing business than to get out of the way as soon as possible. Certainly she would favor the Italian cause, but on condition that she herself should have no sacrifices to make, and no risks to run. To hold the balance equal between reaction and revolution in a Congress was impossible. Determined not to renew the war, Napoleon III. had now but one idea : to prevent the assembling of a Congress which could have no result but the check of the Italian cause or the resumption of hostilities.

An anonymous brochure entitled : *The Pope and the Congress*, published in Paris, December 22, was about to change the face of things. Announced to the sound of trumpets by the semi-official journals, this sensational brochure was plainly instigated by Napoleon III., even if he were not its author. "I did not write it," he said to various persons, "but I approve of all its ideas."

Nothing could be more disagreeable to Pius IX. than this publication which paid him abundant homage but demanded that the Romagnas should be taken from him, and which said concerning the temporal power: "The smaller the territory, the greater will be the sovereign. . . . The power of the Pope will result less from his strength than from his weakness." Cries of wrath were uttered. Mgr. Dupanloup, Bishop of Orléans, published an indignant refutation of the brochure. December 30, the *Journal de Rome*, organ of the Vatican, declared that it "was a veritable homage to the Revolution, an insidious thesis for weak minds incapable of recognizing its hidden poison, a cause of pain to all good Catholics." The Congress had become impossible. The Pope could not be asked to send a representative to a diplomatic assembly where there was question of recording his expropriation as an accomplished fact. With the exception of England, the non-Catholic powers themselves blamed the pamphlet which brought the whole question up again.

The Duke of Montebello, ambassador of France at Saint Petersburg, wrote to Count Walewski, December 31: "The brochure *The Pope and the Congress* is producing a deplorable effect. Prince Gortchakoff said to me last evening: 'I do not understand your hesitating to disavow it explicitly in the *Moniteur*. It is a friend who says to you: Europe needs repose; if you trouble it in this way periodically, you will inspire apprehensions in everybody and end by alienating your best friends!'"

The brochure had been published without the knowledge of Count Walewski, all of whose ideas it shocked. The Emperor was governing against his own government. The Ministry of Foreign Affairs was no longer more than a façade, an optical illusion. Unwilling to be the instrument of a policy he disapproved, the minister was about to be forced to hand in his resignation.

After long tergiversation, Napoleon III. had made up his mind. He gave up the notion of an Italian Confederation which nobody wanted, and he despaired of obtaining for Venetia an autonomous Italian régime. Convinced that the dispossessed princes could be restored only by force, he concluded to permit Piedmont to annex their States, but on one condition, namely, that the compensation for this aggrandizement should be the annexation of Savoy and Nice to France. The jealousies of the powers, of England especially, were to render very difficult this combination without which France would rightly regard herself as having been duped and mystified. The task of diplomacy was to be as difficult as that of the army had been, and the realization of the new imperial programme was to encounter obstacles of every sort, not merely abroad, but in the interior of France.

The year 1859 had commenced by the alarms arising from the remarks addressed to the Austrian ambassador by the Emperor. It was closing amidst the anxieties and controversies caused by the Italian question, and chiefly by the Roman question. Minds were greatly disturbed by indecision. Many were asking whether the victories of Magenta and Solferino had not been sterile ones for France. Disconcerted by the problems still remaining to be solved, public opinion continued in a state of bewilderment and trouble. The Emperor did not fail to appreciate the difficulty of satisfying it. He comprehended that France would not forgive him for the blood shed in a war so violently criticised unless, in return for her efforts and sacrifices, she received an enlargement of territory which might flatter her self-love.

INDEX

ALEXANDER II. of Russia, in 1859 his relations with Napoleon III. very cordial, p. 61; why he wished to give Austria a lesson, p. 63; did not desire the unification of Italy, p. 65; delighted by the peace of Villafranca, p. 274; recognizes that Napoleon III. has been a profound politician as well as a great captain, p. 274.

ANTONELLI, Cardinal, on behalf of the Pope, demands the evacuation of the Pontifical States by the armies of occupation, p. 69; protests against the seizure of the Romagna, p. 217.

ARESE, Count, meets Napoleon III. in Genoa, p. 115; his early friendship for him, p. 325; meets him at Saint-Sauveur, p. 327.

AUVERGNE, Prince de La Tour d', minister of France at Turin; his despatches concerning the Hübner incident, pp. 10, 11, 12; concerning Prince Napoleon's arrival, pp. 16, 17; opposed to the Italian War, p. 46; his opinion of Cavour, pp. 256–57; on the sensation created at Turin by the peace of Villafranca, pp. 266–67; on Tuscan sentiment, pp. 301, 302; on the appointment of Cavour as plenipotentiary, pp. 340, 341.

BAILLIENCOURT, General de, his curious account of Victor Emmanuel's talk after Cavour's resignation, p. 259 *et seq.*; describes the dinner given at Milan to Napoleon III. and Victor Emmanuel, pp. 264–65.

BANNEVILLE, Marquis de, *chargé d'affaires* of France at Turin; his despatches, pp. 9, 10, 12, 14, 27, 39.

BAROCHE, president of French Council of State; his speech after the Emperor's return from Italy, p. 276.

BISMARCK, possibly the only German who in 1859 shared the views of Napoleon III., p. 56; defends him against the prejudices of Frederick William IV., p. 57; Napoleon III. believed in his star.

BUOL, Count, Austrian Minister of Foreign Affairs, p. 14; praises Napoleon's speech from the throne, p. 40.

BUONCAMPAGNI, M. de, Sardinian minister at Florence, lays the train for the revolution in that city, p. 212.

CANROBERT, Marshal, describes the taking of Ponte di Magenta, pp. 142–43.

CASSAGNAC, A. G. de, describes Napoleon III. as a journalist, p. 29.

CAVOUR, Count, addresses a memorandum to England, p. 69; interviews Napoleon III. by appointment, p. 77; writes the Emperor a letter, entreating him not to adopt a retrograde policy, p. 78; resigns his office after the peace of Villafranca, p. 257; what his compatriots said of his resignation, p. 261; sees Napoleon III. for the last time at Turin, p. 269; appointed Victor Emmanuel's plenipotentiary at the Congress, p. 340.

CHARTRES, Duc de, acts as a Sardinian cavalry officer during the war of Italy, p. 128; La Marmora's orderly officer, p. 157.

CHATEAURENARD, Marquis de, *chargé d'affaires* of France at Saint Petersburg; despatches to Walewski, pp. 61, 62, 65.

CLOTILDE, Princess, her betrothal announced, p. 14; renounces her inheritance, p. 19; her marriage to Prince Napoleon, p. 20; characteristics of, p. 23 *et seq.*

COTTE, General de, his death described, p. 178.

DERBY, Lord, English Prime Minister, quoted, pp. 148, 149.

DONNET, Cardinal, Archbishop of Bordeaux, his address to the Emperor, pp. 333, 334.

DUPANLOUP, Bishop of Orléans, makes an indignant reply to the brochure: *The Pope and the Congress*, p. 344.

ENGLAND, opinions of her public men on the Italian question, p. 48 *et seq.*

ESPINASSE, General, killed at Magenta, p. 145; the Emperor's emotion on recognizing his body, p. 151.

EUGÉNIE, the Empress, regent during the war, p. 202 *et seq.*; witnesses the return of the troops with the Prince Imperial, pp. 286, 288, deeply interested in the Duchess of Parma, p. 304; writes to Arese about the Italian question, p. 326.

FARINI, Piedmontese commissioner at Modena, described, p. 311.

FAVRE, Jules, extract of letter to M. Rothan, p. 7; defends Piedmont and denounces Austria, p. 93.

FLEURY, General, aide-de-camp of Napoleon III., acquaints him with the dissatisfaction of his officers after the battle of Magenta, p. 152; criticises the hasty attack at Melegnano, p. 172; letters to his wife before Solferino, p. 177 *et seq.*; describes the attitude of Prince Napoleon after Solferino, p. 218; sent with a letter to Francis Joseph proposing a cessation of hostilities, p. 230 *et seq.*; regrets changes wrought by a democratic government in the appearance of the French army, p. 245.

FOURCADE, editorial writer in the *Revue des Deux Mondes*, quoted pp. 44, 45, 280.

FRANCIS JOSEPH, Emperor of Austria, sends the Archduke Albert on a mission to the Prince Regent of Prussia, p. 59; establishes his headquarters at Villafranca, p. 176; receives a Prussian note which determines him to take the offensive, p. 180; orders a retreat beyond the Mincio, p. 191; receives a letter from Napoleon III. proposing an armistice, p. 232; incurred fewer risks than Napoleon III. from a continuation of the war, p. 233; accepts armistice, p. 234; meets the French Emperor at Villafranca, p. 242; refuses to cede Lombardy to Sardinia and to abandon Venice, p. 243; agrees to join France in asking the Pope for reforms in his states, p. 244; discusses the conditions of peace with Prince Napoleon, p. 249 *et seq.*; text of his reply to Napoleon III., p. 253 *et seq.*

GARIBALDI, Giuseppe, said to have

placed himself at the disposition of the Sardinian government and renounced all alliance with the Mazzinians in case of war, p. 10; enters Como with his volunteers after the battle of Montebello, p. 123.

GORCE, M. de La, quoted, pp. 64, 281.

GORTCHAKOFF, Prince, admires the French Emperor's sagacity in concluding the Italian War, pp. 273-74.

GRAMONT, Duc de, ambassador of France at Rome, opposed to the war, p. 46; despatch concerning the Emperor's speech from the throne, pp. 68-69.

GUÉRONNIERE, Viscount de La, anonymous author of the brochure, *The Emperor Napoleon III. and Italy*, p. 29 et seq.

HESSE, Field Marshal Baron, Austrian chief of staff, peace commissioner at Villafranca, p. 237.

HILLIERS, Marshal Baraguey d', commander of 1st army corps, p. 162; reports the losses after battle of Melegnano, p. 167; criticised by Fleury for precipitating the attack, p. 172.

HOHENLOHE, Prince, his errand to Napoleon III. at Valeggio, p. 241.

HÜBNER, Baron, Austrian ambassador at Paris, the effect produced by the Emperor's remark to him on New Year's Day, p. 8 et seq.

ITALY, the War of, inaugurated a new era, p. 6; the attitude of French parties after it began, p. 97 et seq.

IVOY, Colonel Paulze d', killed at Melegnano, p. 165.

LA GRAVIÈRE, Rear-Admiral Jurien de, p. 226.

LA MARMORA, General de, writes Cavour that the armistice may lead to peace, p. 257.

LANZA, Sardinian Minister of Finance, proposes a war loan, p. 28.

LA TOUR, Viscount de, speech in the Corps Législatif, pp. 94-95.

LEBRUN, General, describes the sufferings of the troops after battle of Melegnano, p. 171.

LEMERCIER, Viscount Anatole, expresses the anxieties of France concerning the Papacy, pp. 93-94.

LEOPOLD, Grand Duke of Tuscany, abdicates in favor of his son, p. 293.

LHUYS, Drouyn de, favors Austrian alliance, opposes the principle of nationalities, p. 45.

MACMAHON, commander of 2d army corps; report to the Emperor after the battle of Turbigo, p. 134; created Marshal of France and Duke of Magenta after the battle of Magenta, p. 152.

MAGENTA, battle of, p. 136 et seq.

MANTUA, not included in the cession of Lombardy, pp. 251, 254.

MARTIMPREY, General de, second French peace commissioner, at Villafranca, p. 237.

MASSA, Marquis de, describes scenes at Milan after the battle of Melegnano, pp. 170, 171; scenes of the triumph on the return of the troops, p. 285.

MELEGNANO, battle of, p. 162 et seq.

MENSDORF-POUILLY, General Count de, second Austrian peace commissioner at Villafranca, p. 237.

METTERNICH, Prince, his visit to Napoleon III. at Saint-Sauveur, pp. 327-28; made ambassador to France, p. 339.

MODENA, Duke Francis of, shuts himself up in his fortress of

350　INDEX

Brescello, p. 216; his conduct unfavorably compared with that of the Duchess of Parma, p. 306.

MOLTKE, Marshal, states the military condition of Prussia, in 1859, p. 248.

MONTEBELLO, the battle of, described, p. 118 *et seq.*

MONTEBELLO, Duc de, French ambassador to Russia, p. 46; notifies Walewski that the Russian Cabinet thinks negotiations for peace should begin, p. 219; that Russia favors the cause of the young Duke of Parma, p. 307; describes the satisfaction of Alexander II. and Prince Gortchakoff at the conclusion of the war, pp. 273–74; despatch concerning *The Pope and the Congress,* p. 344.

MORNY, Count de, an advocate of peace, p. 43; favors the Russian alliance, p. 46; thinks the principle of nationalities is chiefly supported by revolutionists, p. 46; praises Napoleon III. when he returns from the war, pp. 275–76.

MOSBOURG, Count de, describes the Duchess of Parma's departure from her dominions, p. 305.

MOUSTIER, Marquis de, minister of France at Berlin, p. 46.

NAPOLEON III., full light thrown on him by the Italian War, p. 3 *et seq.;* the anonymous brochure, p. 28 *et seq.;* speech from the throne, p. 35 *et seq.;* replies to Victoria's letter, p. 51; special liking for Bismarck, p. 57; goes to war, p. 109; first order of the day, p. 113; proclamations at Milan, pp. 158–60; directs all military operations at Solferino, p. 193; proclamation after the battle, pp. 198, 199; prepares for war while intending peace, p. 224 *et seq.;* proclamation from Valeggio, p. 238; to the army after the peace of Villafranca, pp. 262–63; reception at Milan, pp. 264, 265; meets Cavour at Turin, pp. 268–69; disagrees with the French estimate of the German *landwehr,* p. 273; replies to address of the great bodies of state, p. 276 *et seq.;* his reply to the Nuncio, p. 279; speech at the Louvre dinner, pp. 289–90; political amnesty extended to all but the Bourbons, p. 291; recommends Modenese autonomy, p. 313; hampered by his antecedents, p. 319; quoted on the attitude of the French Republic in Rome, pp. 319–20; forebodes the difficulties of the Roman question, pp. 322–23; meets Arese and Metternich, p. 327; his article in the *Moniteur,* pp. 328–29; dissatisfied with the Pope, p. 333; his reply to Cardinal Donnet, pp. 334–35; convinced that a European Congress would embarrass him and concludes to dispense with it, p. 341 *et seq.;* instigates the brochure which makes it impossible, p. 343 *et seq.;* abandons the notion of an Italian Confederation and demands the annexation of Savoy and Nice, p. 345.

NAPOLEON, Prince, marries Princess Clotilde of Savoy, p. 20; relieved of ministerial functions, p. 71; commands 5th army corps during the war, p. 211; antagonizes in Leghorn the minister of France, p. 213; the bearer of the conditions of peace, p. 249; discusses the separate paragraphs with Francis Joseph, p. 249 *et seq.*

OLLIVIER, M. ÉMILE, quoted on the policy of Napoleon III., pp. 31–32.

PAGERIE, Countess Stéphanie de Tascher de La, quoted on the impression produced in France by the ultimatum, p. 84; the Empress on the eve of war, p. 106; the Emperor on his return from Italy, p. 272; the impression produced by the peace, pp. 279–80.

PALESTRO, battle of, p. 123 et seq.

PALLIERI, governor of Parma under Victor Emmanuel, p. 307.

PARMA, Duchess of, sister of Count of Chambord, p. 216; why Francis Joseph did not defend her rights at Villafranca, p. 253; leaves Parma, pp. 304–5; her cause favored by Napoleon III. and Alexander II., but disregarded by Piedmontese government, p. 307.

PERSIGNY, Count, ambassador of France at London, favors English alliance but opposes principle of nationalities, p. 15; repulsed by Palmerston when he urges him to assist Napoleon III. in making peace, p. 223.

PESCHIERA, fortress of, not included in the cession of Lombardy, pp. 251, 254.

PIUS IX., under an illusion concerning his temporal power, p. 68; proposed as honorary president of an Italian Confederation, pp. 243, 250; will not consider it unless the Romagna is first restored to him, p. 333.

PLICHON, speech before the Corps Législatif, pp. 94–95.

PONIATOWSKI, Prince Joseph, pp. 298–99.

RICASOLI, Baron, pp. 293, 295.

ROCCA, Count della, Sardinian peace commissioner at Villafranca, p. 237.

ROMAIN-DESFOSSÉS, Vice-Admiral, pp. 226, 235.

RUSSIA, its attitude toward Italy in 1859, p. 61 et seq.; its moral support the chief object of Napoleon III. in the Stuttgart interview, p. 62; flatly opposed to Italian unity, p. 66; diplomatic situation in, after Solferino, p. 219.

SAINTE-AULAIRE, Count de, criticises the political condition of the Romagna in 1831, p. 318.

SAINT-JEAN D'ANGÉLY, Regnaud, created marshal of France after battle of Magenta, p. 153.

SCHOUVALOFF, Count, sent by Alexander II. to follow the operations of the Italian campaign, p. 220.

SOLFERINO, battle of, p. 182 et seq.

THIERS, M., describes Piedmont in 1852, p. 45.

THORANE, Grand, French consul at Chambéry, describes the Emperor's reception there, pp. 269–70.

TROPLONG, President of French Senate, compares Napoleon III. to Scipio, p. 275.

TROUBETZKOY, Princess, wife of Count de Morny, p. 75.

TURBIGO, battle of, p. 131 et seq.

TURIN, angry demonstrations after peace of Villafranca, pp. 265–66.

ULTIMATUM, the Austrian, p. 82 et seq.

USEDON, M. d', Prussian minister at Frankfort, p. 59; his motion in the Diet that the German army contingent should be put into marching order, p. 60.

VAILLANT, Marshal, French peace commissioner at Villafranca, p. 237.

VANDAL, Count Albert, extract from speech when received into the French Academy, p. 6.

VAYER, Marquis de Ferrière le, minister of France at Turin, p. 46; despatches concerning Prince Napoleon, p. 213 *et seq.*; concerning Tuscany, pp. 294-97.

VICTOR EMMANUEL, aggressor in the Italian War, p. 5; makes a war loan, p. 28; letter of, after battle of Palestro, p. 129; fights at San Martino during battle of Solferino, p. 192; proclaimed dictator of the Romagna, p. 217; disappointed by the peace of Villafranca, p. 247; did not like Cavour, p. 258; curious remarks after Cavour resigns, pp. 259-60; replies to Tuscan delegation, p. 301; forebodes the difficulties of the Roman question, pp. 323-25.

VICTORIA, Queen, extract from speech from the throne in Feb., 1859, p. 48; writes to Napoleon III., pleading for peace, and warning him that England will not assist him, p. 51.

VILLAFRANCA, armistice of, pp. 237-38; interview of the French and Austrian emperors at, p. 240 *et seq.*; text of the articles of peace of, pp. 253-54; articles of, signed by both sovereigns, p. 255.

VITU, M., journalistic collaborator of Napoleon III., p. 29.

WALEWSKI, Count, Minister of Foreign Affairs, seeks to lessen the importance of the Hübner incident, p. 9; opposed on principle to the Italian War, p. 46; telegraphs Pélissier, pp. 81, 82; a convinced partisan of Tuscan autonomy, p. 214; sends Napoleon III. alarming reports to induce discontinuance of the war, p. 221; despatch concerning Tuscany, p. 294.

www.ingramcontent.com/pod-product-compliance
Lightning Source LLC
Chambersburg PA
CBHW020220240426

43672CB00006B/365